The Bahamas in American History

The Bahamas in American History

From Early European Contact to
Bahamian Independence in 1973

Keith Tinker

Library of Congress Control Number:		2011961480
ISBN:	Hardcover	978-1-4653-1083-5
	Softcover	978-1-4653-1082-8
	Ebook	978-1-4653-1084-2

On the cover, Continental Marines Land at New Providence, March 1776, oil painting on canvas by V. Zveg, 1973. Courtesy U.S. Navy Art Collection.

Cover design by Jane Schultheiss.

This book was printed in the United States of America.

To order additional copies of this book, contact:
Xlibris Corporation
1-888-795-4274
www.Xlibris.com
Orders@Xlibris.com
104179

CONTENTS

This book is dedicated to that very special person, the one who truly lifted me up so that I now stand on that figurative mountain where I am now able to more clearly view my *raison d'être*, the one who taught me the true meaning of life and inspired me to research and to write and to be the very best I could possibly, under God, be!

PREFACE

The Commonwealth of The Bahamas and the United States have shared historic linkages in economic, political, and social exchanges that have lasted for more than 200 years. These connections have continued almost without interruption despite the obvious fact that the United States is vastly superior to The Bahamas in geographic size, demographic diversity, natural resources, global political positioning, economic and military prowess, and cultural advancement. Both countries share a common British colonial heritage that ultimately created a variety of reasons for the connections over the centuries. On the 4th of July 2010, the United States of America celebrated 234 years of independence from Great Britain. In comparison, on July 10, 2010, the Bahamas celebrated 37 years of independence from Great Britain. It is, however, primarily that common British heritage that created an environment for these historic connections to happen.

Geographically, the estimated 700 islands, cays, and rocks (30 are inhabited) that make up the archipelago commonly called "the Bahamas" extend northward to 55 miles off the southeastern coast of Florida and the southeastern United States and southward over an estimated 100,000 miles of mostly subtropical, turquoise-colored Atlantic waters to within 50 miles of the northern coast of Cuba. Globally, the islands are known as popular vacation destinations for mostly Americans seeking the excitement of casinos, the pleasure of almost eternal sunshine, constantly flowing warm breezes, beautiful beaches, and investment opportunities in international financial centers. In general, few persons, regrettably including most Bahamians, are aware that the rich and vibrant history of the islands that has evolved over the centuries is the primary result of evolving global politics and commerce, migration, and immigration experiences that have significantly impacted relations between the United States and the Bahamas.

In the early 1500s, shortly after the epic voyages of Christopher Columbus to the Americas, Spanish colonial administrators removed and subjected many of the Lucayans, the aboriginal Bahamians, to forced labor elsewhere in the Caribbean. For the most part, the islands were generally neglected. By the 1640s the islands were sparsely settled by transplanted English colonists who had decided to leave Bermuda for religious reasons. This small group of early settlers brought their enslaved Africans with them. The leader of this group, William Sayle, later became the proprietary governor of South Carolina. They were joined by free Africans deported from Bermuda on charges of conspiracy in treason. Later, in the 1700s, thousands of British Loyalists, slaves, and free blacks migrated via New York and St. Augustine primarily from Virginia, the Carolinas, and Georgia to the Bahamas. This group of political dissidents was led by the former English governor of New York and Virginia, Lord Dunmore. In addition, during the American Revolutionary War, three of the first expeditions of the fledgling United States coast guard and navy occurred in attacks against and the eventual capture of the town of Nassau, capital of the Bahamas.

In the 1800s, groups of Black Seminoles and fugitive slaves escaped Jacksonian ethnic purges via the Florida underground railroad system to freedom in the Bahamas. With the abolition of the British slave trade, thousands of Africans, some destined for slavery in the United States, were freed and resettled in the Bahamas. During the 1860s, the Bahamas became an important *entrepôt* for the shipment of vital supplies to the Confederate forces during the American Civil War. By the 1880s, increasing numbers of American tourists heading for vacation or convalescence in Cuba began to stop in the Bahamas, thus giving impetus to the beginning of tourism in the islands. As new hotels were built, the racial discriminatory practices of the South were adopted to accommodate these visitors.

In the late 1800s, mostly American steamers destined for ports in the Caribbean, Central and South America stopped over in the southern Bahamas to recruit Bahamians as stevedores. During this same period, hundreds of Bahamians from the northern Bahamas began to migrate to south Florida in search of economic opportunity. The labor of these early Bahamian immigrants contributed significantly to the emergence of cities like Key West, Miami, Delray, and West Palm Beach. Bahamians also contributed to the development of the sponge industry so vital to the economy of Florida before the emergence of tourism. Consular offices were established in strategic areas of the colony, and the American diplomatic presence in the islands began to evolve.

Bahamians played a significant role in the growth of the United States during the twentieth century. Early in the century, they were active in the development of the United Negro Improvement Association, fostered by Marcus Garvey and the precursor of the later civil rights movement, and in the New York-based Harlem Renaissance that showcased black culture and literary talent. During the experimental Prohibition years, ports in the northern Bahamas were used to store and smuggle large quantities of illegal liquor to centers located along the eastern seaboard of the United States. Thousands of Bahamians were employed by American companies during the Second World War to supplement the agricultural labor shortage created by the mass recruiting of Americans for military duties and as laborers in the development of naval defense systems in the Carolinas.

The following pages will attempt to demonstrate how the United States and the Bahamas developed in an incubator of symbiotic relationships fashioned by political, economic, cultural, and historical circumstances. Of necessity, this book is to some minor degree an examination of the ways in which both countries have responded to that ideology in terms of respective national histories, political ideals, and national psychologies. This work is by no means an exhaustive treatise on the subject of American-Bahamian historical relations, nor is it the intent of this author to cover every aspect of that subject in this volume. Additionally, the work draws heavily from existing sources and relies on research in the respective subject areas already included in the historiography. It ends with Bahamian independence in 1973 and as such allows for the possible publication of a sequel that can treat the subject up to the present. It is hoped that this book will create greater awareness in Bahamians in particular (and others interested in the subject) of the need for a revision of Bahamian historical and cultural identity as we Bahamians complacently and often smugly exist completely enveloped in an aura of relative security in the "benign" shadow of our giant neighbor to the north.

1. EARLY EUROPEAN CONTACT

Spanish Colonial Connections

On October 12, 1492, Christopher Columbus and a motley group of mostly Spanish adventurers landed on an island in the southeastern Bahamas, claimed the islands for Spain and thus officially instituted Spanish colonial influence in the New World.[1] The Spanish were not the first recorded adventurers to land in the Americas. This feat is accredited first to groups of nomadic Asians crossing the Bering Strait some 1,000 years before, followed around AD 1000 by Norsemen who reportedly established a colony on Newfoundland.[2] It is accepted, however, that for more than 300 years the Spanish-led European invasions resulted in the systematic exploration and mapping of the newly "discovered" lands.[3] Subsequently, the arrival of the Europeans eventually led to mass adulteration of the early American cultures, which were arguably equally as (or in some cases more) noble and celebrated as the contemporary cultures that existed in Europe. The series of events that followed this accidental encounter between the two hemispheres were to indelibly impact the course of history for the civilization of both the worlds in a significantly redefining fashion.

For the purpose of this book, it is sufficient to state that the Spanish encounters created an environment of social, political, and economic intrigue that placed the future United States of America and the Commonwealth of The Bahamas on a course of both collision and cooperation. To better understand how this environment was created, however, it is necessary to glimpse the role of the Spanish in this age of exploration. David Weber, in his work titled *The Spanish Frontier in North America* (1992), succinctly outlines the magnitude of this significance:

> In Columbus' wake, white-sailed vessels from Spain conducted a remarkable
> reconnaissance of the new-found lands—a reconnaissance that lasted, in
> a sense, for over three hundred centuries, as Spaniards probed ever more

13

deeply to understand the secrets of the American landscape . . . . Whether
one understands the first significant encounters between peoples from
the two hemispheres as discoveries or as invasions, it is clear that those
encounters were remarkably swift and pervasive. Spaniards, who stood
in the vanguard of European westward expansion, penetrated some
of the most remote corners of the hemisphere within a half century of
Columbus' first landing.[4]

In April 1513, the Spanish conquistador Juan Ponce de León traveled through
the northern Bahamas and landed on the east coast of Florida. Ponce de León was
a veteran of Columbus's second voyage and a former governor of Puerto Rico. He
had, according to myth and legend, embarked on an expedition to find the fabled
Fountain of Youth allegedly located in the northern Bahamas on the island called
Bimini.[5] The indigenous people reportedly claimed that the waters of this fountain
had health-restorative properties. Ponce de León also reportedly hoped to capture
unsuspecting Lucayans to supplement the increasing demand for slaves in Spanish
America. However, in 1513 the Spaniard was already the wealthy owner of large
landholdings and many slaves. Ponce de León's official mission was to search for
the fabled, wealthy land called Beniny and in effect to extend the geographical
boundaries of the Spanish Atlantic empire. Whatever the reason for the expedition,
Ponce de León was apparently impressed by the lavish landscape and beautiful
beaches of the land he stumbled upon reportedly near present Daytona Beach.
He claimed it for Spain and named the place La Florida, or "place of flowers," in
honor of the day he went ashore, which was Easter Sunday, or La Pascua Florida.
Interestingly, as will be discussed in later chapters, this first recorded travel between
The Bahamas and Florida has continued almost unabated.

In the sixteenth and early seventeenth centuries, the European imperial
powers showed very little interest in colonizing the Bahama Islands. The
inconsistent interest shown by the Spanish was focused largely on sporadic
slave-catching raids and expeditions to discourage attacks against Spanish
maritime commerce. Generally, it was determined that the islands were ill suited
for commercial agriculture, they had no gold or silver, and their waters produced
an insignificant number of pearls. After the founding of the English colony of
Jamestown, however, it became more important for Spain to secure its claims
in North America, especially along the Atlantic coast. Of vital importance was
control of the Bahama Channel through which Spanish commerce flowed, and
where many ships were wrecked each year on the numerous often-hidden shoals
or doomed to the fury of hurricanes. Florida provided a base from which relief for
shipwrecked victims and supplies for general maritime commerce were provided.
With bases in Cuba to the south and Florida to the north, Spain could better
protect its commercial interests as its ships plied the alluring turquoise-hued but
treacherous, pirate-infested waters of the Bahamas.

The Eleutheran Adventurers

In 1629, the English temporarily wrested control of the islands from the Spanish and officially claimed, but made no serious attempts to settle, the Bahama Islands. In the mid-seventeenth century, civil war raged between the forces of King Charles I and Parliament, represented by Puritan Oliver Cromwell. The conflict, which caused Puritan dissidents like the Pilgrim Fathers to eventually immigrate to the American colonies spread to Bermuda. Supporters of the Royalists prevailed, and many who refused to swear allegiance to the Crown were banished. The early American—Bermudan colonists soon used the Bahama Islands as a convenient place for the exile of convicts and other undesirables.

The events of the mid-1600s that witnessed the arrival of the Pilgrims aboard the *Mayflower* at Plymouth Rock in English North America were mirrored in the Bahama Islands when a group of English Puritan refugees left the island of Bermuda aboard the *William* and settled on an island originally called Cigateo in the northeastern Bahamas. The immigrants renamed the island Eleutheria, the Greek name connoting freedom, in commemoration of their new-found religious and political freedom.[6] The group was led by William Sayle, who later, at the age of eighty, was elected governor of South Carolina.

The early European-Bahamian colonists were economically hard pressed and initially sheltered in a cave, where they held church services. In 1648, the indigent immigrants dispatched William Sayle and eight others in a small boat to seek assistance on the American mainland. After nine days of navigating treacherous shoals and the Atlantic Ocean, the group arrived in Virginia, where sympathetic brethren immediately formulated plans for assistance. Samuel Eliot Morison, a member of the Harvard University class of 1908 and one of the most renowned American historians of the mid-twentieth century, tells the story in *Harvard in the Seventeenth Century*. He notes that in 1650, the derelict Eleuthera immigrants were providentially sustained by £800 worth of supplies sent by benevolent Boston settlers from various local churches throughout Massachusetts. In gratitude, the Bahamian "Pilgrims" sent a shipment of ten tons of valuable brazilwood to Massachusetts as a contribution to the development of Harvard College.[7]

Morison notes that Harvard alumnus Nathaniel White Jr., son of the Eleutheran preacher, returned to the island with the relief provisions and led the return expedition to Boston with a shipment of hardwood. He reportedly was awarded a scholarship to study at Harvard. The Bahamian gift was accompanied by a letter signed by Sayle, Robert Ridley, and Nathaniel White senior, replete with biblical verses illustrating the ever-abiding grace and mercy of God. The significance of the gift is demonstrated in remarks by then Havard president Dunster, who said, "And when the Colony [Massachusetts] could not relieve us, God sent supplies even from poor Cyguotea to enlarge our room."[8] In 1957, Harvard University presented to the island of Eleuthera a brass plaque mounted on brazilwood commemorating that historic contribution some three hundred years before.[9] The wood was sold for £124, which was used to purchase land and develop a residence for students.

Proprietary Connections

In 1670, the political relationship between the English colonies of the Carolinas and the Bahama Islands was strengthened when the administration of the islands was granted to the Lords Proprietors of the Provence of Carolina. The five proprietors—the Duke of Albemarle, Lord Craven, Lord Ashley, Sir George Carteret and Peter Colleton—appointed proprietary governors to represent their collective political and economic interests. These colonial investors also had proprietary administrative responsibility for the island of Barbados, where most of the available arable land was devoted to the cultivation of sugarcane. This scarcity of land for the production of food encouraged emigrants from Barbados to settle in the Carolinas with the primary responsibility of producing a constant supply of food for the Barbadians and other English sugar-producing Caribbean islands.

In the 1670s, the English colony of Barbados was arguably the richest, most highly developed, and most populous English colony in the Americas, boasting a lucrative sugar industry controlled by an estimated population of 50,000 inhabitants, including some 30,000 mostly enslaved Blacks.[10] In 1663, eighty-five prominent Barbadians, under the leadership of Sir John Yeamans, signed a document requesting authorization to establish settlements in the province of Carolina. Barbadians were considered suitable colonists because of their proven success in agriculture as well as their adaptability to warm climates. Proprietor Lord Ashley Cooper, in a letter to Sir John Yeamans in South Carolina, noted, "I am so glad to hear soe many considerable men come from Barbados for we find by deare experience that noe other are able to make a Plantation but such as are in condition to stock and furnish themselves."[11]

The initial attempt at colonization of Cape Fear was an economic failure; however, migration from Barbados to the Carolinas continued, until by 1672 many of the settlers of Charleston were of Barbadian origin. The Bahamas, which very early were proven unsuited to commercial agricultural activity, were left virtually unsupervised. It was knowledge of this administrative vacuum that later prompted some of the most renowned pirates to establish bases in The Bahamas. Interestingly, a century later, it was some of the descendents of these early Barbadian immigrants to the Carolinas who migrated to the Bahamas in the 1780s and indelibly changed the course of history of those islands.

2. IMPACT OF THE AMERICAN REVOLUTION

Emergence of the American Navy

The events of the American Revolution underscored tenuous relations between Bourbon Spain, France, and the fledgling United States of America in their cooperative on-again, off-again alliance against their initial common foe: Great Britain. These events significantly impacted life in the islands of The Bahamas. More commonly called in the eighteenth century New Providence, the Bahamas were a British possession almost as radically affected by the American Revolution as were the Thirteen Colonies. David Weber summed up the situation as follows:

> When thirteen of England's American colonies rebelled in 1775-6, they presented Spain with a chance for revenge after the humiliating defeat of the Seven Years' War, as well as opportunities for gain from England's distress. Spain's primary interest lay in Europe, particularly in regaining Gibraltar and Minorca, which it had lost to England in 1713. In North America, however, war with Britain also gave Spain a chance to drive England out of the lower Mississippi Valley and regain the Floridas.[12]

In the late eighteenth century, the heretofore neglected British Bahamian colony became significant in European political and commercial affairs because of its geographical position almost as a series of stepping-stones connecting Spanish America to its possessions in North America and to the revolting British colonies. What happened in Philadelphia, New York, or Charleston often had significant implications for the island chain.

The story of the Continental Navy of the United States and the role it played in determining the results of the American Revolution is one of intrigue. Early in the Revolutionary War, the patriots decided to develop a navy with which to protect their

17

maritime interests. Tracing the evolution of the Continental Navy, however, presents difficulties for determining an exact starting date for the process, because many different proposals for naval expeditions and commercial maritime exercises were under discussion almost simultaneously. It may be safe to presume, however, that a valid starting date would be October 1775, when the Continental Congress voted an appropriation of $100,000 to identify and outfit ships to become the nucleus of a naval force. Later in November, the Naval Committee voted for the establishment of a Marine Corp. Shortly afterward, an appropriation of $1million was voted to build a fleet comprising thirteen ships—one for each of the revolting states. The Naval Committee, chaired by Stephen Hopkins of Rhode Island, emerged as the most authoritative agency engaged in the deliberations. The evolution of the American navy was to have an almost immediate direct impact on the affairs of the Bahama Islands.

The Naval Committee was developed to implement strategies by which the rebels could harass the enemy, provide supplies to the American forces, and "begin a system of maritime and naval operations."[13] The Naval Committee, not to be confused with the Marine Committee, was established in 1775 by members of the so-called Secret Committee of Congress in a secret meeting held in a tavern in Philadelphia. The Marine Committee, with its thirteen representatives and direct association with the Board of Admiralty, secured the funds with which to build the navy. The varied egos and interests of the thirteen states often resulted in disagreement. Each state, although having its own navy at different stages of development, still demanded equal representation and access to available federal resources. Into this mix were thrown the privateer factions squabbling over policy decisions for the distribution of prizes to be awarded, and merchant marine owners demanding protection for their commercial interests. Adding further to the confusion, the various states constantly changed representatives responsible for naval affairs.

The Secret Committee, initially called the Committee of Secret Correspondence, was established to explain American ideals to various European interests in hopes of soliciting support for the revolutionary cause. The committee, consisting of Benjamin Franklin, Benjamin Harrison, John Dickinson, John Jay, and Robert Morris, authorized Silas Deane to meet with the French Foreign Minister to plead the American cause, assure the French of the rebels' intentions toward independence, and request military supplies. The French surreptitiously and unofficially arranged for the provision of ships and military supplies for the Americans. Additionally, Gilbert du Motier, Marquis de Lafayette, was dispatched to provide military expertise and training to the officers of the Continental Army. It was not until the American defeat of the British at the Battle of Saratoga in 1777, however, that the French were convinced of the possibility of success of the American revolutionary cause. Eventually, Benjamin Franklin became American ambassador to France and ultimately assumed direct and almost sole responsibility for the solicitation and procurement of supplies for the Americans. The direct impact of the American

Revolution on the Bahama Islands began with the appointment of Ezek Hopkins as the first commodore of the American Continental fleet.

Commodore Ezek Hopkins

Ezek Hopkins was a veteran Rhode Island merchant captain whose naval experience was largely as a privateer in the French wars. He was a brigadier general in the Rhode Island militia and participated in the plan to construct the seawall defenses. Perhaps because of the influence of his brother Stephen, who was chairman of the Naval Committee, Ezek was commissioned as the commander-in-chief of the Continental Navy. His initial instructions were to proceed to "Chesapeake Bay in Virginia . . . enter said bay, search out and attack, take or destroy all naval forces of our enemies that you may find there."[14] It appears that Ezek Hopkins, despite the fact that his brother was chairman, held the committee in very low regard, referring to its members as "a pack of fools, ignorant as lawyers' clerks, who thought the navy could help pay for the war."[15] Hopkins decided on a different course of action: to attack and raid the British colony of the Bahama Islands.

In February 1776, Commodore Hopkins summoned the commanders of the Continental naval forces to a meeting aboard his ship, the *Alfred*, where he explained his intention to countermand the instructions of the Naval Committee and instead initiate a preemptive strike against New Providence and capture a cache of ammunition reportedly stored on that island.[16] William Fowler Jr., in his *Rebels under Sail* (1976), describes the action that followed:

> The fleet sailed from Newcastle, Delaware, on February 14, 1776. By March 1, six of the eight vessels lay at anchor off Great Abaco. *Hornet* and *Fly* had disappeared during the voyage. For two days the fleet waited for them using the time to further train men and refill their water casks. Two small vessels were taken when they blundered into the anchorage filled with warships, and from the prisoners Hopkins received intelligence about New Providence. From this information and his own knowledge of the place, Hopkins drew the specifics of his raid . . . . [He] decided to use subterfuge and send in the marines.[17]

Two hundred marines, packed into the two captured vessels along with fifty seamen, discretely sailed into Nassau harbor. The plans called for the amphibious force to initiate the first attack against Fort Nassau, to be supported by invasion by the fleet in short order. Although the plans were not executed exactly as expected, the outcome for the invaders was satisfactory.[18] The marines came ashore on a beach located immediately west of the fort, where, after a brief skirmish, the British capitulated and Fort Nassau was captured.[19] Unfortunately for the Americans, the success of the raid was limited by the fact that the Bahamian colonial administration, with advance warning of the impending invasion, removed most of the ammunition from the forts.[20] Still, the invaders were able to raid the town and seize significant stores of supplies, including eighty-eight cannons, mortars of various sizes, and thousands of rounds of shot and other ammunition. Additional fortune occurred when the damaged *Fly*, which had collided with the *Hornet* in a storm, sailed into Nassau harbor. Since Hopkins had no plans to capture the town of Nassau, he promptly ordered his fleet to return to Rhode Island; however, another raid on Nassau by American forces was soon to follow.

John Peck Rathburn

On January 27, 1778, Captain John Peck Rathburn of the sloop *Providence* launched a surprise attack on the town of Nassau. Rathburn, who had initially served as an officer in the Continental Navy and later in the United States Navy, hailed from Rhode Island. He was first lieutenant under John Paul Jones and had participated in the initial raid on Nassau led by Hopkins. The *Providence* approached Nassau harbor at night disguised as a merchant vessel. Twenty-six marines under the command of Captain John Trevett went ashore by small boat equipped with scaling ropes. then scaled the walls of Fort Nassau and subdued the two unsuspecting guards. While some of the invaders routinely signaled the "all is well" call to the guards outside the fort, others repositioned the fort cannons toward parts of the town from which reinforcement could come.

At dawn, Nassau awoke to the sight of enemy forces patrolling the walls and the American flag flying atop Fort Nassau, significantly for the first time since the Continental Congress had adopted that flag as a symbol of American national pride. Trevett sent a delegation of three marines to Fort Montague, which guarded the eastern entrance to Nassau, with the report that American forces numbering 250 marines had captured Fort Nassau. Unable to immediately verify this claim, the British forces surrendered and evacuated Fort Montague. The marines, with the assistance of American merchant seamen, spiked the cannons and curiously dumped the seized gunpowder into the sea.[21] The combined American forces, in turn, seized five ships anchored in Nassau harbor as prize. It was later that afternoon, after the town was secured, that Rathburn sailed the *Providence* into Nassau harbor. The confiscated ammunition was immediately loaded on the *Providence* and on three of the ships captured and manned by the freed American merchant seamen. The two other ships, which the American personnel were too few in number to command, were burned. On the morning of the following day, Rathburn and his convoy sailed from Nassau harbor without having fired a single shot or shed a single drop of blood.[22]

The third expedition of the Americans against the Bahama Islands is, perhaps, the most intriguing of the three. To fully appreciate the significance of the impact of this event requires a brief overview of role of imperial Spain in world affairs at that time. Geographically, the islands of the Bahamas are situated along the trade routes that even today dictate that much of the commercial back-and-forth flow in the north Atlantic pass the islands. The geography of the islands was especially significant for the transport of commerce throughout the Spanish empire. Tuckman notes,

> In the eighteenth century, war typically followed the routes of commerce. Fated to be so close to much of the action of the war, they were often part of the action. Occupied four times in eight years of war by invading forces, the Bahamas fell to new masters often. The most significant of these temporary masters was Spain, which invaded, occupied, and lost the colony during the last year of the war from 1782 to 1783.[23]

Mario Rodriguez states that in 1775, Spain was initially conservative in its reaction to the erupting rebellion in English America.[24] Obviously, Bourbon Spain was mindful of the prowess of the British navy, which had repeatedly thwarted plans by other European imperial powers to unite military forces against them. The memory of the events of 1762-1763, when Spain lost both Havana and Manila to the British, was not easily forgotten; however, developing events in 1775 colonial America had forced Great Britain to divert significant forces in an effort to confront the colonial disturbances. For imperial Europe, colonial disturbances of this magnitude were unprecedented. France, a historical nemesis, was first to take advantage of a distracted Great Britain by declaring war in 1778. The French could not know that within fewer than thirty years it would be confronted with similar rebellion in its sugar-lucrative Caribbean colony of Saint Domingue.

Spain declared war against Great Britain in 1779 and thereupon planned the capture of British Florida and the reconquest of their Bahamian possessions. In the fall of 1781, the Spanish plan to reconquer the Bahama Islands was launched. Spanish officials targeted New Providence as a secondary measure because they determined that the reconquest of the islands would contribute to more secured Caribbean commerce. Plans to capture Pensacola, capital of British Florida, however, was a primary objective, initiated the previous year, but which failed when the expedition launched from Havana was nearly destroyed by a hurricane. The delayed attack against British Florida allowed time for a Bahamian expedition to begin in January 1782. The attack against New Providence was, however, temporarily delayed and may not have happened, but for the coincidental intervention of the American naval frigate the *South Carolina*.

Saga of the **South Carolina**

Because of the weak position of the Spanish navy, protection was required from European allies for its various commercial and military expeditions. An agreement with France allowed for this accommodation; however, France, which was engaged in its own global struggles with Great Britain, did not (perhaps at times for strategic military reasons) always immediately comply with Spanish requests. The needed escort came unexpectedly when Commodore Alexander Gillon sailed the frigate *South Carolina* into Havana harbor on its maiden voyage.

During the American Revolutionary War, the *South Carolina* was one of the prized ships under direct American command and part of the state navy of South Carolina. The ship mounted 40 cannons and carried 550 men, including 330 marines. Even the *Bonhomme Richard* under the command of the American naval icon John Paul Jones was considered inferior to the *South Carolina*. Its passengers included a list of prominent Americans, such as Charles Adams, son of John Adams (then American ambassador to Holland, later to become president of the United States); New England painter John Trumbull; and distinguished Harvard University scientist Benjamin Waterhouse. The ship was on a voyage from the Netherlands to New England when circumstances caused it to stumble into Havana harbor that fateful day in January. Few then knew that the ship would eventually earn the distinction of leading a successful American revolutionary maritime expedition against the British colony of the Bahamas.

The saga of the *South Carolina* and the way in which its intended cruise to New England came to include the capture of Nassau makes an interesting story of intrigue and at times controversy. The ship, commissioned to be built in neutral Holland by the French government, was clandestinely intended for use by the belligerent Americans. Because of Holland's neutrality, the Dutch would not release the frigate directly to the Americans. The French, however, hoping the ship would in some way still be used against the British, allowed the prince of the Kingdom of Luxemburg to take possession of the vessel. The prince, in turn, placed the ship on auction to the most politically ideal and financially capable bidder. Perhaps, through a prearrangement with the French, the auction was apparently rigged in favor of the American revolutionary cause, as only Americans were facilitated in the exercise.

On May 30, 1780, Alexander Gillon, a prominent Charleston merchant, commissioned commodore, and an agent for the state of Carolina, won the auction, and, under a three-year contract with the prince, took command of the ship, changing its name from *L'Indien* to the *South Carolina*. Interestingly, Gillon won against the odds of significant other bidders, including the venerable John Paul Jones. What may account for Gillon's success were the advantages he held over his competitors. Alexander Gillon was born in Holland and raised in a Dutch-Scottish household. In 1776, he migrated to Charleston and then soon married a prominent widow. During the American Revolution he distinguished himself as a sympathizer of the rebel cause and a very capable mariner. Gillon was one of several agents commissioned by the rebel colonies to travel to Europe to purchase and outfit ships suitable to engage the British and to become the nucleus of the fledgling Continental navy and coast guard. He was multilingual and understood the idiosyncrasies of the various imperial courts. Perhaps most important was the fact that Gillon was wealthy and able to provide adequate security for the commercial agreement.

Under the terms of the agreement, Gillon could not use the ship for direct naval combat. He could, however, use the frigate as a privateer to plunder booty from enemy commercial ships and sell the plunder to the French. The prince was to receive 25 percent of all monies received from the sale of the plunder. The state of Carolina received another 25 percent, and the remaining 50 percent was to be divided among the crew. Upon completion of the three-year contract, the ship was to be returned to the prince along with a final compensation payment of 100,000 livres. If the ship was lost, however, the state of Carolina and its commissioned agent were obligated to pay compensation in the amount of 400,000 livres. From a business perspective, it was in the financial interests of Gillon and the state of Carolina to employ the vessel in any way possible under the terms of the contract to make a lot money and turn a profit. And so it was under these circumstances that the American-Spanish fleet of fifty-nine vessels led by the *South Carolina* sailed against New Providence.

The fleet included 13 American merchantmen outfitted as armed privateers, conveyed 1,531 sailors and 2,000 soldiers, and boasted a combined 311 guns. Juan Manuel de Cagigal, governor and captain general of Havana, led the armed forces, while Commodore Gillon was contracted to lead the naval expedition. The fleet entered Bahamian territorial waters, traveling up the Bahama Channel without obstruction, perhaps because the pilots of the fleet were residents of the Bahamas and reportedly the same pilots who had guided the Hopkins raid against Nassau in 1776. The pilots, William Woodside, Downham Newton, and William Jeremiah Newton, were actually natives of Charleston who lived in Philadelphia during the Revolutionary War, but operated businesses from Nassau as commercial opportunity dictated. In any case, Bahamian Governor Maxwell, in his deposition on the affair, complained that the Spanish fleet was guided into Nassau harbor by traitors.[25] In the events that followed, the Spanish fleet under American convoy sailed into Nassau harbor without incident, even after observing and being observed by several other vessels.

The Spanish, intent on remaining in the Bahamas, made generous efforts to spare the islands from political and commercial disruption. Their communications to the Bahamians were essentially to surrender without resistance and to escape direct and deliberate plunder. Additionally, the Spanish promised that with surrender, they would confiscate only public property and seize private ammunition. In return for compliance, the Bahamians would also be granted the privilege of continuing business as usual under British laws. Privateers would be left in the care of their owners as long as they were not used to disrupt Spanish commerce. The leading Nassau merchants, many owners of privateers, took positive note of the Spanish promise to spare their businesses from plunder and urged Governor Maxwell to surrender. Faced with overwhelming odds and personally unwilling to engage in military conflict on behalf of a people he actually despised, Governor Maxwell surrendered control of the islands to the Spanish on May 8, 1782. The American convoy of privateers, loaded with commercial goods from Havana, sailed from Nassau harbor five days later intent on selling their cargoes at markets in New England. The

Spanish occupation of the islands proved short-lived, however, as another American invasion, this time led by Andrew Deveaux, was to happen one year later.

Andrew Deveaux

In July 1783, a Loyalist expedition under the command of Andrew Deveaux Jr. attacked and captured Nassau. Unlike the previous American invasions undertaken on behalf of the revolutionary cause and against the British, the Deveaux expedition was a Loyalist initiative undertaken on behalf of the British. When Deveaux enlisted in the Continental army at age 17, his father, who stoutly supported the British, objected, much to the anger of his neighbors in Beaufort, South Carolina. In retaliation for attacks against his father, Deveaux Jr. switched political allegiance, gathered a band of young rebels of like sentiment and set about disrupting life in and around Beaufort.[26] In 1779, Deveaux Jr. joined forces with British Major General Augustine Prévost, distinguished himself in the British victories at the Siege of Savannah and the Siege of Charleston, and was rewarded by Lord Cornwallis with the rank of colonel and given command of a company of Loyalist irregulars. In 1782, however, the British were forced to evacuate Charleston, prompting Deveaux to retreat to St. Augustine, capital of British East Florida. While there, he began to develop a plan to recapture Nassau for the British.

From the beginning of the American Revolution, the British garrison at St. Augustine had offered security for thousands of Loyalists driven from nearby Georgia and the Carolinas. The stream of immigrants swelled in 1782, when thousands of civilians accompanied British forces retreating first from Savannah and then from Charleston. Soon after his arrival, Andrew Deveaux held public meetings in St. Augustine to explain his plans for the recapture of Nassau. He hoped to encourage the financial and military aid of sympathizers wishing to see the islands recaptured from the Spanish and returned to British control. Perhaps more appealing to many in attendance, some of whom had been displaced from significant acreages of private lands, was the promise of prize and large tracts of arable virgin land in a tropical paradise just a few nautical miles from their former homes. Deveaux seems to have attracted a small band of like-minded mariners, including one William Lyford, after whom the most affluent gated community in The Bahamas is now named.

In March 1783, Deveaux and his band of seventy men sailed from St. Augustine aboard six vessels toward Nassau. He was joined at sea two days later by the privateer brigantines *Perseverance*, under the command of Thomas Dow, and *Whitby Warrior*, under the command of Daniel Wheeler.[27] The ships anchored off the coast of Harbour Island, where an additional 170 Bahamian volunteers were recruited. Ironically, the Spanish sloop *Flor de Mayo* was on its way from Havana to Nassau to inform authorities that a peace agreement had been concluded between Spain and Great Britain that included the restoration of the Bahamas to the British in exchange for East Florida. Deveaux and his force nonetheless captured Fort

Montague through the use of elements of surprise and trickery. Deveaux's exploit was described in a letter to a friend back in St. Augustine.[28] Lt. Colonel Roderick MacKenzie also reported a contemporary account of the invasion:

> When Deveaux landed his modest force at the eastern end of Nassau, it appeared to the Spanish that a large and dangerous force had invaded. Deveaux made so many trips back and forth to his vessels, each time seemingly returning with boatloads of men, that [caused] the Spanish [to] spiked their cannons and abandoned Ft. Montagu. Some troops were dressed like Indians, their war whoops designed to strike terror in the heart of any Spaniard, and long bundles bound together sticks (fascines) used in strengthening ramparts, looked like men. On each return trip, the troops crowded in the bottom of the long boats ready to pop up again.[29]

On April 17, 1783, Don Antonio Claraco Sauz surrendered Spanish control of the islands to the Americans. British colonial authority was reestablished and remained in effect until the islands became an independent country in 1973.

Evidence suggests that Deveaux and his associates were fully aware of the treaty between Great Britain and Spain. A May 1783 correspondence from East Florida Governor Patrick Tonyn to British home secretary Lord Townsend supports this assertion:

> I have the honour of acquainting you, of the reduction of the Island of New Providence, by the intrepid and spirited conduct of Major Deveaux, of the South Carolina Militia. A young Gentleman who resided here for some time as a refugee, having lost the greatest part of his fortune in South Carolina, with the remains, he fitted out and collected a small fleet of Privateers, and about two hundred Loyalists; with these, and by an allowable artifice he subdued the Spanish Garrison. As I was doubtful of his success, I claim no credit for countenancing the Expedition. I am confident that his spirit and success will, Sir, recommend him to your favor and protection.[30]

The British rewarded Andrew Deveaux and his invaders with large land grants in The Bahamas. The participating islanders received land grants on the island of Eleuthera totaling some 6000 acres. Lyford received two grants that included 448 acres of land on the western tip of New Providence and 592 acres on southern Cat Island, near Port Howe. John Braddock, Lyford's nephew, received two grants of a combined total of 140 acres on Long Island. Deveaux was given a large land grant at Port Howe, Cat Island, where he built a mansion, the ruins of which remain today. The risky expedition against The Bahamas, which proved profitable for the Deveaux group, was to open the doors to thousands of other loyalists who migrated to the islands shortly afterward.

The invasions of Nassau were relatively minor campaigns in the saga of imperial global conflict; however, they are significant because the initial campaign is recognized as the first naval expedition by the fledgling United States Navy. More significantly, the invasions demonstrated "the most ambitious [rebel] challenge to the colonial empire of Great Britain during the Revolution."[31] McCusker opined that despite the limited direct military success of the campaigns, they portended a greater significance:

> The threat inherent in this surprise attack for the trade-rich West Indies and, more strategically and logically important, to Great Britain's very ability to carry on a victorious war 3,000 miles from home, struck forcibly. Caron de Beaumarchais reported from London to the French Minister of Foreign Affairs, Comte de Vergennes, that the North government was so perplexed upon learning of the news of the American descent upon Nassau that it did not know which way to turn.[32]

The British responded by concentrating the majority of their naval resources in and around Atlantic ports, primarily to protect their lucrative Caribbean sugar colonies from attack. This shift in resources, however, resulted in weakened British defenses in the Mediterranean, the Straits of Gibraltar, and, even closer to home, the North Atlantic. On May 16, 1778, the unimaginable happened when a major French fleet sailed from the Mediterranean Sea, through the Straits of Gibraltar, into the Atlantic Ocean and on to the Chesapeake Bay, where a naval blockade of access to the heart of New England was established. Consequently, this French blockade, with the tacit collaboration of the American rebels, prevented British access to the area, without which supplies and reinforcements were denied, and certainly played a major role in the decisive turn of events that resulted in the British defeat at Yorktown. As McCusker notes, "had not the Royal Navy been so occupied in the Western Atlantic as a consequence of the actions of the American forces, the freedom of the seas could have been denied to the French and perhaps the course of the war materially altered as a result."[33]

Loyalist Migration

Beginning in the late 1780s, thousands of disenfranchised Americans migrated to The Bahamas in the wake of the American Revolution. Thelma Peters succinctly describes the situation as follows:

> Supporters of the British Crown found life in the colonies rigorous in the years prior to, during, and after the Revolutionary War. The hazards of war and the inequities of peace forced many Loyalists into Bahamian exile. In the wild and turbulent Carolinas in the 1760s, colonial officials

battled the first stirrings of rebellion. The Sons of Liberty were born. Tarred and feathered Loyalists were paraded in dung carts through the streets of Savannah and past the bustling shops of Charleston. Their fortunes reduced, Loyalists retreated behind British lines at New York and in East Florida . . . . Many refugees rejected the cold regions of Nova Scotia in favor of the warmer Bahamas . . . . The situation encountered by the loyalist refugees on their arrival in the Bahamas was more than depressing. The memory of the dense Carolina woodlands became the reality of the Bahamian scrub, the rich soil of rice and indigo plantations replaced by rock.[34]

The economic plight of the Loyalists was dictated largely by the enforcement of the 1778 Banishment Act, which allowed states to banish persons who refused to publicly declare allegiance to the new republic. One year later, as the financial capability of some states became increasingly depressed, Congress allowed states to enforce the Confiscation Act, which allowed for the seizure and subsequent sale or lease of the property of the banished Loyalist, often at basement bargain prices, as a means of defraying some of the cost of the war. On June 13, 1782, for example, the five-hundred-acre estate of Georgian Alexander Wylly was sold by the state to a Thomas Stone, together with a house on the waterfront for £355. Reportedly, "In New York alone over $3,600,000 worth of property was acquired by the state."[35]

Most Loyalists from the Carolinas and Georgia had escaped the hostilities of once civil neighbors in the wake of the British retreat from Savannah and Charlestown. Now in St. Augustine, many attempted to ride out the revolutionary storm by establishing new (presumably temporary) lives in hopes of someday returning to their former familiar domiciles. The news that the British planned to evacuate St. Augustine as well and return control of East Florida to Spain was extremely devastating. In fact, the preliminary articles of peace between Spain and Britain, signed on January 20, 1783, allowed just eighteen months for the British subjects to dispose of their properties, collect their debts, and evacuate. Not everyone, however, was prepared to accept the drastic change in politics without resistance. Very early, the process became bogged in a quagmire of political and economic intrigue.

The announcement of the cession prompted bands of armed vigilantes to raid Loyalist properties, adding to the troubles faced by the mostly defenseless refugees. The bandits focused primarily on the capture of blacks, slave or free, because of the premium value they brought on the auction markets in the neighboring southern states. Raids were particularly pronounced north of the St. Johns River in north Florida, where British authority was not vigorously enforced because of limitations in available resources. Patrick Tonyn, the governor of East Florida, dispatched a small force of mostly Loyalists headed by William Young, formerly of the South Carolina Ninety-Sixth District, to encounter the bandits. This group had several skirmishes with the raiders and remained on the defensive until full evacuation was completed.[36]

The British subjects of East Florida were ultimately faced with the options of remaining and placing their fate in the hands of the Spanish or of being relocated to Great Britain, Nova Scotia, the Bahamas, or elsewhere in the West Indies. The option of retaining control of the province by force, however, continued to be entertained by a more desperate group led by John Cruden.

John Cruden hailed from North Carolina, where, before the war, he and his family were merchants and traders. During British occupation of coastal Carolina, he served as commissioner of confiscated estates under the authority of General Charles Lord Cornwallis, with specific duties to supervise the distribution of lands and slaves confiscated from hapless rebels. Now, proclaiming himself president of "The British American Loyalist who took Refuge in East Florida," Cruden sought to rally Loyalists to support his cause against the Spanish and in direct defiance of the articles of peace. When his plans for insurrection failed to gain significant support, Cruden presumed to throw the plight of the refugees on the mercy of the Spanish. His admonishment to the Spanish king Carlos III was explicit:

> We may it please your Majesty are Reduced to the dreadful alternative of returning to our Homes, to receive insults worse than Death to Men of Spirit, or to run the hazard of being Murdered in Cold Blood, to Go to the inhospitable Regions of Nova Scotia or take refuge on the Barren Rocks of the Bahamas where poverty and wretchedness stares us in the face Or do what our Spirit cannot brook (pardon Sire the freedom) renounce our country, Drug the religion of Our Fathers and become your Subjects.[37]

Vicente Manuel de Zéspedes y Velasco, the newly appointed Spanish governor and captain general of East Florida, was assured by outgoing British Governor Tonyn that the threat of raids by bandits was to be of more concern that the ranting of Cruden. Tonyn, in a correspondence to the Spanish authorities, termed the Cruden affair "merely chimerical, and such as deserves no kind of serious consideration."[38] Zespedes, noting the British commitment to honor the terms of treaty, yet sensing the difficulties the British encountered in effecting the evacuation, granted an extension for the process to continue until July 1785.

The evacuation was plagued by continued obstacles, chief among them the reluctance of the refugees to leave for a number of reasons. First, rumors and false reports in newspapers about the possibility of a British reversal of policy and their ultimate retention of control of East Florida kept hope of remaining in the United States alive for most Loyalists. Second, some merchants who had extended lines of credit to the Spanish to supply provisions to the garrisons were hoping that payment on those outstanding debts would arrive on ships from Havana. Certainly, they were not eager to leave without collecting on those debts. Third, some farmers had crops in their fields they wanted to harvest and sell to capitalize their resettlement efforts.

In vain, persons impacted by the Banishment and Confiscation Acts lingered in hope that the acts would be reversed and their properties returned.[39]

Significantly, the sluggish state of the real estate market in St. Augustine resulted in disappointment for many Loyalists who were forced to settle for submarket prices for the sale of their properties or outright abandon them. Some Loyalists hoped that the Spanish occupation would result in a boost to the real estate market, in which scores of newly arrived Spaniards needing affordable housing would speculate in the market and purchase properties at bargain, but still reasonable rates. This hope, however, was dashed as only a small group of officers initially accompanied Zéspedes during the early years of occupation. The case of Thomas Courtney of South Carolina provides a typical example of the dilemma faced by the Loyalists.

Courtney claimed he had purchased a house and lot in St. Augustine for £400 and refurbished the property for an additional £25. The property was placed on auction, but since no bid was higher than £40, it was pulled from the auction. Courtney eventually and reluctantly sold the property to a Spaniard for £53.[40] Household goods and livestock were also difficult to dispose of at market value. A claim case was recorded of a set of finely hand-carved chairs, which in 1782 sold in Charleston for £20, but sold for six shillings in St. Augustine during the evacuation period.[41] Livestock was either traded for items essential to life outside the metropolitan United States, or otherwise left unsold, as in the claim of Benjamin Springer, who reportedly was forced to leave behind fifty horses, forty head of cattle, and forty hogs.[42]

The plight of the ill-fated Loyalists was further exacerbated by the fact that the relatively small size of the cargo ships and scarcity of resources, mostly exhausted by wars, limited the quantity and type of cargo shipped to allow primarily the more essential slaves and luggage to be transported. Most other movable property had to be left behind. Some Loyalists like Peter Edwards, who had dismantled his house and moved the cargo to the St. Mary's River for shipment to the Bahamas, were outraged at the limitations placed on them.[43] Fourteen of the twenty-five transport ships assigned to the evacuation were committed to government cargo consisting mostly of building supplies, artillery, and public personnel. In all, fifteen ships made thirty-four trips laden with Loyalists and their property, the last sailing in September 1785.

Most Loyalist slave owners went primarily to Caribbean destinations and the Bahamas. Nova Scotia was not favored because of a dread of the harsh winters with which to contend there. One Loyalist who initially went to Nova Scotia but eventually settled in the Bahamas explained his reason for relocation: "I fear that it is to[o] cold for us to bear it now we have [been] so long in this hot climett."[44] Another claimed he had lost a slave who ran away when confronted with the prospect of relocation to Nova Scotia.[45] The Reverend James Seymour requested the Society for the Propagation of the Gospel to appoint him to the Bahamas so as to avoid the harsh Canadian winters. Sadly, Seymour died on his way to the islands.[46]

Most Loyalists chose to be evacuated to the Bahamas, not because of a burning desire to live there, but because it was the British colony nearest to East Florida and it had a tropical climate that was pleasant, soil that could at best support some measure of a plantation lifestyle, and a significant military presence augmented by the evacuation of troops from East Florida garrisons. 1n 1783, Lewis Johnson, a planter and member of the Georgia aristocracy, traveled to the Bahamas to assess its suitability for plantation life. He expressed his disappointment as follows:

> My expectations by no means sanguine being so cruelly disappointed I intend to embark for St. Augustine in 7 or 8 days as much at a loss as ever where to direct my steps . . . . The West Indies would on many accounts be the country I would prefer, but the great expense of living there and the uncertainty of being about to employ my few Negroes to any advantage deters me from it, so that after all if better prospects do not open on my return to St. Augustine it is probable I will return to this poor Country on the evacuation of Florida.[47]

The official reaction of the Bahamians to the anticipated arrival of the Loyalists was totally unflattering. Bahamian governor Powell publicly voiced his disapproval of the mass migration of the Americans as a potential social burden to his government and favored, if any, only migration of the more wealthy. Powell's position arguably reflected that of the Nassau ruling merchants, who did not welcome potential competition to their established mercantilist monopoly. The governor relayed the Bahamian sentiments in a letter to Tonyn:

> I understand a large number of back Country Loyalist may be expected by the next Transport that arrive here, these Islands are by no means calculated for these people, who mostly subsist on the Continent by Hunting and like Arabs removing their inhabitants, and stock from one place or province to another, and therefore could your Excellency order them to Nova Scotia or some other Province on the Continent, or should your Excellency be inclined to send them this way, you may think it more of His Majesty's service to empower me to forward them to the Moskito shore.[48]

Tonyn ignored Powell's request, and in the ensuing months thousands of Loyalists migrated to the islands. The impact of the migration significantly affected life in the Bahamas and the colony was never the same again.

The Loyalists who migrated to the Bahama Islands toward the close of the American Revolution represented a variety of professions and ancestral backgrounds as well as social stratification reflecting a cross section of people of European and African descent living in the United States, especially in the southern states, at that time. Lydia Austin Parrish conducted a study of eighty of the Loyalist families with a focus on the aristocratic planter-merchant class.[49] Parrish notes that most of the eighty families could trace their ancestry to English or Scottish ancestry. The few exceptions included Isaac Baillou (French), David Zubly (Swiss), John and James Armbrister (Polish), and William Wylly (Irish). Based on Parrish's research, the professions of the families included medical doctors, surgeons, finish carpenters, ship builders, mariners, and school teachers.

Thelma Peters notes that the contrast in lifestyles and ideology that existed between the old Bahamians and the new Bahamians was a formula for conflict: "The superimposing of this essentially landlubber culture upon that of the canny but uneducated seafaring Bahamians, the Conchs, led to inevitable conflict."[50] Peters concludes, "Those refugees who represented 'the rich, the well born and the able,' many of whom had held office in the American colonies, were determined to gain power in the Bahamas, [and] they succeeded but only after plots and counterplots which brought the downfall of two successive governors, John Maxwell and John, Earl of Dunmore."[51]

It was perhaps a shock to some and a puzzle to many others to learn of the appointment of John Murray, Earl of Dunmore, peer of the venerable British House of Lords, former colonial governor of New York and Virginia, to the post of governor of the often ignored and politically insignificant Bahama Islands, which in the 1780s could not boast of a combined population of whites and blacks comparable in size to any of the major cities in any of the North American colonies. Some answers to this question, however, may be gleaned from a cursory review of British politics of that period, particularly with regard to Spanish North America, and from an insight into the ambitions of Lord Dunmore.

In 1782 Britain was at war with France, Spain, and Holland—the most powerful nations on the continent. The war with the American rebels was only one arena of many in the European wars of the period. That the enemies of Britain directly and indirectly supported the rebels was not based on support of their political ideology, but rather a convenient method of distracting the British and forcing that nation to spread its resources more than was economically or militarily convenient. In fact, the European antagonists, all colonial superpowers, regarded the American resistance as a negative image for the continued control of their respective global empires. Equally noteworthy is the fact that in the late 1700s, the British, as did other European powers, favored protecting their growing interest in the sugar islands of the Caribbean, and the exploitation of Spanish colonial commerce with more than thirteen colonies that produced primarily tobacco and cotton, but very little sugar. So, it was perhaps not a surprise that in the 1780s Britain adopted a policy to restrict military action in North America to defensive measures. The wars, especially with France, for domination of most of the world's resources demanded more urgent British attention elsewhere than the American colonies, which, after all, were predominantly white and generally English in culture, and whether independent or not would presumably still maintain ties to the motherland.

The series of events of the post-American Revolution years left Great Britain in control of most French interests in North America, including a colonial presence in the Mississippi Valley, along the St. Lawrence River and the Great Lakes, and in the Floridas. The policy was, however, inconsistent as to how to proceed with the administration of the vast territories. J. Leitch Wright Jr. explains the situation as follows:

> Throughout the 1783-1815 period the British government was simultaneously pulled by a desire to reach an accommodation with former colonists and a willingness to ally with various red, white, or black Americans to constrict the boundaries of the new republic or to bring about its downfall . . . . [however], what the [British] minister in the American capital proclaimed was Britain's official policy and what Charles Jenkinson, Lord Hawkesbury, and what William Wundham, Henry Dundas, Lord Melville, and Robert Banks Jenkinson, the second earl of Liverpool (among the most influential statesmen in London) were up to frequently differed.[52]

Furthermore, as Wright asserts, in America "there was the paradox that, though liberty flourished in America after 1783, the policies of George III's allegedly despotic government seemed to many American Indians and Negroes more identified with liberty than measures adopted by the new United States."[53]

In the cessation of conflicts with the American rebels and France, Britain was faced with the dilemma of finding new homes for thousands of loyal American subjects, all of whom were politically, socially, and economically disenfranchised, but many of whom could not (or outright refused to) return to Britain. And while thousands eventually migrated to colonies outside the continent, thousands of others remained, some hoping to be resettled in frontier lands to the west. The Old Northwest, in this regard, became increasingly interesting to British policy makers as a possible colonial refuge or even a neutral zone.[54] Wright notes that while the new republic assumed that the 1783 Treaty of Versailles had given them perpetual sovereignty over the Old West in fulfillment of the American ideal of "manifest destiny," the European powers had dismissed that idea as contrary to their respective political objectives. According to Wright, "It was the Mississippi Valley's final disposition that made the [two] Floridas so important. Whoever had these provinces was likely to have New Orleans and command of the Lower Mississippi, and whoever controlled the Mississippi's mouth had the key to North America's interior."[55]

Complicating the matter further was the fact that after the American Revolution, the lands in contention were ceded to Spain, which had planned to systematically colonize Kentucky and Tennessee as its resources allowed. In anticipation of a French takeover of the American West, scores of Acadians began to migrate to Louisiana and

West Florida. Bahamian Loyalists, consumed by their own perspectives of "manifest destiny," protested what they determined to be French encroachment on lands they viewed as preserved exclusively for British expansion and, of course, primarily for themselves.[56] In summary, Wright comments, "The disturbing French involvement, internal strife in the United States, entreaties from Canadian authorities and fur traders, and the prospect of a Spanish revolt forced Britain to take a second look at [the idea of colonization of] the Floridas and the Mississippi Valley . . . . [As a result, debate of] the concept of a unified Mississippi Valley, economically and politically dominated by Britain, linked to Canada and a refuge for loyalists, reemerged in the latter part of the 1780s."[57]

Consideration for retention of this large frontier area was heightened by entreaties to this effect made by merchants, Indian allies, and land speculators.[58] The Indians were on the warpath against the Americans for repeated encroachment on their ancestral lands. According to Wright, the American attitude toward the noble savages was somewhat dismissive, and their perspective was essentially that "the Indians were not British subjects but wards of the United States living on American soil."[59] On the other hand, the British did not take the presence of the Native Americans lightly. Reports in the *London Times* stated that the Creeks and Cherokee, some 35,000 strong, were planning to retake Georgia and South Carolina and that a confederacy of all the Indian peoples ranging from Canada to the Gulf of Mexico were preparing to create an independent state.[60] In 1789, in an attempt to emphasize the importance of alliance with the Indians, Thomas Dalton, a sometime—resident of the Bahamas, appeared in London dressed as a Native American, reportedly with a message to King George III from the Creek and Cherokee nations, petitioning the English monarch to establish a treaty with those peoples, build a fort to protect common English and Indian interests, and create a trading post for mutually beneficial commercial exchange.[61] It was into this cauldron of political and economic stew that the seemingly indomitable Lord Dunmore emerged as a leading advocate of British retention and possibly even acquisition of lands in the American west and southwest.

Dunmore had initially retreated to England during the revolutionary wars, but he returned to America in 1782 in the wake of the Cornwallis victories, expecting to resume his position as governor of Virginia. The British defeat at Yorktown, however, forced him to land at Charlestown instead, where the British still maintained a tentative measure of control. The British political resolution, which spoke only to hostilities with the rebel Americans, provided an opportunity to recoup some of its losses in the Americas by concentrating attacks against the less formidable Spanish.[62] Dunmore urged his peers to initiate or otherwise support a campaign that might eventually lead to recovery of the lower Mississippi, Alabama, and West Florida.[63] He understood, like many other British officials, that the fate of Florida was particularly important to the thousands of loyalist refugees forced to leave their homes and seek asylum in those provinces. A British—controlled Florida would provide a permanent home for thousands of angry people still loyal to Britain and willing to support the recapture of confiscated properties and restore British authority by any means necessary should the opportunity arise. Furthermore, there was the prospect of arming and enlisting thousands of free blacks and slaves, especially from the southern regions in the campaign.

Dunmore's military record suggests that he recognized the potential of arming and incorporating blacks—free and enslaved—in military campaign against the rebels and Spanish. As governor of Virginia, he had encouraged the enlistment and arming of slaves, promising freedom to those who escaped to join the British ranks and the possibility of land to those already free. Between1775 and 1776, his predominantly black Ethiopian Regiment had already played an important role in the effort to retain control of Virginia.[64] Dunmore conferred with knowledgeable sympathizers, such as John Cruden, the commissioner responsible for confiscated property in South Carolina and a supporter of Dunmore, about the status of the many blacks of whom he was responsible for disposing. They agreed on a plan to create a loyalist force of ten thousand blacks to be deployed as political expediency dictated.[65] Both Dunmore and Cruden as well as senior British officials were convinced that a large black loyalist force would be sufficiently motivated by the prospect of freedom and access to land to assist in the capture of Spanish West Florida and possibly even New Orleans and ultimately create a British loyalist sanctuary for themselves and other blacks and whites wishing to remain loyal to the Crown, but unwilling to leave the United States.[66] For students of Bahamian history, this information on Dunmore arming blacks is important as it perhaps explains the contemporary precedent set by William Wylly, Bahamian solicitor general in the early 1800s, to use his armed black slaves to protect his personal interests.[67]

Dunmore's wish to mobilize armed forces primarily of blacks against the Spanish was intriguing, but not an entirely altruistic expression of concern for the thousands of black Americans living either in slavery or in other situations of economic marginalization. Very early, Dunmore, while governor of Virginia and in collaboration with influential associates, used his position before the conflict to speculate in the acquisition of large areas of western lands, particularly in the Mississippi Valley.[68] His co-conspirators included Alexander Ross, Moses Franks, Adam Chrystie, John Murray (Dunmore's son), John Miller, and John Smythe, all of whom followed Dunmore to the Bahamas and made indelible marks on the future development of that colony.[69] The Revolution obviously interrupted their plans, but the group still hoped to establish a base in the Bahamas, which was near in geographic approximation to the action in North America. With Dunmore as governor of the islands, they hoped to continue their plans to promote British control over Spanish territories in the south and be rewarded with huge land grants in the virgin areas in the wake of an anticipated westward expansion.[70]

In 1783, Dunmore was unemployed and faced with the financial burden of supporting his family and maintaining his large estates in Scotland and elsewhere.

He had lost an estimated four million acres of land located mostly in the Ohio Valley, which rebels had confiscated, but which the Dunmore-led Illinois-Wabash Company unrelentingly claimed as its legal property. Dunmore and his associates reasoned that the establishment of a Loyalist state on the Gulf coast would provide an opportunity for the group to recover the land they had previously claimed or otherwise allow them to claim acreages of equivalent proportions in other areas.[71] In order to position themselves to accomplish their land speculation objectives, the group had to be close to the action and capable of influencing decisions on the mainland; therefore, Dunmore accepted the post of governor of the Bahama Islands, where he reigned as a king for a decade, placing some of his most loyal West Florida cronies in positions of authority, in the process alienating an increasingly powerful group of influential East Floridian refugees.

In 1796, Dunmore was unceremoniously recalled from the Bahamas for reasons that remain unclear. Perhaps the numerous charges of corruption and nepotism levied against him had finally taken their toll. While governor of the Bahamas, Dunmore schemed to have his salary doubled; he also gave himself and his associates large land grants and arranged to be paid certain "fees" for facilitating favorable salvage rulings. Dunmore, in reaction to his misfortunes, blamed his political enemies, especially the Duke of Portland, for orchestrating his fall from power and grace.[72] A more likely, though often overlooked, reason was the fact that the marriage of Dunmore's daughter Augusta to Augustus Frederic, the Duke of Sussex and King George III's son, perhaps because of pregnancy, became a scandal of major political and social proportions in British circles. One thing is certain: the King had the marriage annulled and shortly after, the Earl of Dunmore was suddenly dismissed from his position as governor of the Bahama Islands.[73] Dunmore's political adversaries in the Bahamas were elated by his recall, as it provided an administrative vacuum they moved quickly to fill.

In 1784, the largely merchant-professional Loyalists of East Florida established the Board of American Loyalists in Nassau with a primary aim to advance their personal interests and power base in the colony.[74] In 1785, the Board petitioned the governor to dissolve the Assembly and call a new election so that their interests might be better represented through the election of some of them to the Assembly. Their petition concluded with these words: "Resolved: That we do not consider ourselves represented in the present assembly, and of course not bound by any laws they may think proper to pass."[75] The petition was signed by twenty-two East Florida Loyalists, including John Wood, William Moss, James Hepburn, Peter Dean, John Tattnall, and John Wells, all destined to be among the most important shapers of Bahamian history, economics, politics, and culture. The association of this group with the colonial Florida trading conglomerate of Panton, Leslie Company will be discussed further in the next chapter.

To simply state that the Loyalists who migrated to the Bahama Islands in the wake of the American Revolution significantly impacted life in those islands and also in the provinces of Florida would be an understatement. John Wells, for example, the former publisher of the *East Florida Gazette*, published the *Bahama Gazette* as probably the first newspaper in the islands. The paper became an excellent source of information about the Bahamian perspective on the affairs of the colony, as well as on events on the mainland and in Europe.[76] Joseph Eve, a cotton planter on Cat Island and a contemporary rival of Eli Whitney, invented a machine capable of separating the seeds from the fiber of up to 360 pounds of cotton per day. Eve advertised his machine as versatile and capable of being optionally powered by water or cattle.[77]

Porcher and Fick, authors of *The Story of Sea Island Cotton* (2005), tell the story of the cultivation, harvesting, and sale of sea island cotton, which reportedly became of pivotal importance to the economy of the southeastern United States beginning in 1790 and extending into the Civil War years, and how it was significantly influenced by Bahamian intervention. The authors quote Thomas Spalding (1835), who outlined how sea island cotton, *Gossypium barbadense*, was introduced as a commercial crop in the Bahamas:

> She [England] therefore from her many colonies, selected Nova Scotia and the Bahamas Islands as the colonies where a provision of land was to be made for the loyal men who had clung to her fortune through blood and in ruin . . . and when the southern colonists were land with their faithful slaves upon the Bahama Island, in looking around for something upon which might employ themselves, the new interest in which cotton had awakened, in consequence of Arkwright's machinery, reached them . . . . There is a small island in the Caribbean sea called Anguilla, which had long been known to produce the best cotton in the West Indies. The new settlers in the Bahama Islands procured cotton seed to commerce the culture with Anguilla. They had in the year 1785 introduced the culture of cotton upon several of the Bahama Islands successfully, particularly upon Long Island.

Spaulding's account continues:

> The first bale of Sea-Island cotton that was ever produced in Georgia, was grown by Alexander Bissett, Esq. of St. Simon's Island, and I think in the year 1778. In the winter of 1785 and 1786, I know of three parcels of cotton sent from the Bahams, by gentlemen of rank there, to their friends in Georgia; Col. Kelsall sent to my father a small box of cotton-seed; the Surveyor-general of the Bahamas, Col. Tatnall, sent to his son, afterwards, Governor Tatnall of Georgia, a parcel of cotton-seed; Alexander Bissett's father, who was commissary Genl. to the Southern British Army sent a box of cotton seed to his son, in the year 1786; this cotton gave no fruit, but the

winter being moderate and the land new and warm, both my father and Mr. Bissett had seed from the ration, and the plant became acclimatized.[78]

By all accounts, the successful introduction of sea island cotton cultivation to the southeastern United States from the Bahamas was based on the following circumstances:

> The above-ground parts of the plant froze back during the winter, but—the winter being mild—the roots were not killed. The following spring, new plants developed from the rations, flowered in July and produced fruit throughout the fall. Subsequent crops, grown from seeds selected each year from early-blooming plants, became acclimated as day-neutral plants. Planters then grew sea island cotton as an annual, and by the 1790s, its fiber characteristics gained a high reputation in the English market. A few years after 1786, sea island cotton was commonly planted and exported from Georgia . . . . By 1793, many coastal South Carolina planters, enticed by the high prices at Liverpool, England, began experimenting with the crop on the sea islands."[79]

Bahamians, besides introducing the seed, also assisted Southerners with improvements in planting the sea island cotton. Michael Edwards credits Spalding with first noting the use of the innovative and highly successful ridge method:

> In 1794, a new ridge method of planting the seed more thickly was introduced by a planter from the Bahamas. The method was first adopted by Thomas Spaulding [sic], an influential Southerner, who had been one of the first to see the possibilities of Sea Island cotton growing on a large-scale. Within a short time he had increased the yield from 100 to 340 lb. per acre, and his success encouraged others to use the new system, making possible a sharp jump in the output of Sea Islands from 1799 onwards.

Early ginning was initially done by a manual process called "pinch ginning" or "finger ginning." The practice was adequate, although time consuming and labor intensive, and relatively adequate for local consumption demands. As the industry grew, however, the old method, which produced only about four pounds of cotton fiber per week, became grossly unsatisfactory.

The introduction of the "Eve's gin," however, proved very significant to the development of the cotton industry in the South:

> In 1790, Joseph Eve (1760-1835) introduced a modified roller gin into Georgia that was run by animal, wind and water power . . . . It was brought to South Carolina in 1797 or 1798 (Burden 1844b, 201). Eve

was living at the time in the Bahamas and may have gotten the idea for his gin from gins used there. Eve had been encouraged to develop a gin as financial compensation was offered by the governor of the Bahamas for improvements in cotton culture. His gin proved to be an important breakthrough since it cleared large amounts of cotton more quickly and efficiently than the traditional methods.[80]

Some East Floridians who became prominent in Bahamian political and social circles included Henry Yonge, a London-born and trained barrister, formerly attorney general in East Florida and later clerk of the executive council in Nassau. Among other things, one of Yonge's duties was to note losses and claims filed by his fellow refugees and to submit these memorials to the British authorities for consideration for reparations.[81] Yonge was rewarded with a crown grant of 400 acres on the island of Exuma. Peter Edwards was another notable East Floridian refugee who gained prominence in the colony. Originally from Georgia, Edwards became clerk of the Bahamas House of Assembly, eventually serving thirty years as a judge of an inferior court and the important vice-admiralty court. Interestingly, when Georgia repealed its banishment laws, Edwards refused to return to the United States. Daniel McKinnon met Edwards while the former was on his tour of the islands and flatteringly reported the latter to be "an amiable and very estimable gentleman of the [legal] profession."[82]

The three Armbrister brothers, James, John and Henry, all formerly of South Carolina and refugees via East Florida, are worthy of note, as they established one of the most influential families in Bahamian history and factored significantly in the early history of Florida. James, in particular, served as assistant registrar general to Adam Chrystie, and their apparent friendship is reflected in the fact that James named his son Robert Chrystie. It was this ill-fated Robert Chrystie who was executed by orders of Andrew Jackson for treasonable interference in affairs of the Indian wars and the associated turmoil that eventually brought Florida into statehood.

West Florida refugees in the Bahamas were generally rejected by their East Florida counterparts as socially inferior and a cultural degree above the indigenous Conchs. Many of the West Florida exiles were trappers who, in their dress, cuisine, and social lifestyle compared unfavorably with the elitist civility demonstrated by the southern East Florida gentry. In 1763, shortly after Spain ceded Florida to England, geographic boundaries for the division of the territories into two Floridas were declared by Royal Proclamation of the British monarch: "The part between the Apalachicola and the Mississippi Rivers, extending as far north as the 31st parallel, was called West Florida, with Pensacola as its capital, while land east of the Apalachicola up to the St. Mary River become known as East Florida, with its capital at St. Augustine."[83] West Florida was largely populated by Native Americans and regularly traversed by rough and crude frontiersmen, and life in those mostly lawless areas resembled the wild wild West of cowboy lore.

West Floridians were justifiably upset and resentful of their eastern immigrant counterparts when they were declared ineligible by the British authorities for compensation for property loss as a result of the conflict on the grounds that the western province had been "conquered by Spain in war, whereas East Florida had been given over in a time of Peace."[84] In response, some westerners formed vigilante groups that raided the South Carolina and Georgia woodland areas and captured cattle and slaves as compensation for the losses many had suffered at the hands of the rebels. Many others chose to tie their fate to that of the Bahamian government in hopes of gaining favor with the governors and as a result receive land grants or at best employment in a government post in a place where positions of importance often commanded respect and held promise of upward mobility.

This hostility may perhaps in part be explained by the fact that some prominent West Floridians supported the administration of governors Maxwell and Dunmore, and as such were accorded certain privileges. The ranks of the West Florida refugees included John Miller, a merchant, who was appointed to the Bahamas Council by Maxwell in 1785. Then there was former British army doctor Michael Grant, who was appointed commissary and granted membership in the Council by Dunmore in 1788 and later become vice-admiralty court judge. Occasionally, Grant practiced medicine, which his East Florida compatriots held in contempt, because they regarded the doctor as nothing more than a quack.[85]

In the years following the revolution, Bahamian-loyalist Indian traders and filibusters played pivotal roles in impacting the Indian Wars and military decisions of Andrew Jackson that led to the eventual establishment of the state of Florida. These events and other issues will be discussed in another chapter, when the role of the Bahama Islands in the emerging Atlantic economy will be presented.

3. THE EMERGING ATLANTIC ECONOMY

The Intrigues of Piracy and Privateering

The Bahamas, largely because of its geographic location at the crossroads of the Americas, played a pivotal role in shaping the course of the development of global commerce in the emerging Atlantic economy. During the sixteenth through the eighteenth centuries, the islands were consistently used (or allowed to be used) by various European (and later American) interest groups as a base from which the commercial activities of respective adversaries could be undermined, and from which some of the most infamous pirates and adventurous privateers operated. As noted in the previous chapter, some British politicians and influence peddlers plotted to use the colony as a base to undermine the expansionist policies of the United States.

The Bahamas, as with the rest of the British West Indies, does not have a depth of historiography comparable to that of the thirteen rebel mainland American colonies now known as the United States of America, because superior resources and favorable conditions of fate allowed the latter to develop into a significant industrialized nation boasting major metropolitan centers. On the other hand, the former British West Indies, which remained colonial possessions until the 1960s, evolved into a myriad of microstates with fragmented identities, demonstrating traditional traits of underdevelopment, poverty, and general social failures, all a direct consequence of centuries of excessive colonial exploitation. It is important to note, however, that any economic history of the emerging Atlantic economy must include reference to the Caribbean and The Bahamas, which were arguably indispensible to the development of the mainland colonies, and as such an appreciation of development in one is almost impossible without an appreciation for the other.[86] As Perkins notes, "The West Indies interacted with the mainland colonies in several ways; they served as major markets for colonial exports, particularly foodstuffs and wood products; they supplied a variety of goods that the continental colonist imported, processed, consumed, and re-exported; and they provided an important source of foreign exchange that helped balance colonial accounts and pay for British manufactures."[87]

The expansion of Europe into the Americas and the resulting effects of respective colonial commercial policies helped create a framework of mercantilism based on the belief that colonies existed primarily to enrich the parent country. Variations of this commercial policy were generally adopted by all the superpowers of that era, and the policy became the motivation for many of the policies and laws passed by the countries and enforced in their global possessions. In practical terms, the application of mercantilism was to establish trade arrangements under which colonies produced and exported raw materials to the parent country, from which finished products were produced and graded, with the higher quality goods traded to the more lucrative markets in the major metropolitan cities, while comparatively inferior goods were sent to the colonies, often on lines of credit that kept the colonists in perpetual economic servitude.[88]

Colonial industrialization was discouraged by the parent country through the enforcement of high tariffs, exorbitant taxes, and other restrictive laws intended to control the flow of the huge profits monopolized by the merchant investors. It was rejection of this policy of mercantilist protectionism without equitable representation (together with greed) and political expediency that encouraged piracy and privateering, and motivated colonial retaliatory actions such as the "Boston Tea Party" that eventually led to the American Revolution and subsequent attacks against Nassau, the Haitian Revolution, and the migration of thousands of émigrés to Philadelphia, New Orleans, and Nassau, and more directly related to this study, Bahamian interference in the implementation of the presumed American "manifest destiny" in the Floridas.

In 1763, at the close of the Seven Years War, Britain was saddled with a national exceeding £135,000 ($8.8 million). Impacting this debt was the continuing expense of defending the newly won territories of Canada, midwestern frontiers, and, most importantly, the Atlantic maritime trade routes, all of which required an additional £400,000 ($26 million) per annum. Tax rates in England had skyrocketed, with land taxes rising from 10% to 20%, arguably one of the highest in the world at that time. Prior to 1764, the colonial contribution to servicing of the national debt was practically negligible. The application of a series of Navigation Acts, intended to directly impact colonial trade and raise revenue through taxes on the importation of certain foreign products, was often ineffective. Perkins states that "colonists evaded the royal customs collectors or settled with them for a fraction of the total due; in Boston, [for example,] one-tenth was reportedly the standard rate for looking the other way."[89]

Gary Cash's research revealed significant facts about the level of urbanization of New England cities just before and immediately after the American Revolution.

According to Cash, until the 1740s, Boston was the leading commercial center in North America, and its merchant families were among the wealthiest on the continent. By the late colonial period, however, Philadelphia had emerged as the most active port city, boasting a population of some 30,000 residents, which was twice that of Boston. By 1770, the port of Philadelphia reportedly handled 15% more foreign commerce than Boston and had become a major clearing port for finished goods (legal and sometimes contraband) that were systematically distributed to shopkeepers in area towns and villages.[90] By 1770, New York had emerged as the third major port city, followed by Norfolk and Baltimore.

By the beginning of the American Revolution, the thirteen rebel colonies boasted a combined population estimated at 2.7 million, including 1.9 million whites, 520,000 blacks, and an estimated 100,000 Native Americans. The combined population was equal to almost 33% of that of Great Britain, with economic output comparable to almost 40% of that of the mother country. Still, the factor that significantly influenced the development of politics and economics in the Americas was the existence of colonies outside the mainland. The Bahamas is included in this equation primarily for the part that colony played as a significant entrepôt for the facilitation of pirate and privateering activities.

Acts of piracy and privateering in the Atlantic began in earnest during the Elizabethan Era (1558-1603) when England initiated an approach to counteract the policy of mercantilism imposed by Spain. The English developed a naval and merchant fleet capable of challenging the Spanish commercial monopoly in the Americas—the area they considered unjustifiably deeded to the Spanish by Pope Alexander VI under the terms of the Treaty of Tordesillas. The Spanish and Portuguese, as a result of their feats of exploration in the Orient and the Americas, had disputed the extent of their respective geographic spheres of sovereignty over these newly "discovered" lands. On May 4, 1493, the Pope settled the dispute by creating an imaginary line dissecting the mid-Atlantic within 100 leagues of the Cape Verde Islands. Spain was granted sovereignty over all unclaimed lands west of this line, and Portugal could possess lands east of the imaginary parallel. Of course, emerging superpowers England, Holland, and France rejected their exclusion from access to these potentially lucrative markets and formulated reactionary policies to circumvent the papal decree. The resultant English Trade and Navigation Acts gave orders-in-council to the Admiralty to both protect and promote English maritime interests. The French had adopted similar policies also designed to protect and promote their maritime interests. This authority, as we shall discuss later, provided opportunity for piracy and privateering through the issuance of Letters of Marquee and Reprisal.

A Letter of Marque and Reprisal was a government license authorizing a private vessel to attack and capture vessels belonging to the enemy, or in the process of providing aid to, or even suspected of giving potential aid to the enemy, as a national duty combining patriotism and profit. Admiralty courts were established to adjudicate cases of captured vessels and decide on the division of the spoils. The

French used the term *Lettre de Course,* which gave rise to the term *corsair*—a relatively small, easily maneuverable, heavily armed and crewed vessel almost exclusively intended for quick attack. The Letter of Marque, used by all major countries of the day, allowed vessels to ignore international borders in order to effect reprisal operations outside territorial borders. In times of peace, however, actions of reprisal once authorized by respective governments were condemned as acts of piracy. In most cases, for those engaged in the trade, the lines of authority were often blurred by the prospect of gaining enormous wealth.

Between 1774 and 1776, prohibitions on trade by the British and the American Congress, together with the closing of traditional markets, effectively curtailed foreign trade and subsequently created acute shortages in foreign goods. Congress attempted to enforce all trade restrictions through embargoes and boycotts. Once the fighting began, however, the restrictions were eased and eventually removed in April 1776, primarily to facilitate trade with France, the Caribbean, and the Bahama Islands. Preoccupation with military campaigns had the effect of slowing production in many states, while frontier warfare severely disrupted Indian trade. McCusker and Menard, commenting on the situation, state that

> the naval conflict crippled the New England fishery. Moreover, troop movements through settled areas interfered with farming, workers being called into service diminished the supply of labor and capital goods and resources once devoted to the export sector (such as sailing ships) were converted to meet the demands of war. Traditional markets in Great Britain and the British West Indies were closed and long-established trading partnerships suspended, with singularly severe consequences for the trade in foodstuff and for the shipbuilding industry, while British bounties on indigo and naval stores came to an abrupt end.[91]

Conditions of high taxes on freight and a significant decrease in ships available for commerce created imbalances in commodity trade. The economic recession in the mainland colonies that followed was alleviated, in part, by a vibrant, officially sanctioned and highly lucrative privateer industry that sometimes demonstrated traits of blatant piracy.

Piracy

George Woodbury, in his research on the subject of American frontier expansion, states the following concerning piracy:

> Much of [American] national history is written in terms of . . . westward-expanding frontier—that momentous century of migration from the eastern seaboard sweeping over prairie, plains, deserts, and mountains

toward the west. But this frontier and its development were preceded by
an earlier and quite as significant human migration. For the West Indies
were the frontier of Europe for three hundred years. It was a maritime
frontier, unique in history. Its pioneers were the same adventurous, often
outlaw, breed that gravitates toward all frontiers, but with a distinction:
they were seafaring men. The buccaneers and pirates of the Caribbean
were the counterparts of the "mountain men" and desperados of the
American West. The great national tree so portentously inclined in the
winning of the West had its first twig bent in the expansion of Europe into
the West Indies. One of the conspicuous features of that expansion was
the rise and development of piracy.[92]

Piracy, it should be noted, was established in antiquity, and well organized
centuries before Europeans imported the practice to the Atlantic. The Aegean Sea
was infested with pirates before the introduction of Christianity to the world stage,
and even the great Julius Caesar suffered capture by Aegean pirates and was freed
only after a handsome ransom was paid. Caesar's contemporary Pompey is reputed
to have waged an unrelenting and apparently successful war against piracy in the
Aegean Sea, eventually clearing the maritime routes from Rome to the Levant of
pirates.

The early settlement of the Bahama Islands was constantly interrupted by
sporadic Spanish and French raids designed to disrupt the development of English
settlements and discourage acts of indiscriminate wrecking and piracy by early
Bahamian settlers.[93] In 1684, a Spanish expedition of two hundred men from
Cuba inflicted a devastating attack against the colony, destroying the settlements
and capturing many settlers. Some settlers escaped by sailing to Casco Bay near
Portland, Maine, which in the early colonial period was part of the Province of
Massachusetts. They appealed to the residents of Massachusetts for help. In turn,
Governor Andros of Massachusetts was petitioned to intervene on behalf of the fifty
destitute Bahamians who had sought refuge in the town of North Yarmouth.

Riley's research includes a 1786 petition that tells the story of their plight:

> . . . in July last past, arrived at this Town of Boston from Eleuthera,
> one of the Bahama Islands, many families having been spoiled by the
> Spaniards of all their possessions and driven off naked and destitute, who
> on their arrival here were like to be continued charge unto this place.
> Your petitioners . . . made application upon the President and Council
> offering that if the interjacent land . . . might be granted unto us, who
> have each of us some land upon the place, that we would advance money
> for their support and supply and settlement on said land. We were pleased
> thereupon to have an order for removing the said distressed people
> unto that place, declaring they would recommend our request unto his

Majesty for his Royal favor therein. Whereupon we were at the charge
of removing them about *nine families* of the distressed people and have
been at considerable charge in furnishing them with necessaries for their
supply and support this winter.[94]

The Bahamian immigrants apparently barely survived the winter of 1786, for the
next year they again petitioned the government of Massachusetts for disaster relief,
complaining that their benefactors had reneged on their part of the bargain to
provide them with adequate relief assistance. Eventually, the disgruntled immigrants
returned to The Bahamas.

The brief sojourn of the Bahamians in Maine marks one of the earliest examples
of Bahamian migration to the United States. Why the group sailed past the Carolinas,
Virginia, and even Boston to Maine remains a mystery. Riley attempted to unravel
that mystery by suggesting that perhaps

> . . . it was because many of the Eleutherans were whalers, an occupation
> they had in common with New Englanders at the time . . . . It is reasonable
> to infer that at the Peace of 1783 American Loyalist refugees came [to
> the Bahamas] from New England to settle Eleuthera and Abaco . . . .
> New Englanders as well as Loyalists from other American colonies would
> naturally migrate to the areas where they had kin . . . . Since so many of
> the early Bahamians were seafarers, it is possible that they maintained
> a constant connection with the American colonies from the early days
> of settlement."[95] This assumption helps to explain to a large extent
> the connections established with the mainland that were necessary for
> Bahamians, especially Harbour Islanders to successfully facilitate black
> markets for goods purchased from pirates and eventual sale to merchants
> in and from New England during the period that became infamously
> known as the Golden Age of Piracy.

The Golden Age of Piracy lasted from 1715 to 1725 and involved perhaps no fewer
than seven thousand persons led by twenty to thirty captains, all generally acquainted
with each other through reputation and mutual service aboard merchant vessels
or pirate ships. Their common base of operation was the heretofore insignificant,
sometime-Spanish, often British colony of The Bahamas. As noted already, the
Bahama Islands are geographically located along the Florida Straits through which
eastbound and westbound Atlantic commerce sailed. New Providence harbor, in
particular, was well sheltered and could accommodate as many as five hundred of
the relatively small pirate ships, yet was too shallow to accommodate the much larger
ships of the European royal navies. The islands were sparsely inhabited and had a
loose form of governance; by 1716, however, New Providence had become a thriving
colony of about three thousand residents and visitors, catering primarily to the

social and commercial desires of the pirates. There, the pirates brought their prizes and auctioned of their cargoes to merchants who thrived from marketing the stolen goods. Most of the merchandise eventually was exported to markets in Jamaica, and to the mainland cities of Charleston, New York, Boston, and Philadelphia. Other goods, such as naval stores, sails, pitch, tallow, and cordage were kept for local trade among the nefarious brotherhood.

Most accounts associate the origin of piracy in the Bahama Islands with the auspicious arrival of Henry Avery in New Providence on April Fool's Day, 1696. Avery reportedly sailed into Nassau Harbor aboard a ship familiar to the local residents as a trading vessel from neighboring Harbour Island accompanied by a small crew all dressed in Indian and African attire. The delegation was escorted by the owner of the vessel, a well-known Harbor Island merchant, to the home of Governor Nicholas Trot. The strangers, who had arrived in the islands aboard the privateer *Fancy*, requested permission of the governor to enter the local harbor to rest, refit their vessel, and replenish supplies, all for a significant recompense. The strangers reportedly offered a personal gift to the governor of "twenty Spanish pieces of eight and two pieces of gold . . . a bribe worth some £860 at a time when a governor's annual salary was but £300. To top it off, the crew would also give him the *Fancy* herself, once they had unloaded and disposed of the (as yet) unspecified cargo."[96]

Trott reportedly convened an emergency meeting of the local council at which he outlined the conditions of the request and the advantages to the colony that could result, and he urged the members to agree to welcome the strangers as a blessing to the islands in a number of ways. In the absence of the minutes of that meeting, which were lost, one can presume that Trott argued that the presence of the strangers represented additional security for the island in terms of able-bodied, seasoned fighters, a well-armed ship to protect the harbor, and lots of money for merchants to make from patrons eager to pay generously for the services of women, wine, and song. The members agreed and the strangers were officially welcomed to Nassau.

Woodard described the events that followed that forever changed the course of business in The Bahamas:

> Not long after, a great ship rounded Hogg Island, her decks crowded with sailors, her sides pierced with gun ports, and her hull sunk low in the water under the weight of her cargo. Adams and his party were the first to come ashore, their longboat filled with bags and chests. The promised loot was there: a fortune in silver pieces of eight and golden coins minted in Arabia and beyond. Longboats ferried the landing party: ordinary-looking marines dressed in oriental finery, each bearing large parcels of gold, silver and jewels. The man calling himself Captain Bridgeman also came ashore and, after a closed meeting with Trott, turned the great warship over to him. When the governor arrived aboard the *Fancy* he found they had left

him a tip: The hold contained more than fifty tons of elephant tusks, 100 barrels of gunpowder, several chests filled with guns and muskets, and a remarkable collection of ship's anchors.[97]

Captain Bridgeman was actually Henry Avery, arguably the most successful pirate of his day, who was also one of the most wanted men in England. He had in essence gifted his pirate ship to a royal governor presumably for the defense of the colony and included a significant bribe, besides. During the ensuing days, the pirates were allowed unrestricted access to the island and its "tropical treasures," thus establishing conditions of cordiality between the Bahamians and the pirates and opening the doors for an expansion of that cordiality to others. Word of Avery's welcome in the Bahamas spread and influenced the subsequent actions of Benjamin Hornigold and his mate Edward Thatch, aka Blackbeard.

The end of the War of Spanish Succession in 1713 left thousands of sailors unemployed and destitute. Many who had served on privateers found themselves competing with thousands of others for scarce jobs on the few merchant ships still in operation, where wages were very low, and "those lucky to find work had to survive on twenty-two to twenty-eight shillings (£1.1 to £1.4) a month."[98] Those employed in the Caribbean were constantly harassed by the Spanish coast guard, which in its search for smugglers of goods from Spanish colonies, disrupted British shipping en route to and from Jamaica. An estimated thirty-eight Jamaican ships were confiscated between 1713 and 1715, costing the owners some £76,000 in losses.[99] Crews of confiscated ships were regularly incarcerated in jails in Cuba for months and sometimes years. Some were executed as examples to others of the illegality and consequences of smuggling from Spanish ports and of the futility of resisting arrest. Discouraged and mostly destitute, many Jamaican seamen decided to retaliate against the Spanish abuses by attacking Spanish shipping and enriching themselves in the process.

According to Woodard,

> By the summer of 1713, they [Horngold, Thatch and associates] had had enough of poverty and Spanish coast guards. Hornigold suggested to a number of former shipmates and drinking buddies that they put their skills together to solve both problems. They should go back to attacking Spanish shipping, avenging and enriching themselves at the same time. All they needed was a small vessel, a few good men, and a secure nest from which to launch their raids. Hornigold knew just the place . . . . The Bahamas, [which] every Jamaican knew, was a perfect buccaneering base.[100]

The Jamaicans reasoned that the Bahama Islands had no real government to prosecute them for violations of Spanish maritime trade since the joint Spanish-French invasion of 1703 had devastated the island and scattered its residents. In 1713, many sailed from Port Royal for the Bahamas, thus establishing the humble beginnings of what was to evolve into virtually a pirate republic in The Bahamas.[101]

The pirates, fewer than one hundred strong, organized themselves into three groups of twenty-five each, headed by Hornigold, John West, and John Cockram, respectively. Armed with cutlasses, muskets, pikes, and cudgels, the men engaged initially in small-time piracy, attacking lightly armed Spanish trading ships and small plantations located along the shores of Spanish Florida and Cuba. The level of their success was apparent in news of the pirates' feats recorded in New England newspapers. A report in the *Boston News-Letter* of 1714 noted that the pirates returned to Nassau with prize that included slaves, bales of expensive linens from Prussia, Asian silks, and a assortment of rum, sugar, copper, and silver coins, together valued in excess of £13,000, many times more than the annual imports of the sister Atlantic colony of Bermuda.[102] The pirates needed a means of fencing their stolen goods without the trouble of traveling the 450 miles south to Jamaica, which was a treacherous journey even for them, and where Jamaicans officials might demand exorbitant sums as bribery for protection. Fortunately for them, they were accommodated by a few wealthy Harbour Islands merchants who had no love of the Spanish and even fewer scruples about turning a quick profit by any means necessary.

Harbour Island lay some fifty miles north of New Providence and in the early 1700s boasted a population of about two hundred. The village, so named for its large, well-sheltered harbor, lay on the northeastern coast of the mainland of Eleuthera. The capital of the village is still Dunmore Town, named in honor of the former governor of Virginia and later the Bahamas, the Earl of Dunmore, who maintained a summer home there. The geographical location of Harbour Island in close proximity to the other main islands of the colony and to the mainland American colonies influenced its role in the development of early Bahamian maritime trade and migration. By the 1640s, the island was used by sailors as a significant navigational landmark for plotting travel between New England and the West Indies. Jim and Anne Lawlor contend that, "despite its diminutive one and a half square miles, Harbour Island was well known to the traders and mariners plying the Atlantic waters in the eighteenth century."[103] Interestingly, one of the earliest maps of Harbour Island was contained in a manuscript by John Cockram, the former deputy of pirate chief Hornigold, who became a well-respected member of society, marrying the daughter of the wealthiest of the local Harbour Island merchants, Richard Thompson.

Harbour Island deputy governor Richard Thompson was one of several wealthy merchants who were also traders of legal and illegal goods sold to and purchased from pirates, some of which were destined for New England markets. Thompson reportedly operated a lucrative trade from Harbor Island, where pirated goods were shipped to the Carolinas and sugar and provisions were imported back to the Bahamas with the concurrence of the residents, who "welcomed the pirate presence . . . as it added a measure of security to the island against constant incursions by the Spanish . . . . Thus in the absence of government to protect them from the harsh reality of their Spanish foes, the Harbour Island people had little choice but to embrace the pirates."[104]

Virginia governor Alexander Spotswood warned that the Bahama Islands had become "a nest of pirates[, a situation which would] prove dangerous to British commerce if not timely repressed."[105] The governor of Jamaica lamented that the economy of his island and that of neighboring Hispaniola were virtually crippled by pirates who had attacked and captured more than half of the ships destined for those ports.[106] Even the British Royal Navy was challenged by the intensity of the pirates' attacks. The captain of the six-gun sloop *Swift* reportedly was afraid to venture out of Port Royal, and Leeward Islands. Ann and Jim Lowlar notes that the "Governor Walter Hamilton was forced to cancel an official tour of the Virgin Islands on the sixth-rate frigate HMS *Seaford* for fear they would be captured by pirates."[107] By 1717, a number of American-based ships from Boston were reported at Harbour Island with the intent of selling provisional supplies to the resident pirates, who "were frequently coming and going to purchase provisions for the pirate vessels at Providence."[108]

From the Bahama Islands, practically every major pirate launched numerous attacks against American shipping, and few colonies were spared the ravages of piracy. Hornigold and Blackbeard achieved their initial success as partners in waters off the coasts of Delaware and Virginia. In May 1718, Blackbeard terrorized Charleston, holding the city hostage in what later became known as Blackbeard's Blockade of Charleston. Governor Johnson reported the events of that fateful day to the Council of Trade and Plantations:

> The unspeakable calamity this poor Province suffers from pyrats obliges me to inform your Lordships of it in order that his Majestie may know it and be induced to afford us the assistance of a frigate or two to cruse hereabouts upon them for we are continually alarmed and our ships taken to the utter ruin of our trade; twice since my coming here in 9 months they lain of our barr taleing and plundering all ships that either goe or come in to this port, about 14 days ago 4 sail of them appeared in sight of Town tooke our pilot boat and afterwards 8 or 9 sail with several of the best inhabitants of this place on board and then sent me word if I did not immediately send then a chest of medicines they would put every prisoner to death which for their sakes being complied with after plundering them all they had were sent ashore almost naked. This company is commanded by one Teach alias Blackbeard has a ship of 40 od guns under him and 3 sloopes tenders besides and in all above 400 men.[109]

In June 1718, Blackbeard left South Carolina with his medicine, taking cargo from all the ships in port he could plunder and sailing for the friendly shores of North Carolina and the protection of its governor Eden, from whom he was sure "he could obtain a pardon for this heinous act . . . . He was sure Governor Eden still welcomed rogues such as himself." And he was right. Since North Carolina had no cash crops, the pirates were too good for the economy to be turned away. The buccaneers sold their ill-gotten goods at a deep discount to the citizen, while they, in turn, sold their goods and services to the pirates.[110]

The alleged relationship between Governor Eden and Blackbeard is the subject of speculation and lore, yet there is evidence suggesting they were "business associates" and perhaps even friends. Legend has it that a tunnel ran from the basement of the governor's mansion to Bath Town Creek, where smuggled goods were stored for redistribution. Blackbeard temporarily lived on a farm just outside Bath, and ironically (or coincidentally), the governor's mansion was reportedly situated between Blackbeard's farm and the home of Tobias Knight, the collector of customs. Allegedly, the governor performed one of Blackbeard's many weddings, to the daughter of a local planter.[111] Blackbeard attacked and seized two French merchant ships sailing out of Martinique carrying a cargo that included sugar and cocoa, items scarce in North Carolina. He presented the prize to the authorities at North Carolina with the story that he had just happened to find the ship deserted and took possession of it. Both the customs collector and the governor accepted the story, "declared the ship a derelict, and the three split the booty."[112]

Blackbeard established a base for his smuggling activities on Ocracoke Island, located in the Outer Banks barrier islands of North Carolina. There, he reportedly threw a huge party that attracted pirates from throughout the region:

> Notorious pirates such as Calico Jack Rackman and Charles Vane began arriving at Ocracoke Island. It soon became the site of a huge continual party that has also been described as the 'Orcracoke Orgy'. For one week, the biggest gathering of pirates on the eastern seaboard took place . . . . Good food, lots of drink, and anything desired was plentiful. Wild and wicked sea villains chased women around the beach, while musicians played all night . . . . Panic spread that Ocracoke was to be the new pirate headquarters, replacing former safe havens Madagascar and the Bahamas.[113]

After a week of revelry, however, the pirates left Blackbeard alone in his North Carolina headquarters, some perhaps aware that plans were underway to rid the Americas of pirates. While piracy created employment opportunity for many unemployed seamen and stimulated the economy of many colonies, residents had grown increasingly tired of living in fear of the often unscrupulously cruel plunderers. Prominent citizens and high-ranking officials began to protest the illegal trade. In the Bahamas, for example, Thomas Walker led the charge against piracy.

Thomas Walker served as a judge in the Bahamian Vice-Admiralty Court, and later as acting deputy governor. Walker's story is interesting for several reasons, not the least of which was his marriage to a free black woman. From this marriage, mulatto children Thomas Jr., Neal, Charles, and Sarah were born. Young Sarah eventually married William Fairfax, for whom Fairfax County, Virginia is named. Their daughter Anne, who married Lawrence Washington, brother of George Washington, was for several years surreptitiously, albeit awkwardly, allegedly the mistress of the first president of the United States of America.[114] Thomas Walker waged an unrelentless war against piracy in the Bahama Islands, dispatching letters of protest to "everyone he could think of—the lords of the admiralty, the lords of trade, the Duke of Beaufort, and the other Proprietors of the Bahamas, even the *Boston News-Letter*—informing them of the increasingly dangerous situation [and threatening that] . . . Until a new governor was appointed, he would take it upon himself to 'curb the exorbitant tempters of some of the people of these islands and to execute justice upon Piratts.'"[115]

Protests came from official quarters on the mainland as well. Governor Spotswood of Virginia began a crusade against piracy, especially against Blackbeard, by sending repeated correspondence to London containing reports of the villainy of the pirate, in hopes of soliciting assistance from the Royal Navy. Governor Johnson of South Carolina, embarrassed by the pirate assault of 1718 on his town, collaborated with Spotswood to rid the area of pirates. In response, the British government commissioned Captain Woodes Rogers, a former pirate, with the following official instructions: "Whereas by reason of the great neglect of the Proprietors of the Bahama Islands, the said islands are exposed to be plundered and ravaged by pirates and others, and are in danger of being lost from our Crown of Great Britain . . . . We . . . By these present do constitute and appoint you, Woodes Rogers, to be Our Captain General and Governor in Chief."[116] The commission of Rogers signaled the beginning of the end for piracy in the Atlantic. Blackbeard was killed in battle with the Royal Navy off the coast of South Carolina. William Fly was convicted in a Boston court and, together with his pirate crew, executed, after which their tarred corpses were publicly displayed near Boston Harbor. Stede Bonnet, the "Gentleman Pirate," and most of his men were hanged at White Point in Charleston, Carolina.

Some pirates were more fortunate and lived respectable and successful lives in their communities. One such case is that of Thomas Tew, one of the few pirates who held the distinction of being an American, from Newport, Rhode Island, and who made a fortune raiding ships in the Indian Ocean. In April 1694, Tew and his crew returned to Newport to a hero's reception: "The seamen were welcomed like conquering heroes. The success they had achieved was stupendous. The local economy flourished with the influx of trade. Governor Fletcher became a good friend of Tew's, reveling in his stories at sea . . . . With his wealth, the sea robber established his own shipping fleet with vessels in North Carolina, New York, Pennsylvania, and Rhode Island."[117] In similar fashion, pirate Captain John Redfield benefited from absconding with Captain Kidd's buried treasure. He and his bride moved to Charleston, where they secured palatial dwellings in one of the most upscale districts. The community presumably assumed Redfield had secured his immense wealth through shrewd business dealings. Freelance piracy, historically considered to have ended in the 1720s, was to be replaced by a legal form of piracy that, among other things, brought great stimulus to the depressed Atlantic economy and created many of America's institutions of wealth.

Privateering

Events of the American Revolution demonstrated the effectiveness of the fledgling American Navy in successfully confronting the British government and its powerful Royal Navy through the use of privateering as a major response to the excess of imports over exports and severe imbalance in commodities the British policy of mercantilism tried to force on the Atlantic colonies. In the final analysis, privateering became a potent weapon used by the rebels to thwart British military and economic designs for the colonies and stimulate the American economy. McCusker and Menard drew on the research of several papers on the subject to sum up the situation:

> Privateering emerged as a major American enterprise during the war; over the entire conflict, Great Britain lost 2,000 vessels and 12,000 sailors. The lost vessels, with their cargoes, were worth an estimated £18,000,000 sterling. At such levels, privateering gave an enormous boost to an economy staggering under the impact of wars and also made major contributions to the war effort. By diverting the British naval fleet away from military action and toward the protection of commerce and by capturing military stores, privateering had a destructive effect on British shipping. In addition, privateering supplied consumers with a variety of goods, provided employment for ships and seamen, expanded the size of the American fleet, and earned impressive fortunes for enterprising merchants and ship captains.[118]

Patton, in his work *Patriot Pirates* (2008), writes that during the American Revolution, more than two thousand private ships were commissioned by Congress to prey on enemy shipping. The mostly merchant vessels were converted into fast-sailing and easily maneuverable warships that defied the British Royal Navy, arguably the greatest maritime power of the age, and plundered enemy merchant shipping in a massive seaborne insurgency that significantly interrupted British commerce, contributed to increased economic recession in the mother colony, and helped to pave the way to American independence. Patton notes that privateering impacted all categories of social and economic life in the colonies, giving rise to a network of merchants and brokers who bought and sold captured goods, often without scruples, but from which fortunes were made by many who speculated in that market. He cites instances where sailors made more money in one month of privateering than they otherwise made in one year. The author concludes that the genesis of the fortunes of some of New England's more renowned families hail back to this period.[119]

Molyneux Shuldham, former governor of Newfoundland and a vice admiral of the Royal Navy, replaced Admiral Graves as head of British naval forces in the Atlantic. This was a face-saving move in the wake of the embarrassing success of the American privateers against the formidable Royal Navy in the bold capture of the *Nancy*. The capture of the *Nancy*, a 250-ton British munition supply vessel, while downplayed by the British press, was cause for celebration in America. General George Washington commented on the occasion that "Surely nothing ever came more apropos."[120] Patton noted that some Americans derisively applauded the move: "What excuse can be found for a British admiral who tamely and supinely looks on and sees fishing schooners, whaleboats and canoes riding triumphant under the muzzles of his guns and carrying off every supply destined for your [British military] relief?"[121] The rebels were successfully challenging the British policy that allowed any American vessel, whether military or privately owned, to be seized "during the continuance of the rebellion."[122]

Shuldham was directed to evacuate British naval forces from Boston as well as the one hundred ships stationed at Staten Island, New York, to stations in the south, including the Caribbean and the Bahamas. This change in policy was designed primarily to address the shift in maritime warfare from the northern colonies to the Caribbean. During the course of the war, Britain systematically channeled thousands of troops and tons of munitions from bases established in Jamaica, Antigua, and the Bahamas, with the situation becoming a virtual chanced roll of the dice:

> Waters from Trinidad to Canada teemed with warships and transports under opposing flags chasing or fleeing one another. Captured British prizes were sailed to Massachusetts for trial, American prizes to Antigua or Halifax. On the way, all were vulnerable to recapture and redirection to any enemy port; and all, quite commonly given the great distances involved, might be recaptured yet again, requiring the courts to balance claims and counterclaims in order fairly to distribute prize money.[123]

The U.S. involvement in promotion of privateering during the American Revolution is a story worth recounting that revealed acts of conspiracy to advance the cause of revolution and amass personal fortunes at the same time. Central to all this intrigue was the indomitable statesman Robert Morris, a member of the Secret Committee for Trade and the Committee of Secret Correspondence, the latter established to promote and maintain a Franco-American *entente cordiale*. A prominent and ambitious Philadelphia merchant, Morris became the financial guru of the Revolution, first helping to outfit Washington's fledgling Continental Army through his vast European business contacts. Later, as Superintendent of Finances, "he would keep the American economy afloat by stabilizing its worthless currency through a juggling act of money austerity, foreign trade, hat-in-hand international borrowing, and cash infusion from his own holdings."[124]

In 1776, Morris influenced Congress to appoint Silas Deane as undercover emissary to Paris, and William Bingham as an undercover private business operative to the French authorities in Martinique. The job of the latter was to "secure military wares for shipment home on Congress' account, disseminate American propaganda and upbeat reports to French officials, and begin monitoring activities of the French fleet in the West Indies" to determine whether the French intended to harm or help the rebel cause.[125] Although only twenty-four years old at the time, Bingham, who was from a wealthy family, was well educated and cautiously efficient in the execution of his duties, displaying none of the traits of financial speculation exhibited by Silas Deane.[126] Nevertheless, he arranged for the shipment of a mixed load of munitions for the patriot cause and housewares for Morris, earning him a personal commission of some £742. This transaction "set him on a course to become, on his return to Philadelphia four years later, one of the richest men in America at age twenty-eight."[127]

The intrigue that followed in the wake of the establishment of this clandestine American official yet private venture foreshadowed the role Morris was to epitomize as the public official who speculated with government money and manipulated prices to increase commissions in what the Virginia-born diplomat Arthur Lee not so subtly insinuated was "some deep design against our independence at the bottom. Many factions are, I know, actuated by the desire of getting or retaining the public plunder."[128]

The role of the French in the American affair is easy to understand when one pauses to consider the depth of French antipathy toward the British over its ignoble defeat in the Seven Years War and the national humiliation following the signing of the Peace of Paris in 1763. Perhaps no Frenchman felt the sting of this humiliation more than Charles Gravier, Comte de Vergennes, French foreign minister, and arguably the most powerful man in France. It was to Vergennes that Silas Deane was sent under the most clandestine circumstances:

> His [Deane's] assignment was twofold. First, he was to arrange weapons shipments from French suppliers on the promise of future remittance with American commodities, which is to say on unsecured credit extended to lone agent who had few funds, no official title, no political power, and no authorization from the full Congress, which had been kept in the dark about his mission. Second, he was to parlay a letter of introduction from Benjamin Franklin, internationally famous for his study of electricity, into face-to-face meetings with French officials in order to gauge their willingness to strike a military and commercial alliance with America.[129]

The French response to Deane's overtures was equally clandestine and without full and proper authorization. Vergennes convinced French king Louis XVI that to assist the American cause was in the interest of France, and any initiative to distract or even weaken British prominence in the Americas was beneficial to French political and commercial interests; however, the French king, only nineteen at the time, was not prepared to openly interfere in the Anglo-British conflict for fear that French intervention at that time would disrupt the delicate balance of power and international neutrality agreements officially governing the affairs of the European powers. The wily, fifty-eight-year-old Comte de Vergennes, however, was prepared to manipulate French foreign policy, otherwise.

> Out of deference to his monarch's sensitivities . . . the foreign minister couldn't yet openly back the American rebellion . . . . Even before meeting Deane he'd approved a loan of 1 million livres (about $10 million) to Roderigue Hortalez & Company, a dummy firm created to funnel covert aid to America. Spain, as eager as France to see Britain beaten, matched the loan, as did a consortium of friends of the company's founder, Pierre-Augustin Caron de Beaumarchais."[130]

The intrigue and apparent conflict of interests deepened in May 1776, when a Spanish ship, intercepted and boarded by Maryland privateers in Delaware Bay, was found to have strongboxes hidden in its hold bearing the marks WM and containing $14,000, presumably the property of the Willing and Morris Company. Patton commented on the event and the public apathy applied:

> Willing, Morris & Company was a Philadelphia merchant house named for its founder, Thomas Willing, and for Robert Morris, the Liverpool-born financial wizard Willing had plucked at age twenty from the counting room and made partner in 1754. Concealing its money in the hold of a foreign ship caused no great surprise. The firm was known to engage in extensive trade on behalf of Congress, one-fourth of whose cash disbursements between 1775 and 1777 went to one company—Willing & Morris. No one expected the breadth of the trade to be limited by the fact that Morris ran Congress' procurement efforts through the Secret Committee, negotiating with himself in many transactions.[131]

Morris, through the influences of his public offices, used Silas Deane and the Willing, Morris business connection to personally amass a considerable fortune. In a letter, he encouraged Deane to facilitate the trade for the cause and make a fortune for himself, "citing huge markups on 'every kind of goods' and also on the ships that delivered them (by 1777 merchants and private investors, who sought to convert them to warships, were paying £4,000 for vessels that months earlier had gone for

£1,000), [Morris] urged Deane's 'utmost exertion' in dispatching European cargoes '2/3ds on account of Willing, Morris & Company and 1/3d on your account.'"[132]

Deane, after some disappointments, responded to the appeal of his political master with unparalleled success. In 1777, with the assistance of Beaumarchais, he was able to secure and send eight military transport ships to Boston. The first two ships to arrive, *Amphitrite* and *Mercury*, brought "no less than thirty thousand stands of arms, four hundred tons of gunpowder, five thousand tents, and sixty-four pieces of field artillery."[133] The significant value of the shipments of supplies to the patriot cause is reflected in the words of John Bradford to John Hancock as he reviewed the inventory in Boston, calling the shipment "a smile of heaven on us, for we were really distressed for want of them."[134] Congress paid for the shipment of war supplies by reloading the transport ships with lumber and tobacco, valued at more than 4 million livres, which was received in France as remuneration via Hortalez & Company.

The significance of the shipments of 1777, and in particular the French-manufactured field artillery, was demonstrated in the Battle of Saratoga. American general Gates used French cannons to defeat a British force and capture some six thousand British soldiers and forty-two British cannons, marking the greatest American victory in the war to that point, causing stocks on the British stock market to fall sharply and British Parliament to reconsider its policy on the American agenda:

> After Saratoga, the French-American negotiation took a new dynamic. The British position clearly had weakened, improving the likelihood that peace offers might follow . . . . British officials in London decided to float the possibility, through secret contacts with the commissioners of reconciling with America. The concessions in mind were short of total independence but offered much of the political and economy autonomy the colonist had sought at the start of the war.[135]

As the British military campaign in New England stalled, Whitehall gave increasingly serious consideration to shifting the campaign to the south and southwest, where the growing Native American confederation held the promise of distraction and the possibility of stretching of rebel resources.

Bahamians, Native Americans, and Old Southwest Trade Alliances

During the American Revolution and its aftermath, the political fate of "Florida" was significantly impacted by competing economic struggles that at times were instigated by Bahamas-based vested interests for dominance of the lucrative Native American trade markets. In 1763, Britain divided the vast territory known as Florida into East Florida and West Florida, a division retained by the Spanish when they regained the territory in 1783. West Florida, in particular, was geographically extensive and highly coveted, spreading from the Apalachicola River to the Mississippi River. Most of the area was traditionally populated by Native Americans, mainly Creek, Cherokee, Chickasaw, Choctaw, and Seminole. In the eighteenth century, the most powerful Native Americans in the southeast were the Creeks and Seminoles, who collectively were known as Muscogulges. These peoples were primarily hunters and gatherers who since early Spanish encounter had adopted aspects of European material culture and adjusted to whites and blacks living among them. It was the commercial hunting importance of this people and their inherent reluctance to succumb to white authority that became the subject of international intrigue and led to the Jacksonian purges.

According to Wright,

> Many Americans in the Southeast . . . fought for, rather than against George III, and after 1783, despite their defeat, they still were the typical whites who lived among the Muscogulges. Their presence illustrated that though Britain had lost much of her political control over the southeastern Indians she still dominated their economy, and her influence over the Indians was considerable. Muscogulges had not been much concerned with the Boston Tea Party and taxation without representation, but they understood clearly enough that after 1783 some English—speaking whites disliked each other and were now rivals, subjects of either the United States or of Britain. In an attempt to escape from being treated as inferiors or dependents and to retain their culture and lands, Muscogulges played off British subjects against citizens of the United States.[136]

Early trade of Muscogulges with Europeans centered primarily on the exchange of manufactured goods for mostly Native Americans slaves and peltry. Peltry commodities included the skins, hides, and meat of raccoon, bear, buffalo, and beaver and the highly prized white-tailed deer. Wright notes, "Many Europeans had gone to the West Indies, Africa, and the Far East in search of sugar, slaves, and tea . . . . In the Muscogulge country, however, . . . it was deerskins that enticed Europeans; and southeastern Indians, whose numbers had finally stabilized and perhaps even were growing, consumed their share of European wares."[137] Growing European and American market demands saw an increase in the trade of deerskin leather used in the production of clothing, saddles, harnesses, whips, and aprons, and the employment of thousands of Native Americans, blacks, and whites in the industry. The magnitude of the peltry trade is noted in recorded data, which indicate that "on the eve of the American Revolution 250,000 pounds of deerskin—306,000 pounds in 1768—most of which came from the Creeks, were exported annually from Georgia, and those exports approximately equaled those of Charleston."[138]

It was into this milieu of conflicting territorial claims and lucrative trade alliances that William Augustus Bowles attempted to create a Muskogee state independent of both European and American control.

William Bowles, also known as Estajoca and sometimes affectionately called Billy Bowlegs, was a Maryland-born adventurer who, with the assistance of British interest-groups in the Bahamas, successfully organized groups of Native Americans into a short-lived confederation in northern Florida known as the State of Muskogee. Bowles was attached to the British Army during the American Revolution reportedly when only thirteen years old. In 1781, while stationed at the garrison of Pensacola, he absconded from the fortification to escape punishment for an alleged charge of subordination. Outside the garrison, Bowles eventually made his way to the safety of the Indian country north of Pensacola, where he subsequently married the daughter of a chief of the Creek Nation and very early began to wield increasing influence in that community.[139] For an uncertain period of time, Bowles lived in the Bahamas, from where he launched his campaigns against the Spanish and, more specifically, initiated plans to smash the trade monopoly with the Native Americans traditionally enjoyed by Panton, Leslie & Company.[140]

In 1781, Spanish forces attacked British garrisons along the Gulf coast in an attempt to recapture areas of Spanish Florida encroached upon by the British. Bowles convinced his Creek allies to support the British against the Spanish; the fall of the British garrison at Pensacola, however, was a devastating blow that forced Bowles and the few survivors of the attack to make a hasty retreat into the woods. Bowles soon afterward migrated to the Bahamas. At that time Bowles was either sixteen or seventeen years old. In the Bahamas, Bowles plotted with local interest groups anxious to undermine the economic monopoly long sustained by the Panton, Leslie & Company.

Between 1788 and 1799, Bowles led several expeditions from the Bahamas into Florida, where he organized the Creeks and Seminoles into the confederate State of Muscoge, declaring himself "director general" on account of his marriage into the royalty of the Creek Nation. In 1790, Bowles led an entourage from the "independent State of Muscoge" to London to seek British political recognition for his cause. He conferred with British home secretary William Grenville, outlining his plans to use his position of "director general" to establish free ports accessible to British commerce and to establish direct trade with Nassau and a useful alliance with the British as a result. Grenville reportedly saw merit in Bowles's schemes, and insofar as political decorum permitted, he encouraged the director general to pursue his ambitions. While advising Bowles against expecting open aid, the home secretary stretched the intent of the Free Port Act of 1787 to assure him that ships flying the Muskogee ensign would be welcomed in Nassau.[141]

Bowles declared war against Spain and began to lead and support other privateers in preying on Spanish commerce. His forces soon included two ships and four hundred men, including runaway slaves and Native Americans; however, there were signs that Bowles's position was under threat of being surreptitiously destroyed. Nassau merchant and trusted Bowles supporter John DeLacy sailed to the mouth of the Apalachicola River, presumably to warn Bowles of the turn in political events and of dangerous elements seeking his demise. In actuality, DeLacy was a spy who, with other Nassau merchants, had found the turn of events increasingly unfavorable and determined Bowles to be expendable. They colluded to use any means necessary to protect their threatened economic and political interests by selling Bowles out to the Spanish.

DeLacy had been in contact with some of Bowles's Native American allies and convinced them to abandon Bowles and form a new political alliance with the Spanish and a trade alliance with the "other" Nassau merchants. In August 1802, major Seminole groups signed a treaty with the Spanish at Apalache.[142] In the spring of 1803, the Native Americans of the southeast called a congress at Hickory Ground, near present-day Montgomery, Alabama, to discuss the ever-changing political and economic landscape in West Florida and the implications of the changes for their future. The meeting was attended by a delegation of Bahamian traders led by John Forbes and none other than the indomitable William Augustus Bowles.

Britain signed the Peace of Amiens with France and Spain just as Bowles was engaged in a siege of the Spanish fort at Apalache, creating a reversal of fortune for the adventurer and privateer; it dashed his hopes for continued British support in more ways than one. First, the peace agreement meant that the Bahamas could no longer legally provide support as a haven for outfitting and supplying his cause. Second, the East Florida Loyalists succeeded in having Lord Dunmore, Bowles's political patron, replaced by Robert Hunt as interim governor of the colony. Third, the Spanish promised a reward for his capture, enticing even his Native American allies to betray him. He was eventually captured, but he was first courted by the Spanish to change alliances and support them against American interlopers. Bowles reportedly spurned these overtures, escaped, and continued his hostilities until he was recaptured with the assistance of disenchanted Creeks eager to collect the reward money and jealous of Bowles's influence in their circles. Bowles was incarcerated in the Spanish fortress Castillo San Felipe del Morro in Havana and eventually died in 1805 in a military hospital.[143]

The Bahamian connection with William Augustus Bowles provides interesting insights into the political and economic order of the day in that island colony on several accounts. First, as governor of the Bahama Islands, Lord Dunmore supported Bowles's ambitions because they dovetailed with his own personal political and economic schemes, which essentially were to promote campaigns against the Spanish that would drive them from Florida, paving the way for Dunmore and his cohorts to reestablish British authority in the region, after which a grateful Crown would grant the schemers massive land grants and associated monopolies on mining, forestry, and other trade concessions. Consequently, Bowles's expeditions were outfitted in the Bahamas with supplies and trade goods, uninterrupted. Second, there was no love lost between Dunmore and the Board of American Loyalists, the group of primarily East Florida Loyalist immigrants to the Bahamas, whose primary objective was to have Dunmore removed from the colony and replaced with a governor more sympathetic to their plans to control affairs in the colony by any means necessary. And in this regard, they met publicly at the Nassau home of sympathizer William Panton of the firm Panton, Leslie & Company to discuss their varied schemes to claim their inalienable rights "for which they had left their homes and possessions."[144] Conversely, a rival Bahamian trading company comprising mostly West Florida Loyalist refugee investors had the backing of Governor Dunmore and was determined to destroy the Panton Company's Indian trade in Florida.

Panton, Leslie, & Company was the leading "Indian" trading company in southeastern North America in the late eighteenth century. The company, named for Loyalist principals William Panton, Robert Leslie, and four other merchants, had a long-term contract to trade with the southeastern Native Americans. During the American Revolution, William Panton was among thousands of merchants from South Carolina and Georgia forced to leave behind confiscated possessions and flee for refuge in East Florida. Wright commented on the situation:

> During the Revolution, Pensacola had replaced Charleston as the most important port in the southern Indian trade and was the reason that William Panton moved from St. Augustine in East Florida to Pensacola in West Florida at the end of the Revolution. It became the firm's principal establishment on the American mainland. Packhorse trains loaded with munitions, rum, and an assortment of goods were outfitted here and at the company's other warehouses and made their way to Indian villages in the interior, returning with deerskins, furs, bear oil, honey, and foodstuffs. The company's agents, or factors, maintained truckhouses (stores) in Indian villages scattered from the Florida peninsula to the Mississippi River and from the Gulf coast to Lookout Mountain, Tennessee.[145]

Initially, the Spanish authorized Panton, Leslie & Company to trade goods to the Muscogulge people and gave other British merchants at Mobile and New Orleans similar trade rights with the Choctaw and Chicktaw. Over time, however, the Panton firm pushed westward beyond St. Augustine toward Pensacola, Mobile, and eventually the Mississippi River, incorporating most of the Native American trade along the way in an ironclad monopoly that became the envy of other established or want-to-be trading firms. The firm became owners of extensive land grants of huge acreages in towns and cities scattered throughout Spanish Florida. Outside the United States, the firm operated a massive warehouse in Nassau located on Union Street (now Elizabeth Avenue) in which the majority of goods purchased from markets in the southeast were stored for redistribution in mainland markets. Some goods were sold in bulk to local Bahamian merchants for retail to smaller markets in Nassau and the outlying islands. The Bahamian enterprise was managed by John Forbes.

The significance of the economic dominance and political connections of the Panton, Leslie & Company trading firm is demonstrated in the case of the *Aurora*. In 1793, the *Aurora*, a Panton, Leslie & Company schooner, was captured by a French privateer and sent to Charleston as prize. Although it was condemned and valued at £4,000, it was processed through the French consular court, purchased by Panton, Leslie & Company associates, and resold to the Panton Company for a mere £150. The process was repeated two months later, when the *Aurora* was again recaptured transporting goods from the warehouse in Nassau to St. Augustine. This time, the goods valued at £5,000 were resold to the company for just over £3,000.[146]

Competition with the Panton, Leslie & Company trade monopoly came from a variety of interest groups, including Americans from Georgia and South Carolina either squeezed out or otherwise outright excluded from the trade, and from British merchants looking to compete. The role of Bahamian merchants in the trade wars is a matter of conspiracy and fascination:

> With limited success Georgians and South Carolinians after 1783 continued some of their prewar commerce, and in 1796 the United States established the first of its "factories" (subsidized warehouses) designed to capture the Indian market. British Loyalists who were not members of the Panton, Leslie and Company but who had traded with the southern Indians before 1783 were determined to continue their commerce with the Indians despite opposition from Panton and from Spain. Foremost in this group was John Miller, a member of the west Florida assembly, who fled from Pensacola in 1781 and at the end of the Revolution established himself in Nassau. Associated with him was young William Augustus Bowles . . . . Miller, Bowles, the Bahamian governor Lord Dunmore, and other uprooted loyalists hoped to make the Southeast a British protectorate or colony. Whether or not they succeeded in these political objectives, they expected to profit from trafficking with the Indians.[147]

In 1801, William Panton died and was buried on Great Cay in the Berry Islands, Bahamas. John Forbes, long Panton's protégé, emerged as head of operations, whereupon he immediately notified contacts on the mainland of the changing of the guard. Forbes requested the Spanish authorities to reaffirm their agreement with the company to allow continued trade in the southwest. Challenges to the trade monopoly, however, continued almost unabated, led in large part by rival Nassau-based merchants Joseph Hunter and John Delacy.

Joseph Hunter operated an illegal trade establishment in the St. Marks area on the Gulf, where he sold goods at prices lower than those of the Panton firm. He supported the Bowles's attacks against the Spanish fort at St. Marks, which, if successful, would have allowed him and other Bahamian merchants a safe harbor to facilitate their clandestine business. This security was necessary as attacks on the smugglers by Spanish patrol boats were increasing. In 1800 a Spanish patrol vessel chased Hunter and his crew, forcing them to ditch the vessel in Apaláchée Bay. Hunter survived the ordeal and eventually made his way back to Nassau. The following year, one of his ships carrying a cargo of dry goods and a cannon intended for delivery to Bowles was captured by the Spanish and confiscated. In a letter to Bowles, Hunter accused Forbes and Panton agents of informing the Spanish authorities of the movement of smugglers operating out of Nassau and as such the cause of his losses.[148]

John DeLacy, more ambitious than Hunter, had designs to replace the entire Panton southwest operation with one he would head. His intention was to undermine the Panton trade operation at Pensacola with the establishment of his own headquarters near the Chattahoochee River. In preparation for this goal, DeLacy traveled between the Native American communities of the southeast, sharing his plans with the Panton suppliers and promising them attractive business deals for their support of his venture. DeLacy kept his British supporters on the mainland and in the Bahamas interested with promises of millions of pounds sterling in sales of manufactured goods, once his scheme succeeded. He was careful to include Bowles in his plans as long as the latter proved useful. Bowles would become British superintendent of Indian Affairs if the British managed to reoccupy Florida. If the British failed, the Spanish authorities would be bribed to allow their ships to pass without incident.[149]

John Forbes, formerly apprentice to William Panton, mogul of Panton, Leslie & Company, assumed leadership of the firm in 1801 upon the death of his mentor. Interestingly, in 1765, Panton was an apprentice in the firm of John Gordon and Company of Charleston. Gordon was the maternal uncle to John Forbes, and one in a string of American-Scottish immigrants who established businesses in colonial America, and as Loyalists, migrated to the Bahamas. Through this network, John and his brother Thomas became associates of the Panton firm. Thomas died in 1808 at the age of fifty. A brief sketch of John's life in the Bahamas is provided by Coker and Watson:

> Forbes reached Nassau in 1783, where he directed the construction of
> the company warehouses to be used in the Florida Indian trade, before
> leaving for London . . . . Forbes returned to Nassau in December 1785, and
> immediately joined the fight between the "New Settler" and Old Settler
> factions. Before long he was known as one of the "outspoken leaders"
> of the New Settler faction and, as such, became involved in the turmoil
> of Bahamian politics following the arrival in 1787 of Lord Dunmore,
> former governor of Virginia. In 1789, Forbes was elected to the assembly
> and represented the island of Abaco until 1794. The new Governor,

John Forbes—no relation to Thomas Forbes—appointed Thomas to the council, where he remained from 1797 to 1807. He also served as a vestryman for the parish of Christ Church . . . . [D]uring the ensuing years, Forbes successfully conducted the business in Nassau, which served as an entropot for the company. Forbes owned several thousand acres of land scattered among the islands and cays in the Bahamas. He was obviously one of the most successful businessmen in the islands.[150]

The accounts of the activities of Bahamian business interests in southeastern America demonstrate the intimate knowledge these men had already acquired of life in those remote areas long before migration to the Bahamas. For example, it has been noted that Augustus Bowles moved with relative freedom and intimacy between the Bahamas and the Muscogulge peoples. Later, DeLacy reportedly held extensive meetings with Native American groups throughout the southeast in his bid to gain their support in undermining the Panton Company operation. And in 1803, Forbes attended the conference of southern Native Americans at the Hickory Grounds in hopes of negotiating the payment of outstanding debts owed by the native groups to the Panton Company. Equally interesting is the fact that Native Americans traveled to the Bahamas frequently and freely, as was later evidenced in the mission of the Muscogulge delegation to the Bahamian government in 1819 and in the case of the "Black Seminole" odyssey to Andros Island in the northern Bahamas in the 1850s.

With the inauguration of James Madison as president in 1808, the final results of the American Revolution were still virtually resolved, and relations between the United States and Britain remained unstable. Southern states had persuaded Congress to levy embargoes against British trade. The British government added to the intrigue by wavering between a need to reach an accommodation with the former colonist and a desire to form alliances with any Americans—red, white, or black—willing to collaborate in constricting the boundaries of the new republic and confining them to areas along the eastern seaboard or, even better, in systematic disunion. The situation took a decisive turn in 1812, however, when Britain and the United States once again went to war.

In 1812, the United States declared war on Britain for a number of reasons, including resentment of British embargoes and restrictions on American trade with France, the impressing of American sailors into the Royal Navy, the opportunity for American annexation of Canada, and British support for Native Americans resisting American internal continental expansion into their traditional homelands. For the first two years of the conflict, Britain adopted a defensive policy, when its forces moved to protect its empire. After the abdication of Napoleon and defeat of the French in 1814, however, the British adopted a more aggressive strategy that resulted in the British invasion and burning of Washington, D.C. At sea, warships and privateers repeatedly attacked opposing sides. More significant for this research, major land battles along the southern and Gulf coasts resulted in the almost wanton annihilation of British allied Native American communities by American forces. Americans were especially concerned about British support of the Shawnee leader, Tecumsech, and other militants, who had launched attacks against American settlers moving into the northwest hinterlands. Ironically, U.S. policy was based on a continued belief in "Manifest Destiny"—the inalienable right of the white American to the entire continental United States, despite the historical occupation of those regions, which include the modern states of Ohio, Indiana, Illinois, Michigan, and Wisconsin, by Native Americans for thousands of years.

By 1812, the Muscogulge trade alliance with the Panton Company, which at that time bore the name Forbes & Company, had waned following a shift in company alliance from British to American. The Revolution was over and the Americans appeared to be in a stronger commercial position to advance trade agreements with the firm. Forbes & Company began to steadily move the bulk of its business from Nassau back to the United States, creating a vacuum in the "Indian trade" that other interest groups were eager to fill. At the end of the War of 1812, Alexander Arbuthnot, Nassau merchant and trader, sought to fill that vacuum. He established a trading post at St. Marks on the site of the former Forbes & Company depot, and other stores at Tampa Bay and at Cedar Cay just below the mouth of the Suwannee River. The strategic location of these stores provided convenience for agents to send packhorses to deliver and collect supplies and for trade with independent traders.

Over time, as in the case of Augustus Bowles, Arbuthnot gained the confidence of many of the native people and was granted power of attorney by the leaders of the Creek Nation. He became the principal advisor on American and European matters, a position that was later to cost him his life. Over time, he wrote letters on behalf of the native people on matters impacting the fate of the Native Americans: "He wrote letters to the British minister in Washington and to authorities in London, insisting that the United States had blatantly violated the Treaty of Ghent by appropriating Indian lands. Britain should protest, reassert her presence among the southern Indians, appoint him or someone Indian superintendent, and consider acquiring the Floridas."[151] To hedge his bet against British reluctance or refusal to provide support, Arbuthnot wrote a similar letter to Spanish authorities in Havana.[152]

Arbuthnot encouraged a delegation of Native Americans to travel to London and directly petition the British authorities. In 1815 the delegation, led by Hillis Haya, Tuskeegee chief, traveled from the Apalachicola River to London, where they held discussions with King George III. The mission was apparently approved by British southeast authorities, because none other than Colonel Edward Nicholas, commander of British forces in the region, personally hosted the Native Americans at his home and facilitated their audience with the king. Hillis Haya described the plight of his people at the hands of the Americans and begged British intervention for their cause.[153] Despite the fervent pleas of the guests and the obvious American violation of their rights, the British were reluctant to publicly express support for the Native Americans. Instead, the delegation was dismissed with gifts of a silver pipe tomahawk for Hillis Haya, £100 to defray return travel expenses, and vague assurances of assistance at an appropriate time.

Arbuthnot advised other Native Americans to petition the British minister in Washington with limited results:

> Advised by Arbuthnot, [Tallahassee chief Peter] McQueen (Creek leader) wrote Minister Charles Bagot how American settlements at Tensaw and on the lower Chattahoochee had notoriously violated the Treaty of Ghent. Though sympathetic, Bagot was noncommittal, and when the [British] cabinet's position finally became clear, he refused to take any action. Nevertheless the possibility existed that Britain might have a change of heart, that the Union Jack might yet wave over Florida, and that King George might come to the rescue of his old Indian allies. This kept alive the hopes of McQueen, Hillis Haya, Kinache, Abraham, Garçon, and Savannah Jack.[154]

Alexander Arbuthnot was eventually captured by American forces and tried by Colonel Andrew Jackson for espionage and for inciting the Creeks to rebellion against the United States. He was convicted, condemned, and hanged from the yardarm of his own ship.

4. THE AMERICAN CIVIL WAR

The Bahamas and Blockade Running

Running blockades into Nassau during the American Civil War produced a tremendous increase in trade and in the price of consumer goods in the Bahamas. The practice also led to an increase in the local crime rate and sparked significant demographic shifts that began the rapid depopulation of the outer islands. Blockade runners flocked to Nassau in large numbers, increasing the demand for accommodations and hospitality services, and paving the way for the genesis of the now-flourishing Bahamian tourist industry. Relations between the Bahamas and the southern states, which were at an all-time low after the American Revolution, warmed as commercial and social fences were mended in the cozy and mutually beneficial accommodation of the lucrative trade. Once the conflict ended in 1865, the price of commodities, wages, and the crime rate plummeted to pre-Civil War levels. The demographic composition of the islands, however, remained virtually the same.

The American Civil War was waged between the predominantly northern states opposed to the institution of slavery and disunion of the states and the southern states that supported slavery and threatened disunion. Eleven southern states eventually formed the Confederate States of America and declared secession from the union. The Confederacy was supported by five "border states" that also favored slavery. In the 1860 presidential election, voters elected Republican Abraham Lincoln on an antislavery platform. Hostilities erupted on April 12, 1861, when Confederate forces launched an attack against Union forces stationed at Fort Sumter in South Carolina. Lincoln responded by organizing an army of volunteers from pro-Union states to recapture the fort. The president established a blockade of Confederate ports and borders, and in his famous Emancipation Proclamation, he announced the ending of slavery in the United States and cautioned against foreign intervention in the conflict.

The Union naval blockade, which took place between 1861 and 1865, was a monumental and often unsuccessful program to control access to and from the Atlantic and the Gulf coast of the Confederate states. Some five hundred ships were deployed specifically to patrol 3,500 miles of Confederate coastline, including that of Mobile and New Orleans on the Gulf, and the Atlantic ports of Richmond, Charleston, Savannah, and Wilmington. The Confederate response to the Union's economic stranglehold was to encourage small, high-speed boats known as blockade runners to operate between the Confederacy and the supposedly neutral ports of Havana, Cuba, Bermuda, and Nassau, Bahamas. Five out of every six ships reportedly evaded the blockade; however, the Union success lay in the fact that the small, fast boats had very limited cargo space, and during the conflict Confederate cotton exports, the economic lifeline of the south, fell 95%, from 10 million bales three years before the war to 500,000 bales during the blockade period.[155]

Mary Ellison notes that "The once calm surface of international trade was troubled by the ominous ripples of the self-imposed Southern embargo on its own cotton, as well as the Northern blockade of Southern ports."[156] According to Ellison, Lancashire and other English ports were hit hard by the cotton embargo and the blockade. This situation led to widespread unemployment and destitution. By 1862, as the majority of the English cotton mills were finding it increasingly difficult to function, thousands of unemployed were exerting pressure on their political representatives to provide "some kind of aid . . . to the South to help establish Confederate independence and so facilitate the renewal of the flow of cotton."[157]

Owsley states that the warning by Confederate secretary of state Robert Toombs of Georgia that the value of English manufacturing would fall by $600 million was based on the premise that shipments of Southern cotton to British mills would be terminated. This ominous prediction, Owsley states, was made because the Confederates believed that cotton was king in the real world of international relations.[158] Frank Merli notes that after war with the United States over the Trent affair had been averted, Britain tried to maintain strict neutrality. Merli claims that it was Confederate naval agents, scouring Europe in an attempt to purchase badly needed warships, who infringed on British neutrality and thus precipitated the international tension. The Confederate agents contracted warships in English shipyards and received such notable ships as the *Florida* in 1862 and the *Alabama* the following July.[159] The Southerners circumvented British laws of neutrality by purchasing British ships in England and having the ships armed and outfitted at other European ports that did not respect British or American laws of neutrality.

The complicity of some northern merchants to continue trade with the South was evident in the meat industry. Most of the meat supplied to the Confederacy was transported through the blockade from New York by way of Nassau, then reshipped to Confederate ports courtesy of the blockade runners. Interestingly, since the meat was sometimes spoiled in transit, Confederate officials actually debated the feasibility of establishing a meat-inspection agency in New York to protect their interests. It was common to find cases of meat hidden in cargoes of lard and salt and shipped to the Confederacy via Nassau.[160]

Blockade running was a lucrative business that tempted many to participate. According to Strickland, a runner made an average of three or four trips to sea before capture; however, some lucky runners made as many as eighteen trips.[161] One former blockade runner boasted that once a steamer had made the run to Charleston twice with merchandise, and out twice with cotton, enough profits could be made to cover losses sustained if the runner were afterward wrecked or captured by the Union navy.[162] Wait notes that a profit of $300,000 for a round trip was not uncommon, and one ship was known to have carried out 7,000 bales of cotton worth more than $2 million before it was caught.[163]

Bounties paid in sterling to officers and crews of runners were substantial. According to Bahamian runner Captain A Roberts, "a captain received £1,000; chief officers £250; second and third officers, £150; pilots, £750; crew and firemen, £50."[164] Half the total was received in Nassau before leaving port. Once paid, no one was allowed ashore for security reasons. The other half was paid when the mission was completed. Officers were allowed to stow small amounts of cargo for personal use or private sale, and captains were allowed to transport ten bales of cotton; pilots, five bales. Crews took it upon themselves to smuggle goods. In one instance, some crewmen attempted to smuggle tobacco into Nassau. Their method was to cover their bodies with the unfolded leaves as smoothly as possible. Unfortunately, they became extremely ill, with slowing pulses, nausea, and cold sweats. They were found to be suffering from severe cases of nicotine poisoning.[165]

During the American Civil War, Nassau became a primary artery through which life-supporting supplies were pumped to the Confederacy. Tinker notes, "Somnolent, easy-going Nassau was suddenly lifted from semi-tropical lassitude to feverish activity. The colonial capital was transformed into a money-making citadel, and New Providence experienced a brief interlude of prosperity."[166] As British subjects sworn to loyalty to the dictates of the Crown, Bahamians made their interpretation of British neutrality in the American affair very apparent by vigorously enforcing the laws against the Union while demonstrating gross laxity toward the Confederates. Tinker's earlier interpretation of the obvious Bahamian pro-Confederate position was based on the assumption that historical bonds of friendship and commercial ties between the Bahamas and the southern states underscored the active role played by the people in support of the Confederate cause; however, in respect to the role of Bahamians in the early development of commerce in the colonial southeastern United States, and in anticipation of their future roles in the supply of merchandise during Prohibition and later in drug smuggling, it is safe to surmise that Bahamian involvement in facilitating block running was motivated purely by profit.

Both Confederate and Union diplomats vied for British support. The U.S. ambassador to London protested to Lord Russell, the British secretary of state for foreign affairs, of breeches in British policy of neutrality through the use of Nassau as an entrepôt for blockade running.[167] The protest by the U.S. envoy in Nassau of the blatant use of Bahamian ports to supply contraband of war to the Confederate states was met with definitive resistance. On June 8, 1862, Samuel Whiting, U.S. consul at Nassau, complained to William H. Seward, U.S. secretary of state, that he was afraid to leave the consulate premises, because "at night Negro roustabouts serenaded me by standing under my window and singing ribald parodies on the American flag, calling out to me singing, 'Say, you's got too many stars in dat flag.'"[168] On the other hand, Jefferson Davis, the Confederate president, complained that the "impartiality of Her Majesty's Government in favor of our enemies was further evinced in the marked difference of its conduct on the subject of the purchase of supplies by the two belligerents."[169]

In December 1861, Lewis Heyliger of New Orleans was appointed head of the depository of Southern finds in Nassau. His duties were to forward shipments of cotton to England and arrange purchases of return cargoes. His administration in the early years was apparently successful, an assumption based on a correspondence sent by the British consul in Charleston to his superior in Washington: "The blockade-runners are doing a great business . . . . Everything is bought in abundance. Not a day passes without an arrival or a departure. Nearly all trade is under the British Flag. The vessels are all changed in Nassau, where Heyliger is doing a commendable job."[170] As the war progressed, increasing numbers of Confederate agents were openly accommodated in Nassau. S. C. Hawley, successor to Whiting as U.S. consul to Nassau, filed a similar complaint; Hawley reported the arrival of a fleet of schooners, all filled with cotton. Among the fleet was the Confederate runner *Ruby,* which he reported was making her eighth trip through the blockade, many of those trips in broad daylight.[171] Later, Hawley was to report twenty-six different blockade runners plying the waters between Nassau and the east coast. Among this latter group was the *Robert E. Lee,* under the command of Captain Wilkinson, which ran the blockade twenty-one times in ten months and transported thousands of bales of cotton.

Hawley reported to Seward that as fast as one runner was captured or wrecked, another from England took its place. He cautioned that the profits from blockade running were so great that no reduction in the illicit activity should be expected "until our blockade is made more effective or the cities of Charleston and Ft. Fisher, Wilmington are taken."[172] To justify his concern, Hawley stated that "in making the voyages . . . the runners have passed our blockade 112 times in less than 90 days, but only 13 of the 26 runners had been wrecked or captured."[173]

Blockade running between Nassau and southern ports heightened in the summer of 1863. Vice-Consul W. C. Thompson, who replaced Hawley, expressed his apprehension when it was discovered that a fleet of new blockade runners had sailed from England to engage in the lucrative trade. On October 26, 1863, Thompson reported nine arrivals from Wilmington from October 6th to the 24th of that year and eight departures from Nassau from October 8th to the 17th, all with complete success. Thompson noted a particular pattern to the trafficking from Nassau that disturbed him. Tinker outlined Thompson's concerns:

> There was, in addition to this regular blockade-running, a kind of trafficking by sailing vessels which seemed to trouble Thompson. These ships apparently sailed in and out of the Bahamas and left no trace, slipping into the inlets of Florida, Georgia, North Carolina, and South Carolina, but without any record of many of these ships appearing in the official records. Thompson concluded by stating that the apparently uninterrupted Trade with the Confederacy suggested that the United States navy was corrupted.[174]

In July 1863, the *Nassau Guardian* reported that Thompson, in obvious frustration, "refused to hoist the Stars and Stripes on the consular flagstaff on the Fourth of July because the national emblem was so highly disrespected in Nassau."[175]

In late September 1864, Benjamin Kirkpatrick, the consul who replaced Thompson, reported that blockade running out of Nassau continued unabated. In his report to Seward, he noted the arrival of twelve ships from Wilmington and Charleston between August 24 and September 23, and thirteen departures for the blockade during the same period. Like his predecessor, he noted the wreck or capture of several ships, but admitted with alarm that a fleet of new runners had recently arrived in Nassau, with a number of others under sail from Europe. When four runners arrived from the south in one day, Kirkpatrick remarked with apparent resignation, "There appears to be no interruption from that end of the line."[176] The duplicity of federal agents in aiding the southern cause is supported by the fact that Confederate agents were well informed on blockade statistics for the Atlantic coast. The southern agents at Nassau openly published the statistics in a Confederate periodical called the *Index,* partially to influence public opinion against the blockade and partially to encourage contravention of the blockade. The information was reportedly received directly from officers of the blockade and from port records in Nassau, whereupon they were subsequently forwarded to England for dissemination. The *Index,* which carried weekly and monthly reports, became a powerful influence for promoting blockade running and was an effective propaganda vehicle for the Confederacy.[177]

Blockade running in the Bahamas had a profound effect on the islands. The once-sleepy island capital, Nassau, was one of the more obscure British colonial citadels. So obscure was the capital that Craton describes pre-Civil War Nassau as "a poor place almost untouched by the tide of modern progress [and the outer islands as] relics of poverty that [were] almost primeval."[178] Yet, almost overnight, the ordinarily poor and often indifferent Bahamians were once again to host a new breed of reckless, wealthy, and extravagant crowd of pirates from many nations and social ranks. Mary Mosely, Bahamian historian and journalist, gives an excellent resumé of Nassau as it appeared in 1860 in the Centenary Issue of her family newspaper, *The Nassau Guardian*:

> It was a sleepy town of about 7,000 inhabitants still scattered mostly on northern slopes of the ridge and not extending west of West Street, or east of St. Matthew's Church. Its people were a population of idlers with maritime tastes. As yet, few carriages were seen on the streets, though the infrequent visitor could hire a horse foe between four and six shillings a day. There were four small boarding-houses, the most prosperous which, French's, charged eight shillings and four pence without liquors. The existing hard-times propelled the proprietor of that 'grand establishment' . . . to make ends meet by supplying fresh cow's milk from the animals he kept in his yard.[179]

In his annual report to the Colonial Office in 1860, Bahamas governor Charles Bayley told the Duke of Newcastle that "the Statue Book was suited to the eighteenth-century; a poll tax on strangers impedes trade, the poor house at Nassau is the sole public institution and the Militia is but a name."[180] He noted that the islands had no hospital, and an inadequate dispensary and interisland boat service. There was a library, he recalled, but the small public budget was unbalanced, and the public debt was high; the Bahamas was in a sadly impoverished state. Bayley complained to Newcastle that it was a reproach to the British Crown to possess islands in the Bahamian archipelago, many more than a hundred miles in length, in such pitiful state. Bayley was perplexed as to why the Bahamas "should remain in their present state of semi-barbarism removed from the enjoyment of commercial and social communication with the neighboring [American] continent."[181]

The pre-Civil War years were indeed a period of poverty and disappointment for most Bahamians. Still, some Bahamians did not totally despair. This was the age of steam and much was hoped to result from the new form of mobility that allowed steamships to sail against the prevailing winds. Craton observes that farsighted Bahamians had begun to realize the importance of communication as a means by which Nassau could become a winter haven for North Americans: "An Act to encourage steam navigation between New York and Nassau had been passed in 1861, but since the first steamship to attempt the voyage, the *S.S. Jewess*, had arrived on 20 May 1861, and had burnt down almost to the waterline, the project died." A new law was passed in 1857 to again encourage steamship communication between New York and Nassau. Timothy Darling, a successful Nassau merchant, demonstrated confidence in the success of the project by persuading the government to purchase a tract of land south of the public prison to build a hotel sufficient to accommodate the potential winter visitors from the chilly north.[182] Although the tourist industry targeting visitors from the cold north was slow to materialize, the new hotel was destined to become a haven for the variety of visitors associated with the blockade, soon to arrive in Nassau in increasing numbers.[183]

Bahamians were slow to recognize the full impact of the American Civil war on the geopolitics of the time. They were rich and important for the first time, and Craton notes that "in the later 1850s the first muffled drum-beats of the tragic conflict impending in the nearby States were heard in Nassau, but few guessed the sudden focus of attention to make the insignificant capital rich and important for the first time."[184] Frank I. Wilson, who visited Nassau in 1857 and described the island as "a small, dilapidated village . . . scarcely worth a place on our maps," again visited the island in 1862 and was astonished to find "newspaper correspondents, English navy officers on leave with half-pay, underwriters, entertainers, spies, crooks, and bums . . . . There were traders of so many nationalities in Nassau, that the language on the street reminded one of the tongues of Babel."[185]

Starks offered a similar observation of the transformation of Nassau during the period:

> Everyone was wild with excitement during these war years. The shops were packed to the ceilings, the streets were crowded with bales, boxes, and barrels. Fortunes were made in a few weeks or months. Money was spent and scattered in the most extravagant and lavish manner. The town actually swarmed with Southern refugees, captains and crews of blockade-runners. Every available space in and out-of-doors was occupied. Money was plenty and sailors sometimes landed with $1,500 in specie.[186]

In his annual report to the Duke of Newcastle, Governor Bayley complained that the wrecking business, the bedrock of Bahamian commerce before the 1860s, was interrupted by the internal conflict in the United States. Consequently, however, he was to report that "the same cause which has destroyed our kind of employment has given rise to another."[187] He applauded the "vast number of ships, fitted out in England for blockade-running purposes, which put in requisition the services of those inhabitants of these islands who habitually earned their livelihood as wreckers."[188] He added, "The proximity of Nassau to Charleston and Wilmington had made it a kind of out-post for Liverpool, Cardiff and Glasgow."[189]

Residents of the outer islands flocked to Nassau in hopes of grabbing a share of the gold that reportedly flowed like water from a waterfall in the capital. And in that mass migration to Nassau, the population of the other islands was significantly decreased. Bayley lamented the significance of this demographic shift, stating that while he was "pleased to see the natives from the other islands finding a decent employment here [Nassau], I find myself apprehensive by the serious drainage of manpower in those islands, which are in reality the bread-basket for Nassau."[190] The demographic shifts made it almost impossible for those islands, already suffering from rapidly depleted soils, to adequately supply Nassau and its burgeoning visitor population with basic food, as had been the traditional practice. In turn, merchants were compelled to import necessary foods.

The Bahamas Census Report for the year 1860 stated the population of the Bahamas at 33,089, with only 7,920 of that total living on the principal island of New Providence, where the capital, Nassau, is located. Beginning in 1861, however, the population of New Providence steadily increased. The census report for the war years indicated these increases as follows: 1861, 9,328; 1862, 11,831; 1863, 15,070; 1864, 15,156; 1865, 12,734. By 1870, five years after the war ended, the population of New Providence plunged to fewer than 8,000, recording a total of 7,544 residents.[191] Many blacks escaped the rigors of back-breaking subsistence agriculture in their outer-island homes by migrating to Nassau in search of a piece of the bonanza blockade-running brought to Nassau. In 1860, for example, the population of New Providence increased by 1,408 to include 938 whites and 469 blacks. The following year, there was an increase of 1,337 whites and 1,166 blacks. In 1863 the demographic composition reversed, recording only 398 whites and 2,843 blacks. In 1865, an estimated 2,409 whites migrated from New Providence to their outer-island homes or to the mainland. In contrast, only 13 blacks returned to the outer islands.[192]

Trade in the Bahamas in 1860 was relatively small. Governor Bayley reported that "the exportation of pineapples from Eleuthera and salt from Inagua accounted for 70 percent of all trade from these islands during the past year" of 1860.[193] Total export was valued at £157,350, of which the export of salt accounted for £65,947 and pineapples, £44,198. The remaining £47,205 was derived primarily from the sale of sponges, citrus fruits, and conch shells, the latter polished and exported to France and Italy for the production of cameo jewelry.[194] Imports for the period were valued at £234,029. Between 1861 and 1864, the volume of trade in Nassau experienced significant growth, with exports and imports climbing to £195,584 and £274,584, respectively. Exports now included such commodities as coal, fabrics, drugs, wines and rum, gunpowder, and, of course, cotton. By 1862, import and export figures were reported at £1,250,322 and £1,007,755, respectively. Bayley reported to Newcastle that "This increase of 1862 exports of 1,00,755 pounds [sterling] versus the figure of 195,584 pounds is attributable to the important part which this Colony—or more correctly speaking, the harbor of Nassau—had played as an Entrepôt of English goods destined for the ports of the Confederate States."[195]

The exports listed in the 1861 governor's report present telling information on the use of Nassau as a conduit for the flow of foreign-made commodities to the south. For example, the Bahamas exported no brandy, coffee, lead, manufactured leather goods, quicksilver, or paints. Yet, in 1862, export figures included 1,512 gallons of brandy, 5,273 hundred-pound weights of coffee, 7,601 gallons of gin and whisky, 2,836 hundred-pound weights of lead, 164 gallons of paint, and 137 flasks of quicksilver. Whereas, 21 tons of coal was exported in 1861, 100 tons was exported the following year, and gunpowder exports for the same period increased from 189 kegs to 8,336 kegs. The import and export figures for 1863 continued to demonstrate significant increases, recording imports at £4,295,316 and exports at £3,308,567, respectively. Bayley was able to report that the increase in revenue "has enabled me to defray the public debt of 43,986 pounds, 19 shillings, and 4 pence by 8,868 pounds, 5 shillings and 1 penny."[196] Cotton import and export figures for the war years demonstrate, to a large degree, the successes and failures of the blockade. In 1860, the struggling Bahamian cotton plantations succeeded exporting 258 bales of cotton. Obviously, there was no need for the Bahamas, with no mills, to import cotton. With the advent of the war, however, cotton imports increased from 1,587 bales in 1861 to 19,128 in 1864, and exports increased from 3,610 bales to 22,347 bales in the same period.

On May 14, 1862, the *Bahama Herald* report on all the foreign ships in Nassau included eight steamers; one British warship; two barques; six schooners; five topsail schooners; and dozens of smaller vessels of American, British, Spanish, French, and Brazilian registry, signifying that the Bahamas had once again become internationally significant. Colonial governor Rawson, in his annual report on the colony, stated that between 1861 and 1865, an estimated 400 ships entered Nassau Harbor from Confederate ports, with 156 of them coming from Charleston and 164 from Wilmington.[197] An anonymous article in *Harper's* quoted a higher number of ships, stating, "during the conflict, it was reported that 588 ships left Nassau for Confederate ports."[198]

The sudden flood of money transformed Nassau like a poor man suddenly bequeathed an unexpected fortune. Mosley states that the increase in public revenue allowed for the widening of Bay Street at the center of Nassau in 1864 at an estimated `cost of £13,730, and the introduction of curbstones and streetlights along that thoroughfare.[199] Warehouses inundated the waterfront along the north side of Bay Street. Sir Etienne Dupuch noted that "Skippers demanded a speed-up, and the new activity meant additional wharf facilities. Demand for waterfront property became so great that shallow harbor areas were filled in to provide more docking space."[200] The new wealth allowed for the construction of a hospital and dispensary, the inauguration of a regular interisland boat service, upgrade of the public library, a local police force, and increases in salaries for public servants.[201] In the end, however, the ambitious public works programs initiated primarily to impress and accommodate the many visitors, proved to be a millstone around the neck of the government.

The end of the conflict resulted in the bust of the Nassau real estate market. Real estate along Bay Street appreciated in some cases by 300 and 400 percent as the need for warehouse space became acute. Governor Rawson reported to the Earl of Cardwell that "Between 1860-65, of the 182 parcels of land sold in New Providence, only 17 tracts were sold for agricultural purposes. In a classic case, a parcel of land measuring 4,500 square feet was sold to John S. George in 1856 for £128. Seven years later, the *Nassau Guardian* reported the sale of that land to a Mr. S. Hewett of Savannah, Georgia for the sum of £3,500. In 1896, after the prosperity bubble had burst, that very parcel was purchased by Herbert McKinney, son-in-law of John S. George, for a mere £90."[202]

The construction of the Royal Victoria Hotel was perhaps the most ambitious public project undertaken by the Bahamas government during the Civil War. During that period, the social life of the capital swirled around that oasis of hospitality. The project was started in 1859 and called for an estimated expenditure of £6,000. The tide of unexpected wealth as a consequence of the war, however, prompted the government to complete the hotel much more lavishly and for considerably more money than initially estimated. Expensive and elegant china and glassware were standard luxuries, and minute details in furnishing and service were planned and implemented to suit the exquisite taste of the fastidious. The *Nassau Guardian* reported that the hotel was embellished with a grand piano, "the most amazing thing the islands had ever seen."[203] With the turn of a crank, the piano could reportedly be made to perform "any overture, waltz or quadrille with surpassing brilliancy of execution."[204]

Peters noted that there were planned teas and picnics, boating parties and balls that kept Nassau alive with excitement, which "warded off boredom for persons whose schedules alternated fitful activity with periods of waiting."[205] The Civilian Cricket Club was organized in 1863, and "all society turned out to watch the matches, which were played on the grounds of Fort Charlotte."[206] Other sources of entertainment included the biweekly band concerts (seats provided for ladies) on the grounds of the Royal Victoria Hotel, with music provided by the predominantly black Second West India Regiment, described by Wilson as "a parcel of fine looking darkies in bright uniforms who made very respectable holiday soldiers."[207] There was an equestrian show, the first for the Bahamas, introduced and sustained by Southern gentlemen, which provided horse showmanship interspersed with mule racing and other forms of entertainment.

One of the most difficult problems confronting Confederate agents in Nassau was that of obtaining adequate supplies of coal to keep their runners efficiently fueled. Since each steamer required 160 to 180 tons of coal for the round trip between Charleston or Wilmington, the coal supply business became almost as profitable for Nassau merchants as cotton. The coal yards of Henry Adderley & Company, Johnson & Brothers, Saunders & Sons, and the Navy Yard reportedly reached mammoth proportions during the 1860s, causing the *Nassau Guardian* to report that "across the Nassau Harbour is a mountain of coal."[208] Besides coal, the predominantly agricultural South needed a variety of supplies and was willing to pay for them in cotton. England, on the other hand, was in desperate need of cotton and prepared to supply ammunition and merchandise in exchange. The Confederacy was definitely in the market, and Nassau merchants, eager to make a profit, became among the chief suppliers of contraband goods to the South.

The leading merchants in Nassau who profited most from the Blockade were H. Adderley, the Johnson Brothers, Messrs. W. H. W. Weech, G. Renguard, Roker, Palacious, T. Brace, C. Knowles, and J. S. George. The prewar advertisements posted by these merchants provide clues to the profitability of their businesses during the war. In 1853, Adderley advertised a few yards of cloth, 9 boxes of clothing, and pieces of mosquito netting; Johnson and Brothers advertised a few yards of cloth, 11 bales of flour and cornmeal, and 2 cases of boots and shoes; Weech advertised thread, soap, quinine, and 10 bags of rice; G. Renguard advertised an assortment of clothing, rice, and sugar. Both Palacious and Roker advertised a small quantity of clothing; Brace advertised a variety of drugs and potions; Knowles, clothes and stationery; and John S. George, a small quantity of tea, gin, morphine, and quinine.[209]

As the war progressed, the volume of trade transacted by the Nassau merchants underwent a dramatic change. In 1863, Henry Adderley advertised the sale of muslins, linens, and expensive gloves; Johnson and Brothers advertised tweeds, flannels, and 67 cases of boots and shoes; Weech advertised 1,800 dozen coats, 180 bags of rice, 16 cases of opium, 32 cases of calomel, and 14 kegs of cream of tartar sauce; Renguard and Company advertised champagnes, cases of glassware, claret, burgundies, meats, black and gold silks, and cases of macaroni and vermicelli; Palacoius and Roker, hair accessories, toothbrushes, stationery, and fine cloths; Brace advertised Russian salves, syrups, liniments, dolls, pills, and a host of chemicals; Knowles advertised an assortment of silk, woolen, and culinary goods; and John S. George advertised huge quantities of tea, morphine, chemicals, gunpowder, camphor, and salad oils.[210]

Bahamian trade with the Confederacy, together with British political duplicity, soured relations between the United States and the Bahamas Islands. In 1863, Governor Bayley refused USS *Flambeau* entry to Nassau harbor when that vessel attempted to refuel from an attendant bunker-ship stationed there. In retaliation, C. F. James, the American minister in London, protested that Nassau was being used as an entropôt for Confederate war supplies. Much to the frustration of the American officials, Lord Russell, the British foreign minister, merely warned blockade runners that his government would not protect them on the high seas from search and seizure by Union warships. Then the Trent incident occurred, and British sentiment almost immediately turned against the North. The Duke of Newcastle warned Bayley against further antagonism toward the United States, but to little avail, for Bahamian officials and citizens continued to facilitate blockade-running activities.

U.S. authorities disapproved of the attitude of Bahamians toward the blockade and launched attacks against vessels determined to be in contravention of its naval policies, even if that vessel happened to be in British territorial waters. In May 1863, USS *Rhode Island* bombarded the British merchant ship *Margaret and Jessie* off the Bahamian island of Eleuthera. On November 21, 1863, the Bahamian government accused the Union of operating without authorization in the Bahamian islands of Inagua, Exuma, and other sparsely populated islands to the south. In January 1864, the editor of the *Nassau Guardian* expressed pleasure that "the continual presence of Federal cruisers within the waters of this colony, in opposition to that policy of neutrality which had been the desire of the Imperial Government to maintain between the belligerents of America, has met with the strong disapprobation of the authorities at home."[211] Bahamian resolve to support the Confederate cause and profit in the process continued unabated, with the obvious collusion of the local justices, as demonstrated in the case of the *Oreto*.

The *Oreto* was built in England and officially classified as a merchant ship. Union observers, however, protested that the vessel had the unmistakable features of a man-o-war. The *Nassau Guardian* noted that when the ship arrived in Nassau to be outfitted for blockade running, the American consul demonstrated such great interest in the vessel that the local merchants thought it prudent to move the ship to Cochrane's Anchorage, some fifteen miles west of Nassau. According to the *Guardian*, U.S. consul Samuel Whiting allegedly bribed an ex-boatswain to testify that the *Oreto* was a Confederate gunboat. Whiting's persistent allegation that his evidence revealed a violation of neutrality forced the British commander of the HMS *Greyhound*, then in Bahamian waters, to seize the *Oreto* and demand that the case be tried in the local Admiralty court. The case was heard on August 2 before Chief Justice Lees, before a packed courtroom electric with excitement. Henry Adderley, prominent Nassau merchant, testified that the *Oreto* had been consigned to him by the Liverpool firm of Fraser Trenholm and Company for service as a merchant vessel. The *Guardian* reported that the trial lasted less than one hour before Judge Lees, who allegedly owned shares in the Adderley enterprises, ruled that evidence was insufficient to conclude that an attempt had been made to outfit the *Oreto* as a warship.[212] Shortly after the trial, an anonymous letter was sent to the press, titled *Oreto Affair*, alleging that some $80,000 in Confederate currency had been brought to Nassau aboard the *Oreto*, of which $20,000 went to Justice Lees and the remainder divided among other parties in Nassau associated with the ship. Eventually, the *Oreto* sailed to a place where it was transformed into a Confederate warship.[213]

The sudden state of wealth thrust upon Nassau had serious consequences. The "Centenary Issue" of the *Nassau Guardian* reported that "The yellow fever which had ravaged Wilmington in the summer of 1864 was unwittingly transmitted to Nassau. It had already killed 2,500 out of the population of some 6,000 in Wilmington. It eventually caused the deaths of some 1,500 people in Nassau."[214] The epidemic was so devastating that Thomas E. Taylor recalled counting seventeen funeral processions passing his window in Nassau in one morning while having breakfast, and attending three funerals of friends on the same day, all victims of yellow fever. Taylor, himself, fell victim to the deadly disease and was forced to move from Nassau to Halifax to recuperate.[215]

Another adverse effect of the overnight fortune enjoyed by Bahamians was the sharp increase in crime that resulted. The *Nassau Guardian* noted the crime surge in a special editorial dated December 24, 1864: "There is scarcely a night but adds sorrow to the dawn by disclosing the fatal consequences of the orgies which are unblushingly engaged in at the dens of iniquity skirting our otherwise fair city. Prostitution, robberies, and violent crimes, formerly rare in Nassau, have become common occurance. We are a God-fearing people, and we need to awaken to our social responsibilities before it is too late."[216] Indeed, the level of crime in Nassau had increased, and the chief offenders were those engaged in blockade running. Governor Bayley reported on the situation to the Duke of Newcastle: "In a recent report of the Provost Marshal he says that, while in the year 1851 the average number of Prisoners in jail was but 13, they now average 100. Among the prisoners for the above description of crimes [burglary and larceny], many are white seamen, and other strangers must be included."[217] The governor continued, "Concerning English sailors flushed with money, the Militia Police Court for the year 1862 shew an excess of 236 [criminal offences] over those for 1861."[218]

The annual list of court cases published by the attorney general of the Bahamas demonstrated the increase in crime during the war years. In 1860, no first-degree murders were listed; however, 2 manslaughter cases, 7 larcenies, 9 frauds, 4 cases of bodily harm, and 12 misdemeanors were listed. In 1861, the figures increased to include 3 cases of first-degree murder, 1 case of manslaughter, 5 larcenies, 18 frauds, 9 cases of bodily harm, and 26 misdemeanors. By 1863, as blockade running through Nassau heightened, 14 first-degree murder cases were recorded, as were 18 cases of manslaughter, 98 larcenys, 84 cases of fraud, 66 cases of bodily harm, and 130 misdemeanors.[219] Additional judicial personnel were hired to deal with the increase in court cases, much to the frustration of the governor, who reported to his superior that, while the foreigners did bring a substantial degree of prosperity to the colony, their generally lawless behavior was an undesirable element, especially when "it is noticed that during the years 1862, 1863, and 1864, the foreign seamen average more than one half of the total number imprisoned . . . [causing me to] often question the profitability of their presence on the island."[220] On May 2, 1864, the Nassau Legislature voted to create a constabulary organization, which became the forerunner of the present Royal Bahamas Police Force. The *Guardian* commented on the occasion, "The Police Force consists of one senior officer in the form of James Henry Bowe. Other officers are Sergeant Wilfred Monroe and Densel Edwards; Corporals Henry Dean, Orville Evans, William Dillett, Samuel Johnson, Marcus Bailey, Stephen sands, Harold Taylor, Roger Atkins, and Kendal Lloyd. There are, also, fifty-two first class and thirty-two second class Constables."[221]

The prosperity spread around Nassau during the American Civil War trickled down to the mass population. Governor Bayley confirmed this in his annual report for 1862: "Shopkeepers were not the only persons who profited largely by this sudden trade, which has put in requisition almost every kind of skilled and unskilled labour at rates of remuneration far above the ordinary level . . . . [U]nskilled labourers receive $1.00 per day for the loading and unloading of steamers for or from the Southern ports—the discharging and repacking of cotton from one ship to another, $2.00 for a nights duty."[222] In 1860, a ship carpenter in Nassau received 4 shillings per day; stevedores and longshoremen, 1 shilling, 3 pence; watchmen, 1 shilling; masons and plasterers, 3 shillings, 6 pence; house carpenters, 3 shillings, 9 pence; painters, 2 shillings; blacksmiths, 3 shillings; rock cutters, 1 shilling, 6 pence; bricklayers, 2 shillings; dray drivers, washwomen, and domestic servants, 9 pence per day. In 1861, wages soared over the previous year: ship carpenters earned 7 shillings per day; stevedores and longshoremen, 5 shillings; watchmen, 2 shillings and 6 pence; masons and plasterers, 5 shillings; and dray drivers, washwomen, and domestic servants, 1 shilling and 9 pence. By 1863, the rate of daily pay rose even higher, with ship carpenters earning 8 shillings, 9 pence; longshoremen and stevedores, 6 shillings, 8 pence; blacksmiths, 11 shillings, 10 pence; and dray drivers, washwomen, and domestic servants earning an estimated 3 shillings. Many merchants built fine country mansions for weekend leisure. Together with the construction of new warehouses and public buildings, a demand for skilled workers was created.

In his book titled *The Bahamas: a Sketch* (1869), Bacot warned visitors to Nassau "to bear in mind; it is not by any means a cheap place to live." He informed the potential visitor that most of the necessities of life were imported from England or America. Bacot cited milk as an "article difficult to procure, as may be gathered from the advertisements of what one tradesman at Nassau designates 'consecrated milk' and 'desecrated eggs' . . . . Turtle, fish and fruit are to be had cheap and plentiful at Nassau in their natural state, but everything else is to be found confined in tins, from salmon to duck with green peas, and English plum pudding."[223] A quart of milk, which cost 2 shillings and 1 penny in 1860, sold for 3 shillings in 1863; the price of one loaf of bread for the same period increased from 4 pence to 7 pence; one pound of steak rose from 4 shillings and 5 pence to 6 shillings and 9 pence.

In 1865, the Union took Charleston, followed by Fort Fisher, which guarded the entrance to Wilmington, and blockade running through Nassau came to a screeching halt; the bubble of prosperity was burst, and conditions of pre-Civil War destitution returned to Nassau. Michael Craton comments, "In Nassau, the ending of the blockade-running deflated the economy with the speed of a punctured balloon."[224] Surgeon-Major Bacot wondered whether the prosperity had served any lasting purpose:

> There was, no doubt, a good deal of drinking going on . . . . Many a Dinah owed her ruin to the extraordinary temptations offered by reckless sailors with more money than they knew what to do with, and with the lowest notions of morality. A few undertakers have profited, as disease and murders became prevalent and fatal; and the government managed to pay off a small debt, but what became of all that money made is a mystery.[225]

G. J. H. Northcroft reported, "Many persons acquired capital which put them in a position to continue business after the war; many more squandered what they made; while a few took their profits and retired from the colony, intending to live in the *otium cum dignitate* which they considered their efforts had earned for them."[226] The ultimate indignity occurred in 1866, when a violent hurricane and a horrid outbreak of typhoid devastated Nassau with almost wanton destruction of property, including devastating damage to the recent private and public works improvements, and loss of lives. Activity at the blocks of newly constructed warehouses that escaped the fury of the hurricane ground to a halt and stood deserted for fifty years, to be revived when events in the United States once again briefly lifted the islands from the embrace of poverty during the federal experiment with Prohibition.

5. THE ROARING TWENTIES

Prohibition and Rum Running

On January 16, 1920, the Eighteenth Amendment to the Constitution of the United States of America went into effect with the introduction of the Volstead Act, so named for Minnesota Representative Andrew Volstead, who had championed the bill. The law was passed twice by Congress by a two-thirds vote of both the House and Senate, the second time in order to override the veto of President Woodrow Wilson. The law placed a prohibition on the sale of alcoholic beverages in the country and determined to restrict the personal consumption of alcohol. The so-called Noble Experiment, which many considered blatant interference in the private lives of a nation that jealously guarded its inalienable right to "the pursuit of happiness," was the result of several factors.

This was the period commonly referred to as the Roaring Twenties, partly because it reflected the public demonstration of freedom that prevailed following the devastating effects of the global conflict of World War I, and partly because of the rise in violent and organized crime it produced. Second, the wanton gaiety of the period reflected reckless immorality and the blatant rejection of traditional Christian family values, a development vigorously protested by the women's suffrage movement. The new law was largely supported by small-town populations in the Bible Belt who rejected the influence of urban immigrants from the "big cities." Together with the introduction of the automobile and other influences of the emerging modern era, Congress was convinced it had a moral responsibility to reform the country and return it to the principles of the Founding Fathers. In the midst of the turmoil that accompanied twenty-three years of experiment, the Bahamas emerged as a primary conduit through which contraband alcohol flowed into the United States.

One of the ironies of the "Noble Experiment" was the fact that America had acquired a national taste for alcohol almost from historical inception. As early as 1630, pioneer John Winthrop and company had sailed into Massachusetts Bay with more than ten thousand gallons of wine and three times more beer than water.[227] In the 1700s, America's love of the "drink" prompted Benjamin Franklin to twice compile and publish a list of terms in the *Pennsylvania Gazette* that could be used for "drunk", using such descriptions as "juicy", "thawed", and "had a thump over the head with the Sampson's jawbone."[228] In 1763, 159 commercial distilleries were operating across New England, and by the 1820s, a glass of whiskey was less expensive than a cup of tea. Frederick Marryat, in his work titled *A Diary of America*, commented on the situation,

> I am sure the Americans can fix nothing without a drink . . . . If you meet, you drink; if you close a bargain, you drink; they quarrel in their drink, and they make it up with a drink. They drink because it is hot; they drink because it is cold. If successful in elections, they drink and rejoice; if not, they drink and swear; they begin to drink early in the morning, they leave off late at night; they commence it early in life, and they continue it, until they soon drop into the grave."[229]

Daniel Okrent summarized the story of America's love of the "drink" as follows:

> In the early days of the Republic drinking was as intimately woven into the social fabric as family or church. In the apt phrase of historian W. J. Rorabaugh, 'Americans drank from crack of dawn to the crack of dawn.' Out in the countryside most farmers kept a barrel of hard cider by the door for family and anyone who might drop in . . . In the cities it was widely understood that common workers would fail to come to work on Mondays, staying home to wrestle with the echoes and aftershocks of a weekend binge . . . . [The] U.S. Army had been receiving four ounces of whiskey as part of their daily ration since 1782; George Washington himself said 'the benefits arising from moderate use of strong Liquor have been experienced in all Armies, and are not to be disputed.'[230]

George Washington, the first president and founding father of America, had an apparent vested interest in the liquor industry as he owned one of the largest whiskey distilleries in the nation. In 1799, the Mount Vernon operation, comprising five stills and a boiler, produced 11,000 gallons of corn and rye whiskey valued then at a whopping $7,500. This passion of early Americans for their favorite brew is evident in the resistance of Pennsylvanians to federal government attempts to raise taxes on liquor as a method of acquiring additional revenue to finance the costly Revolutionary War. Washington, determined to maintain control of the Pennsylvanians, raised a force of 12,000 troops and threatened to march on Philadelphia in response. Needless to say, the acquiescence of Pennsylvanians was almost immediately pronounced.

The American attitude toward Prohibition was one of general ambivalence and disinterest. Robert Carse summed up the mood of the time:

> Midnight, January 16, 1920, when Prohibition went into effect, passed almost unnoticed. Some few New York City hotels set their tables with black cloths as a gesture of mourning, and yet throughout the country there was nothing like a formal ceremony. Prohibition had been ratified by the legislatures of forty-six states, and forty-three had created enforcement codes of their own to implement the action of the federal government . . . . The work of the Women's Christian Temperance Union, which had lasted for four decades, had come to a successful end. Mrs. Ella A. Boodle, the head of the organization, and her cohorts no longer had to ask the question, "Can you change the mind of your dripping Wet Senator?" The W.C.T.U. answer to this was, "No, but you can change your Senator."[231]

According to Carse, "The nation was in no wise dry. Five major sources of illicit liquor satisfied the popular demand: medicinal, sold by doctors' prescriptions and through drugstores; 'near beer' that was often given a strengthening squirt of alcohol just before it was sold over a speakeasy bar; industrial alcohol from existing stocks; still-made alcohol and its less potent cousins, home-pressed wine; and smuggled liquor from the Bahamas, Bermuda, Canada, Mexico, Cuba, and Europe."[232]

The American liquor market undoubtedly demonstrated significant growth in the effort exerted to satisfy the growing public demand for the "drink"; however, the public very early became wary of the unscrupulous practices of liquor suppliers with the sale of partially converted industrial alcohol sold as genuine whiskey, but often diluted with malt syrups, molasses, or almost anything brown, and tap water. The resulting medical repercussion of consumption of this concoction included cases of blindness, teeth turned black, paralysis, and even death. It became apparent that consumption of most local products was a potential danger to the public health; a leaning toward imports, "the real stuff," increased. Even when cut and recut, the imports brought high prices, and demand for "good Scotch," "old-time rye," "straight bourbon," and "French brandy and champagne," created standard phrases in the vernacular vocabulary. Enterprising merchants reportedly began to "swarm the Canadian border by the hundreds. Mexican women became wealthy overnight after crossing the Rio Grande with a carefully suspended cargo of brandy or even tequila inside the very personal zones of their petticoats. Cabin and table stewards aboard the Bermuda-New York passenger lines were reported to be making more each voyage as smugglers than the regular pay of the captains and engineers."[233]

As was the case with the Union blockade of Southern ports in the 1860s, federal authorities were faced with the uphill challenge of enforcement of the law along the 12,000 miles of Gulf, Pacific, and Atlantic coasts, 3,700 miles of north-to-south border, and countless miles of river frontages using the limited resources of 1,550 prohibition agents, 3,000 customs officers, and a complement of 11,000 Coast Guard. The enormous American thirst inevitably promoted widespread cases of graft and corruption that reached into the very core of the enforcement authorities. Less than sixty days after enforcement of the law, two agents assigned to the Baltimore Prohibition Department were arrested on corruption charges. Within less than one year, "one hundred agents in New York alone [were] discharged from their service because of corruption."[234] Carse notes that the demand for liquor was so huge, especially along the Atlantic coast that "the thirsty from Maine to Florida were willing to pay for what they wanted as long as it looked and smelled and had anything like the effect of pre-prohibition drink. There were men ready to satisfy their demands. Smuggling, like the consumption of alcohol, was an old American custom."[235] And Bahamians, among others, were prepared to supply the lucrative demand.

Enforcement of the law was assigned to the Treasury Department, and the newly formed U.S. Coast Guard was charged with the responsibility of interdiction before the illegal cargo could reach American shores. Lieutenant Commander Frederick C. Billard was selected to command the Coast Guard forces, a position he held for seven years. In early 1924, the Navy loaned the Coast Guard twenty-five aging destroyers that had been placed in storage near the close of World War I in the Philadelphia Navy Yard. The ships were "oil-burners, with steam turbines for propulsion . . . [sporting] main batteries of 4' 50 and 3 rifles and pistols."[236] This "Destroyer Force," as the fleet was dubbed, was to be the first line of defense for almost ten years. The Washington D.C. headquarters was reportedly where "strategy and tactics were drawn up for the imminent blockade against Rum Row with all the studied intensity of a wartime operation . . . . In the map room of Headquarters was a huge wall-size chart with colored tabs denoting the name and noon position of all blacks. This vital information was promptly disseminated to Area Commanders in the field, so that they in turn were kept fully in the picture."[237]

Prohibition proved a very unpopular law forced on a nation with an almost unquenchable thirst for alcoholic beverages of all types and quality, and as a direct consequence of this urge, a myriad of societal irregularities emerged, none more popular and lucrative than rum running. Lieutenant Harold Waters, retired Coast Guard officer and contemporary of the Prohibition era, described the situation:

> They came from out all the seas and flew many flags, rust-streaked tramps, onetime luxury yachts whose palatial accommodations had played host to kings, emperors, statesmen and millionaires, steam trawlers, old gunboats, big schooners, small "bankers". Most had seen better days, many were fugitives from the ship breakers yards, and some were manned by so-called

gentlemen adventurers. All drawn to American shores by the easy money
to be made out of catering to the great thirst which had settled upon the
land following the passage of the National Prohibition Act. They rode
at anchor a few miles offshore, holds wide open, ready, willing and able
to do business with anyone who would come out to buy their alcoholic
wares. The daily quotes on cases of scotch, bourbon, rye, rum, champagne
and brandy were chalked up on blackboards displayed in the rigging for
customers to see. Business went on the clock around, with supercargoes
on hand at the gangways to greet customers as they came alongside. We of
the Coast Guard called this ragtag armada Rum Row.[238]

Aditionally, "Syndicates were formed in Great Britain, Europe and elsewhere.
Shares were sold in smuggling ventures, ships purchased, loaded with cargoes of
liquor, then sailed across the Atlantic to take station off Rum Row. Some of the
larger ships carried as much as 25,000 cases. Faked manifests and clearance papers
stated that they were bound for St. Pierre and/or Nassau . . . . Once off Rum Row
they were boarded by Stateside agents of the owners, who had previously made all
arrangements for the loads to be landed. It was as simple as that."[239] The prophesy
of Professor J. G. Dailey of Philadelphia, who in 1911 had written a song titled *A
Saloon-less Nation in 1920,* was to be fulfilled in the enactment of the Prohibition law
and in the resulting movement of large cargoes of alcoholic beverages from once
idle warehouses lining the docks of Nassau, and later Bimini and West End in the
northern Bahamas.[240] Once again, Nassau was bustling with maritime activities and
was rich.

Frederic Van de Water recounts a description by Bill McCoy (perhaps the most
celebrated of the rum runners) of the Nassau he came to know in the 1920s:

> In the early months of 1921 the little white city was still half asleep. The
> liquor trade was just beginning to stir; the New York gangs with their
> rivalries and gunmen had not yet arrived. Besides her peacock-hued
> harbor Nassau dreamed of her past and did not anticipate her immediate
> uproarious future . . . she has lived, this little tropic town. Most of her days
> she has slumbered, but there had been eras when she has stepped out.
> In her early days the buccaneers nested there, rumming and brawling
> and wenching between forays and the Main. When they passed, peace
> descended and prosperity fled. For a century thereafter, Nassau dwindled,
> living upon her slim exports and loans from the mother country. Then
> Civil War brought her again a brief blaze of fortune. Blockade running
> gave her the stimulus piracy once had afforded. Fast black ships,
> munitions-laden, slid from her harbor, snaked their way through the
> clutter of little islands that run westward like a long broken jetty, and
> then, with lights out and boilers throbbing, streak through the night for

the mouth of the Wilmington River dodging the blockading squadrons in
which my father served. Once again Nassau momentarily was rich. After
Appomattox she relapsed and dreamed away another sixty years. Her next
awakening was to be the most violent and lucrative of all.[241]

On the eve of Prohibition, the Bahamian economy was in a state of depression,
and domestic life was generally one of virtual desperation and survival. The colony
had witnessed a decline in the export of its two main trade commodities, sponge
and sisal, which were affected by U.S. agricultural protectionist policies in the form
of high import taxes and rates of foreign exchange. Public works, many of which
were constructed in the 1860s during the boom days of blockade running, were
generally neglected or, at best, inadequately maintained. The lack of public funds
resulted in frequently unlit street lights in Nassau and roads in various stages of
disrepair, agriculture underdeveloped, and attention to education relegated to
the back burner of the government's priority list. The opportunities for prosperity
offered by Prohibition were, therefore, widely hailed and warmly embraced as an
unexpected but very welcome blessing.

The Bahamas indeed prospered from its position as a primary conduit for the
flow of illegal liquor into the United States, and the advent of Prohibition became
a financial boon for the colonial economy, but at the price of the colony's playing
reluctant host to American syndicated crime gangs. On March 3, 1920, the *Times*
reported that the events of Prohibition had "transformed the Bahamas Government's
financial position as if by magic from a deficit to a comparatively huge surplus,
provided labour for large numbers of unemployed Bahamians and put money in
circulation in this little British colony than has been the case for many years."[242]
David Gray summed up the situation: "Most of the liquid contraband entered Florida
via the Bahama islands. The sale of liquor remained legal there, and rum-runners
pursued their sordid vocation with virtual impunity. The good citizens of the
Bahamas, although outwardly professing alarm at the influx of such evil men into
their midst, were all too willing to share in the proceeds of the lucrative trade."[243]

The government benefited from a liquor tax of US$6 for every case of liquor
exported. The value of liquor exports peaked in 1923 to £1,065,899, two hundred
percent higher than that of the previous year, and five hundred percent higher than
in the June 1919-July1920 government annual fiscal cycle.[244] This huge increase in
revenue allowed for the construction and much-needed maintenance of capital civil
works, a situation that excited the government and merchants of the day and caused
the authorities to adopt a "grin and bear it" attitude toward growing disregard for
the law demonstrated by the newly arrived mobsters. Bahamians of all walks of
life, however, were increasingly confronted by hordes of unruly gangsters, mostly
distinguished as New Yorkers by their sharp nasal speech, common in bars and
gambling dens of the "Big Apple," but now common along Bay Street, the main
thoroughfare of Nassau.

Carse recounts McCoy's description of the new visitors to The Bahamas:

> They wore their hatbrims low, their collars were high and shiny, their suits
> in pronounced patterns, the pants tight, their shoes extremely pointed.
> When, in the heat of the day or an argument at a bar, they opened their
> coats, shoulder holsters could be seen. Those held. 38-calibre revolvers or
> the heavier, recently more popular type of weapon, Colt or Luger automatic
> pistols . . . . Their talk was tough, and they were tough. Blackjacks projected
> from certain hip pockets. Brass knuckles were occasionally brought into
> evidence to prove a point under discussion . . . . They went loud-mouthed,
> irredeemably profane, from bar to bar. This was only the fall of 1921, but
> they already called Bay Street 'Booze Avenue' and delighted in taunting
> local constables.[245]

Bay Street, the commercial heart of the colony, certainly lived up to the title
of "Booze Avenue," where a myriad of merchants, wholesale and retail, hawked
their wares with pronounced clarity. They included McPhersons, who advertised the
highest quality Scotch whiskey; David A. Clarkeson 7 Co. Ltd., purveyor of American,
Scotch, and Irish whiskeys and champagnes; Chas. E. Bethel, "Liquor dealers of very
old stock of wines"; Kelly's, Finest in Scotch, American, and Irish whiskeys; W. B.
North, "Wholesale dealer in all Liquors"; and the Bahamas Produce Corporation,
"wholesale dealers in Scotch, Irish and Rye whiskies."[246]

Frederic Van de Water described Nassau in 1921 in similar fashion:

> The town awoke to find herself involuntary hostess to a new group of wild
> ones, combinations of pirates and blockade runner with a few entirely
> individual traits of violence thrown in for good measure—the rum gang . . . .
> The call of big money had summoned them as the pibroch gatherers clan.
> Nassau suffered a variety of the stampede that always follows a gold strike,
> the opening of new diamond mines, the discovery of a fresh oil field. The
> big money clan rushed in upon her. Adventurers, businessmen, soldiers,
> loafers, and at least one minister, they sought to make their fortunes by
> keeping America wet . . . . These Argonauts differed from kindred groups
> who had followed the call of big money in other quarters of the globe.
> In their ranks, it is true, there were many genuine adventurer type, but
> in general they were a harder, tougher, more unscrupulous crowd . . . .
> Nassau's invasion was composed of city men, New York City men, for the
> most part. Big shots of the underworld with their escorts of gunmen and
> racketeers left their haunts in Manhattan and Brooklyn and moved to the
> Bahamas . . . . Big Eddie, Big Harry, Squinty, and Lefty . . . poured in with
> their retinues of gorillas and for some vivid months proceeded to take
> Nassau apart and remould it closer to their hearts desire.[247]

The local police were especially targeted by the gangsters, most of whom had a disdain for law enforcement in any shape, form, or color. As noted, these were seasoned, hardened criminal veterans of violence, graft, and corruption. In contrast, the local police were mostly blacks, tough in a simple way, and trained to enforce the laws of the land armed with only a small wooden club commonly called a "billie." With their billies, the Bahamian police were certainly out of the league of Elliot Ness and his Untouchables, and, although very well trained to control crime elements common to the colony, they were ill equipped to adequately deal with the armed gangsters creating trouble around town. Although no official records could be found to verify his statement, and the local newspapers were equally conspicuously silent, Carse noted that the enforcement initiatives of the Bahamian police were further frustrated by the prevailing government policy: "The attitude taken at Government House . . . was that no matter how unruly the new visitors might be, their presence meant vast increases in the island's wealth. Orders were issued to the constabulary to stay out of any fracas, refrain from action except for self-protection or if British citizens were involved."[248]

Van de Water offered this twist on the law enforcement challenge for Bahamian officials:

> Bay Street, the waterfront chief thoroughfare of the town, no longer was a sun-drenched idle avenue where traffic in sponges and sisal progressed torpidly. It was filled with slit-eyed, hunch-shouldered strangers, with the bluster of Manhattan in their voices and a wary truculence of manner. The faces that passed your shoulder in ten minutes on Bay Street would have given a New York cop nightmares for a week. Their owners for the first few weeks, made a continual horror for the black constabulary of Nassau . . . . Nothing like these hard guys had ever crossed the trail of the gorgeously uniformed, pompous coons of the Bahama police force. The invaders had no reverence whatever for red and blue coats and pipe-clayed sun helmets. These merely constituted excellent targets for fists or missiles . . . . To save themselves from ignoble extinction, the police finally reached a tacit agreement with the gang-men; a live-and-let-live policy . . . . This truce endured while the gangs stayed. Repercussions of their revelry and business dealings disturbed the nerves of Bahamians, but they suffered, generally in silence . . . . Despite the outrages committed on the peace and dignity of His Britannic Majesty's loyal city of Nassau, protest from the sufferers were few. Nassauvian bankrolls were getting too fat for their owners to kick, no matter what the gangs did."[249]

Despite the large amounts of cash distributed lavishly, although seldom graciously, by the gangster throughout Nassau, some residents did protest their disruptive antics. The Gothic-styled Trinity Wesleyan Methodist Church, located at the corner of

Frederick Street and Trinity Place and adjacent to the Lucerne Hotel, the gangster's unofficial headquarters, was directly affected by the rowdy activities of the smugglers:

> The police authorities were informed practically every Sunday by leaders of the congregation that it was impossible to worship in a satisfactory fashion when one could not hear what the minister was saying. One could not hear because next door, the big shots, the mugs and gorillas and gunmen at the Lucerne, were continuing Saturday night's drunk through the bright Sunday morning. Whoops and yawps, singing that was not even remotely hymn-like, brawls, and now and then a general combat with much shattering of furniture, discommoded the worshipers in the adjacent church. Every Sunday they told the constabulary all about it. Every Sunday the constabulary promised to investigate and did nothing more.[250]

The *Tribune*, one of the most respectable Bahamian newspapers, in several articles criticized the activities of the patrons of the Lucerne, citing the endless "orgies" and continuous partying and dancing of the Charleston.[251] Ironically, one of the highlights of the Bahamian social circuit was the so-called Bootleggers Ball, a formal affair held in July, conducted with pomp and circumstance and attended by some of the Bahamas' "venerable" notables.

Van de Water's description of operations at the Lucerne Hotel during the rum running years provide interesting insights on social and judicial life in Nassau:

> The Lucerne was a rambling framed hotel bowered in palm trees. Before the advent of bootleggers, it had been a prim, quiet hostelry, Precisely run by an elderly New England woman and her daughter. The chief justice of the colony and other folk of great respectability lived there. Most of these departed by one door when the bootleggers entered by the other, and sought more refined quarters. But the chief justice stayed on. No one ever understood why. For a servant of the law, it must have been a hideous existence. Nowhere, outside of a boiler factory, was there a less quiet building than the Lucerne during the gang's heyday.[252]

The proprietor of the Lucerne, a small, gray-haired, bespectacled and matronly looking woman, Mrs. Sweeting, was credited with being, perhaps, the only person in the colony the gangsters truly respected. They affectionately called her "Mother." Carse recounts one of McCoy's recollections reflecting the relationship between "Mother" and the mobsters:

> Their nightly habit was a dice game in the hotel bar. This sometimes reached the peak of a thousand dollars a point and emotions were aroused. Then there was the cursing, the scuffling, the cries of, 'I'll hair-comb ya,

ya bastid!' Blackjacks were flourished; brass knuckles left their imprint, and pistol butts creased skulls. Tommy, the Cockney barman, had a philosophical attitude regarding such expressions of bad temper, and he ducked down behind the already grievously scarred mahogany and rested his feet. But "Mother" was less disposed to allow damage done to her customers and establishment. She came in as the conflicts approached climax, walked to the middle of the room and slapped her hands smartly together. She said then, quite calmly, 'Boys, boys. If this keeps up, I must ask Tommy to close the bar for the night.' The answer was invariably, 'Yeah, Mother.' Then she left. Tommy rose from the rear of the bar and asked who would like what. Blood was stanched. Weapons were put away, and tailoring studied for repair. Drinks were passed, the dice were rattled, bills were tossed and bets covered, but in muted, ashamed voices.[253]

The gangsters had a peculiar fascination with fire-dancing, in which black women from the neighboring free-slave community played integral parts. A contemporary report of one of these events again demonstrates the social proclivity of the period and the indomitable influence of "Mother":

Fire dances were one of the gang's chief recreations, a pastime with no inhibitions that traced back directly to the African jungles from which so many of the Bahamian's forefathers hailed. The component parts of a fire dance were a score of negro wenches, a drum fashioned from a keg by stretching a bladder over one end, and illimitable gin. Put these together and they spell, after the fire and gin have melted away restraint, as barbaric an orgy as the stars ever looked upon . . . . Usually these revels were held in a clearing in the bush not far from Grantstown. Some bright spirit among the gang, one evening when Mother was absent temporarily from her hotel, suggested that a fire dance be staged in the Lucerne's yard. Among the palms. It was well underway when the old lady returned, to find a bonfire blazing; a drum throbbing wickedly; dark, wholly nude bacchantes circling madly in the red uncertain light, and a ring of frenzied white men yelling and patting juba. It was not a scene that the entire police force of Nassau would have dared disturb, but the old lady broke through the ring of lustful men and confronted them. The drums stopped, the clapping died away, the wenches scuttled for their discarded clothing. "Boys', the proprietress of the Lucerne said, 'I didn't think you'd do anything like this. Would you want your mothers to see you this way?' That ended the dance.[254]

The two most notable persons on the Bahamian rum-running scene were William "Bill" McCoy, already noted as arguably the most celebrated character of the Prohibition era, and the impeccably dressed, gun-toting Gertrude Lythgoe, whose reputation as a dealer in a man's business earned her the ignoble moniker "the Bahama Queen." If Lythgoe was queen, McCoy was the undisputed king of rum runners, and unquestionably the most successful and notorious of all. When he finally quit the business, he had reportedly smuggled 175,000 cases of liquor to the United States, inventing many of the innovations in rum running later adopted by others and earning him the reputation of the father of Rum Row. McCoy recounted his story to Frederick Van de Water. The author subsequently noted that, "from that talk with Bill McCoy and many subsequent conversations, this book [*The Real McCoy*, 1931] has grown . . . . Even in print, it remains as closely as possible his story. The hand is the hand of his reporter, but the voice is the voice of William McCoy—the real McCoy." The following are excerpts from that series of interviews.

> Of all that hard, wild, unrestrained crew of rascals who infested Nassau in the early, disorganized era of the rum trade, McCoy was the most personable, the most trustworthy. In a day when a man's word was worth no more than the breath that bore it, when contracts were enforced by lynx-like vigilance backed by firearms; when theft, double-crossing, piracy, even murder were frequent and usually unpunished, McCoy strode his boyishly grinning, zestful way, respected and honored by the underworld rabble through which he went, ruefully admired even by the Unites States Consul, Lorin A. Lathrop, a veteran of the service who in official moments was his firm antagonist and, after hours, his friend . . . . The liquor McCoy's ships carried was always the best. Debts he incurred, whether oral or written were always paid on time and in full. Friends whom he made, he kept. Persistently he struck at the law of the country, but he held to his own not inconsiderable moral code . . . . To Nassauvians, who profited greatly during his rum running years, he has become a glamorous Robin Hood of the Main. His erstwhile associates have epitomized his square crookedness in a phrase that has become a part of the nation's slang: 'The Real McCoy'—signifying all that is best and most genuine.[255]

Gertrude "Cleo" Lythgoe was dubbed "Bahama Queen" by contemporaries out of respect for the reputation she earned as the no-nonsense representative of two London distillers, and the only woman to hold a wholesale liquor license in Nassau during a time when danger and intrigue typified the male-dominated business. Lythgoe, although rumored by some to be a gypsy, a Native American, an Egyptian, Russian, French, or Spanish, was actually the dark-haired beautiful daughter of English and Scottish immigrants and born in Bowling Green, Ohio. Lythgoe's story was widely publicized in syndicated columns in magazines and newspapers that included the *New York Times, Chicago Tribune,* and the *Los Angeles Times,* where she was ceremoniously crowned "Queen of the Bootleggers" and the "Queen of the Rum Row." The *Wall Street Journal* estimated that at the end of Prohibition, Lythgoe had amassed a fortune worth millions of dollars. The story stated, "Grace Lythgoe, Englishwoman, head of probably the largest international whiskey business, admits whiskey worth $1,000,000 will soon leave Europe for the Bahamas, to be smuggled into the United States."[256] The newspaper had picked up on a story featured in the *Paris Herald*.

In 1923, the *Los Angeles Times* carried a story headlined "Liquor Queen Due in the East":

> The veritable queen of the bootleggers will arrive in New York shortly from Nassau, capital of the Bahamas and capital also of the West Indies bootlegging trade. She is coming here to invest some of her wealth in Fifth-avenue finery and to do Broadway as she has always longed to do it, but according to her fellow intimates in Nassau, her chief desire is marriage with 'the right man' and a suburban cottage, for which she would gladly forego the adventure and large income of her present post . . . . [T] here is no flapdoodle or flummery about this novel queen, she carries on a legitimate trade and can snap her fingers at prohibition commissioners and their subordinates . . . . She is Gertrude C. Lythgoe, of California.[257]

On January 13, 1924, the *New York Times* carried a less flattering story of the Lythgoe visit under a caption that read, "She Exports Liquors: Miss Gertrude Lythgoe, Formerly a San Francisco Stenographer, Manages a Successful Business in the Bahamas Supplying the Market with Scotch."[258] Lythgoe's acclaim apparently intrigued the young Englishman Netley Lucas, a juvenile delinquent who later became a respected criminologist. In his work titled *Crooks and Confessions* (1925), he wrote a glowing description of the "Bootleger Queen" and Nassau, from where she operated:

> There was a perpetually moving through crowding, jostling and elbowing one another through the streets-some of them narrow and tortuous. There were Americans, Spaniards, Greeks, half-breeds, men with yellow faces and high cheek-bones, blacks, and an odd mixture of sharp-looking white men. The sun threw heavily-marked shadows on to the glaring white walls of the houses, bringing into prominence the brilliantly-striped sun-blinds and gaily-coloured umbrellas. Here and there was a yoke of oxen drawing their heavy carts; a women with a scarlet flower in her hair; a padre in a rusty cassock; and ever the moving crowd of eager, busy men. Here a little group in ill-fitting slops, exchanging greetings amidst laughter and boisterous joking; there a little knot of men, voices raised to a dangerously high pitch, and any number of idlers and hangers-on, ready to do anything for a tip or a drink. The outstanding figure, and the one which always remains clearly in my mind when I think of this scene,

rising above the heads and shoulders of this mixed mob was—a woman. It would be unkind to divulge her name, but I will call her Grace; that name suggests her personality and will help me better my story. She had a strength of character that enabled her to move in this strange, motley crowd of men, to do business in their trade and by their methods, yet she did not in any way tarnish her honour . . . Most striking of all about her in these surroundings and in such setting was the extraordinary clearness of her skin and the intense darkness of her hair, which was extremely abundant and coiled closely and smoothly around her head. Her eyes were grey, beautifully shaped, and deeply set in a face as remarkable for its beauty as for its repose and quiet strength. An enormous black servant, always closely in her wake, completed one of the most striking pictures I have ever seen.[259]

Lythgoe's biography, *The Bahama Queen* (1964) traces some of the exploits of the adventurous businesswoman, including the rum-running voyage she undertook along Rum Row in 1923 with William "Bill" McCoy. According to the author, Bill and his brother Ben built a lucrative business from rum running, with Bill managing all sea operations and Ben taking care of business on land. She noted that the brothers became the specific target of both the enforcement officials and organized crime and were indicted several times on charges of conspiracy to violate the National Prohibition Act. On November 23, 1923, Bill McCoy was eventually captured and arrested. Lythgoe claimed that "To avoid a prolonged trial, and to allow his brother Ben to go free, he pleaded guilty and served nine months in jail."[260] Lythgoe last saw McCoy in 1944, four years before his death in 1948. Gertrude Cecilia Lythgoe went on to eventually live in Miami, then New York, later Detroit, and finally Los Angeles, where she died in 1974 at the age of 86. Some critics believe the 1975 film *Lucky Lady,* which starred Liza Minelli, Burt Reynolds, and Gene Hackman, was inspired by the exploits of this remarkable woman commonly known as the "The Bahama Queen."

The demand for ships and men to handle the rum-running operation at all levels became a monstrous temptation for Bahamians from all walks of life. A member of a wealthy Bahamian family spoke to me under condition of anonymity to protect the reputation of his family on the subject of Bahamian involvement in rum running. He casually noted that almost every economically affluent Bahamian family of today got their "start" from involvement in some aspect of rum running. He noted that some made money from the supply of vessels, some operated vessels, some operated warehouses, some supplied capital, and a few, like his family, were involved at all levels. My informant verified the report of the white expatriate Bahamian police official who, for example, resigned from his post to join the ranks of the rum runners, allegedly with the covert support of his superiors who, the informant claimed, benefited "in kind." The former law enforcement official reportedly made a fortune with which he retired and lived the "life of Riley" on one of the outer Bahamian islands. The informant noted that many of the old guard politicians of "Bay Street" fame and even certain "men of the cloth" were active participants in the alluring bonanza of rum running.[261]

In 1928, the Coast Guard bolstered patrol of the southern waters with the dispatch of twelve ships, and for apparent good reason, which Harold Waters, a contemporary Coast Guard officer explained,

> Floridian rummies, we soon found, had their own Rum Rows-and they were the kind that defied physical dispersion. Rum Rows down south were the Bahamian Group of islands . . . Bimini, the westernmost fringe of the Bahamas, was only fifty-eight miles across the Gulf Stream from Miami Beach . . . . With fine weather prevailing for the greater part of the year, plus the comparatively short hauls—a fast rummy could make two Bimini-Miami runs during the course of a night—and with two few six-bitters and picket boats to guard the five hundred mile length of the Florida Peninsular, Southern rummies had the very best of good things going for them.[262]

Waters noted that the operation of the battery of navigational aid beacons running along the Florida coast became an inadvertent aid to the runners, as the powerful lights were visible from Bimini. Accordingly, "A homeward bound rummy scarcely needed a compass, all he had to do was steer by those lights flashing up into the Floridian skies. And when he wished to establish his position, he merely took a bearing on two lights, giving him a perfect fix."[263] And as for Bimini, the primary supplier of the lucrative Florida Gold Coast trade, Waters had this to say:

> Bimini itself consisted of two small islands. Before the advent of Stateside Prohibition it was just another poorhouse of the British Empire, with fishing providing the scantiest of livings for its hard-pressed negro inhabitants. But now, because of its close proximity to the Florida Gold Coast, Bimini was waxing fat as a major smuggling base, enjoying a fabulous era of prosperity. Bimini's coral strand, known as The King's Highway, was now a sort of International Queer Street swarming with such representative types as rum barons, gambling kings, counterfeiters, call girls, confidence men, bunko operators, gangsters and promoters of every stripe and hue. Standing back from the waterfront were liquor warehouses open for business the clock around.[264]

In 1920, the *Miami Metropolis* described Bimini as a "supermarket of wet goods where the runner went in and with complete confidence in the quality of the merchandise, ordered his liquor sight unseen."[265]

Other Bahamian islands that actively hosted rum-running operations included the microislands called Cat Cay and Gun Cay, both situated in the northwest of the archipelago. Then there was the community at West End on Grand Bahama Island.

On the eve of Prohibition, West End was just another poor community of predominantly black Bahamians eking out a subsistence living, mostly by fishing and subsistence farming. The community displayed several palm-thatched rove huts lining a dusty road that hugged the coast. Tied up to the little jetty and on the beach were a few small unpainted fishing shacks. Most residents, regardless of age or sex, went along without shoes, because such commodities were unaffordable. Much of the diet of West End would have consisted largely of the local bread called "Johnny cake," home-ground grits, grunts and gravy, a common staple of the masses. All this was to change once the gangsters arrived. In 1921, an article in the *Literary Digest* commented, "West End, the largest settlement on Grand Bahama Island, lay sixty-miles due east of West Palm Beach. There were nine liquor warehouses there in 1921, and in the harbor forty to fifty power boats awaited orders and favorable weather to make their stealthy visits to the Florida coasts. As the smugglers lay around swapping tales and frequently sampling their cargoes, burly Negroes loaded the craft while chanting in sonorous tones;

> Ole man he go in the schooner at night,
> Boss man he campin' down.
> Mammy's boy he countin' gold.
> All right, All right."[266]

West End was ideally situated for the running trade, and runners found the community convenient for getting clearance papers with less costly bribes than they were forced to pay in Nassau. Carse summed up the situation as follows:

> West End prospered, grew rapidly wealthy. A palmetto-log dock substantial enough to bear the traffic was built. Warehouses were erected and filled to the sheet-tin roofs with a broad assortment of liquor. The population, less than a hundred formerly easygoing island Negroes, gave up fishing, sponging and turtle-catching as a livelihood. They handled the rum-runner cargoes, and they no longer went barefoot or considered salted codfish eyes a delicacy. Shoes by the crate lot were imported from Nassau. Meat was on the tables at mealtime. American phonographs played American jazz for the worker's pleasure as they filed back and forth from the warehouses to the dock. Scotch whisky was the favored drink, not shandy brandy, that product of the palm tree which, when distilled and drunk, battered a man into insensibility within the space of a few hours. Per capita, West End was the richest community of its kind anywhere in the Caribbean. Even with the decline of the Nassau commerce it held its place, supported by the Florida-bound boats.[267]

The thousands of discarded wooden liquor crates were used by locals for storage and "patching". Instead of investing precious dollars in imported lumber, many residents repaired their homes, damaged from hurricanes or dilapidated with age or neglect, with the discarded crates. In this regard, many buildings sported the labels of the products responsible for the sudden prosperity, prominently and inadvertently advertising such brands as Johnny Walker, Mumm's Extra Dry, and Monarch Scotch Whiskey. It must have been an interesting and, to the more "pious" parishioners of the St. Mary's Anglican Church, uncomfortable sight on Sunday mornings as they worshipped, sang hymns, and gave tithe and offerings with the constant reminders just outside their windows as to the real source of their blessings.

Quentin Reynolds noted that rum runners sometimes used airplanes to transport illegal liquor to American markets: "West End was also base for a fleet of airplanes that regularly contributed in assuaging the thirst of many an anxious Floridian. Although the planes were small, necessarily limiting cargo space, there was virtually no resistance to aeronautical smuggling. The pilots were swashbucklers of the first order, men who lived dangerously and enjoyed it. Perhaps, the only consolation to one unfortunate enough to ditch his plane was that he was assured of going down in good spirits."[268] In the absence of adequate warehouse space on Bimini, in the West End, and on the cays, cases of liquor were commonly stored on barges. Typically these were about thirty by fifty feet with a house on each end, one serving as sleeping quarters and the other as dining room and kitchen. There was ample space on these commodious craft to accommodate several thousand cases.[269]

British complicity in the smuggling trade strained relations between that country and the United States, with smuggling from the British Bahamian Islands becoming the primary subject of debate. In 1923, the *New York Times* reported that British officials generally refused to suppress their "colonials" in the islands who were involved, either directly or indirectly, in smuggling activities.[270] The newspaper reported that an un-named senator had proposed that should war with Britain result, batteries could be erected on Miami from which missile attacks against the Bahamas could be launched.[271] One reporter opined that since the island was already partially owned and visited by Americans, "it should be easy for the American tourist on the spot to seize and hold the island until help can arrive."[272]

Senator Park Trammell of Florida commented on the massive flow of liquor into his state from the Bahamas in a letter to Secretary of State Charles Evans Hughes: "To increase the effectiveness of prohibition enforcement . . . a treaty with Great Britain under which that nation would prohibit its ships from transporting intoxicating liquors into the United State [is needed]."[273] In January 1924, an Anglo-American Rum Running Convention was held in Washington that resulted in a treaty signed by the two nations on January 23, 1924. Under the terms of the treaty, Britain agreed to allow American authorities to board ships in British territorial waters suspected of illegal trafficking. In turn, the United States agreed that liquor destined for foreign ports, but stopping at American ports, would not be disturbed as long as the cargo remained under seal while in American ports and was not unloaded.[274]

Despite the evidence of prosperity that captured the attention of Bahamians during Prohibition, there was a dark, sinister, and at times fatal side to the business. Gertrude Lythgoe, in her interview with Netley Lucas, reportedly commented on the dangers of the trade:

> Strange things happen in this business of ours . . . . I remember a Greek here in Nassau. I knew him very well. He was of a very old Greek family and he always had an idea that if he could only get rich quickly he could go back to Greece, live in the house of his father, and surround himself with art and beauty for the rest of his days . . . . I think he was getting very near to the realization of his hopes when he brought off his last big deal, and that was a cargo of five thousand cases for 'Rum Row.' When the stuff was landed, every single bottle was found to contain salt water . . . . He was [consequently] dealt with here in Nassau. He is dead now, but he did not die in Greece.[275]

As the trade progressed, acts of violence against Bahamians became increasingly severe. West End was to be rudely jolted into this reality. On a bright sunny day, as West Enders went about their usual routines, some reportedly listening to an Al Jolson record brought in from Key West while others read old newspapers or just loafed in the soft sunshine, three rough-looking white men landed at the local dock. While one kept watch at the dock, the others walked up the dusty street and, with brandished handguns, forced entry into every house and robbed the occupants as well as the people on the outside. According to one report, "Everything that was of value and could be carried in the launch was seized. But cash, either American or British, was the real incentive of the raid. His Majesty's collector of Custom was told to hand over what was in his possession. He pleaded the fact that it belonged to the government and pointed to the lion-and-unicorn seal over the door-way of his office. He was pitched into the street on his head and his safe looted."[276] The looters escaped with some four thousand dollars in cash, but not the hundred thousand dollars they were told the customs collector had collected, which ironically, was almost the amount the officer had had sent to Nassau the day before.

While the affair at West End ended without bloodshed, the crew of the Bahamian schooner *William H. Albury* were not so fortunate. According to reports, the ship was anchored off Cat Cay in the northern Bahamas with a load of liquor waiting to supply interested ships with the cargo. Because of the spate of robberies of supply ships, cautious captains allowed only one boat to approach at a time, whereupon that boar was served and sent away before another was invited to approach. As such, all other vessels would anchor at shouting distance from the supply craft until invited to approach. Bahamian captain Edgecombe, two other white men, and the crew of black deckhands of the *William H. Albury* cautiously serviced the first boat and subsequently saw it push off before inviting the second boat to approach. According to court records, Edgecombe allegedly knew Captain Jimmy Truitt of the second boat well enough to invite him and his crew of two others to breakfast. Upon sight of several thousand U.S. dollars still lying on the table in the cabin, Truitt and his crew reportedly brandished revolvers and stole the cash. In the events that followed, Captain Edgecombe was fatally shot in the back when he attempted to escape to the crew quarters. Further reports at Nassau alleged that Truitt left unaware of some forty thousand dollars made from sales before his arrival.[277]

Perhaps the most celebrated case of murder on the high seas involved the very Coast Guard sent to interdict rum running and enforce Prohibition laws. In 1927, the American and British authorities were becoming increasingly alarmed at the widespread display of counterfeit money in the Bahamas, particularly in Bimini. In August of that year, Robert K. Webster, an agent of the United States Secret Service, was aboard a Coast Guard cutter traveling from Ft. Lauderdale to Bimini to investigate growing complaints of "funny money" in circulation there. Boatswain Sidney Sanderlin was the skipper of the six-bitter *249*. A smaller vessel was sighted supposedly sailing from Bimini and heading for Miami. Sanderlin decided to investigate, first by sounding the general alarm for his crew to prepare for necessary action, then authorizing the firing of warning shots intended to alert the suspect ship to surrender. The boarding party found twenty-five cases of whiskey on the rummy. After their boat was secured, the two-man crew of the runner, Captain James Alderman and his deck-hand, identified simply as Weech, a black Bahamian from Bimini, were escorted aboard the Coast Guard cutter and seated in the pilothouse.

Waters relates the sequence of events that followed:

> Alderman, who had strolled into the pilothouse behind [Sanderlin] seized one of four unguarded automatic pistols lying on the chart desk, aimed it at Sanderlin's back and fired. Sanderlin slumped to the deck, dead. Then, snatching another pistol, Alderman charged out on deck, both guns blazing. One of his bullets hit a young machinist mate, Victor Lamby, who, startled by the firing, had started aft toward the armory to get a pistol. Lamby never made it. Mortally wounded, he toppled down the engine room companionway. The bullet had entered his right side, almost severing his spinal cord. Another of the six-bitter's crew, Robinson by name, bravely threw a wrench at Alderman, whose aim was momentarily deflected as he dodged the flying missile. Before the killer could recover himself and bring his gun to bear, Robinson prudently jumped overboard.[278]

Waters notes that what followed "in lightening fashion was the ugliest piece of cold—blooded murder ever to take place on the deck of a Coast Guard cutter."[279]

Alderman reportedly ordered all remaining Coast Guard crew and authorized passengers up to the bow of the vessel and ordered Weech to cut the fuel lines below with the intent to send the crew to Davy's Locker in an explosion of ignited fuel. Weech threw a lighted match into a heap of water-soaked rags he assumed to be fuel-soaked and at a signal the duo attempted to board their vessel intent on motoring away from the presumably doomed Coast Guard cutter. Momentarily distracted by the backfire of their own vessel, the former prisoners surprised and subsequently disarmed the runners, securing them in shackles until help from the Ft. Lauderdale base arrived. Consequently, Alderman was convicted and sentenced to death by a federal court in Miami and later hanged on a gallows erected in an airplane hangar at the Coast Guard Base in Ft. Lauderdale, home base of the murdered servicemen. Weech turned states witness and received a sentence of 366 days in prison. The event apparently touched a raw public nerve, because shortly afterward, public opinion crescendoed and almost certainly influenced the eventual repeal of what one writer called "the zaniest law ever to befoul the statue books of the land."[280] With the demise of Prohibition, the Bahamas once again declined into its historical mode of somnolence and obscurity, waiting for the next economic boom to burst on the horizon as a result of events unfolding in the annals of her big neighbor to the north.

In her work titled *Bahamian Memories* (2000), which offers the story of the Bahamas as told by those who experienced it, Olga Culmer Jenkins provides an interesting perspective from the viewpoint of black Bahamians. In one interview, Joanna Bethel reported that only a small number of black Bahamians living in West End, Grand Bahama, such as Horatio Wilchcombe and Augustus Hepburn, profited from the illegal trade by establishing bars from which rum runners from the United States could purchase wholesale merchandise and thirsty clients could freely quench their thirsts. Other blacks benefited from providing services as cooks, common laborers, and watchmen. Bethel reportedly lamented, however, that the source of wealth lasted "until some [white] Abaconians—John Murray . . . and his son-in-law Mr. Roberts—came there. They bought property and built bars. They built kitchen, dining room and everything to entertain the bootleggers. Took business right away from the natives, you see?"[281] In another interview, Alfred Love was reported to state, "Coloured people didn't make lots of money out of rum-running. The coloured people ain't had no boats. The whites had motor boats . . . . The coloured Bahamians were in the crew and went along, but they didn't make the money. It was mostly the Conchy Joes (Bahamian whites) took part in rum-running."[282]

Bethel's interview largely reflected the general impact of rum-running on the residents of the islands before and after Prohibition:

> Alcohol became a problem at Wet End for plenty of the young people. After the people from the other island found out that they could come here and get drunk, they started coming from Nassau and these other

island, Long Island and all. And then the girls started being prostitutes. That's how prostitution began in Grand Bahama. A few of the native West Enders were doing the same thing. Once liquor became legal in the United States, the drinking and prostitution in West End stopped. They had to stop because the barrooms then began closing down. There was no sale. People began moving out in 1930. Other than that, the neighbours carried on as normally as usual. They make a little money here and there.[283]

The Bahamas, despite the obvious negative effects, profited from the events of Prohibition in a number of ways. In 1922, a new electrical plant and upgrade to the local communication system were introduced. In 1928, Nassau harbor was dredged to accommodate larger ships and a terminal was constructed to accommodate visitors. The waterfront improvement was summarily named Prince George's Wharf in honor of the October visit of His Royal Highness Prince George.[284] Roads, at least in Nassau and parts of New Providence, were improved to accommodate the spate of vehicles purchased with newly acquired wealth. In 1922, local newspapers advertised the sale of vehicles priced at affordable rates. For example, M. N. Chipman offered Studebakers priced at £300, £400, and £500. Rival Royal Garage offered 14-18-mile-per-gallon, five-passenger Buick sedans ranging in price from £512 to £300. On the other hand, John McKinney offered the more affordable two-seater Ford Runabout touring car at £140.[285] By 1926, the *Tribune*, with apparent pride, reported that the touring sedans had become a status symbol in the colony, as demonstrated by high-profile Sunday afternoon drives.[286]

Dupuch, the editor of the *Tribune*, seemingly ignored his editorial of a few years before in which he complained that a significant increase in traffic was creating a problem along Bay Street, "so much recently that walking and driving in that area between 9 a. m. and 5 a. m. are becoming more and more difficult . . . . [C]arriages and automobiles are parked all along the way, sometimes on both sides of the street. Occasionally, a vehicle has to wait a few seconds before being able to pass."[287] In 1923, 164 vehicles were imported, and, by 1927, this total had risen to 297 vehicles, in contrast to the mere six imported in 1918.[288] By 1930, with the end of Prohibition, however, advertisements for vehicles in local Bahamian newspapers all but disappeared as sales dropped to near pre-Prohibition levels.

As a direct result of Prohibition, many visitors flocked to the Bahamas during the 1920s and indulged in a variety of methods to quench their seemingly insatiable thirsts, thus giving impetus to the development of tourism as a primary industry. The Bahamian government seized the opportunity to improve means of communication between the colony and the outside world, and especially with the United States. In response, weekly passenger and freight services were established between Nassau, New York, Miami, and Havana. In 1922, for example, the Ward Line advertised weekly freight and passenger service to New York at the following rates: $75 per passenger for first-class accommodations, $55 for second class, and $44 per passenger for third class. Interestingly, the cost to travel from Nassau to Havana on that line was more expensive than travel to New York, priced at $95 for individual first-class passage and $60 for second-class accommodations.[289] In addition to sea transportation, in 1929 Pan American Airways began daily scheduled flights between Nassau and Miami during the winter months using a 24-passenger seaplane.

To further develop the tourist industry, the Development Board was created, interestingly under the chairmanship of R. H. Curry, owner of perhaps the most successful steamship in the colony. He used public funds to develop advertisements, tour maps, and flyers about the islands to attract wealthy Americans to enjoy not only the free flow of liquor available in the islands, but also the colonial charm, sandy beaches, and tropical paradise environment the islands had to offer. Emphasis was placed on the promotion of existing and newly developed sports and recreation facilities and other sources of entertainment. Naturally, he took the opportunity to promote his own passenger and freight services as viable means of comfortable and reliable transportation to the colony. By 1926, two new luxury hotels had been completed, and several smaller motels were in full operation. Enterprising white Bahamians with the social wherewithal and political clout were able to obtain licenses to lease their other residences to wealthy visitors, while others operated boarding houses, and a few provided rooms for rent in their private residences. Exclusive members-only establishments, such as the Bahamian and the Porcupine clubs, opened for business. The Bahamian Club, in particular, operated by C. F. Reed, an American with alleged ties to the Meyer Lansky Miami-based crime syndicate, was licensed to operate roulette tables—the first legalized gambling operation in the colony.[290]

As early as 1922, the adverse effect of Prohibition beyond the rise in crime was becoming a cause for concern in the colony and, in particular, in Nassau. One writer to the editor of the *Tribune* succinctly summed up the situation:

> It is gratifying to notice that you are calling attention to the present high
> cost of living in this Colony . . . this matter of the high cost of living has
> been on my mind and I should judge that the difference in cost is quite
> fifty per cent more in Nassau [than in Florida] . . . At present time there
> is another question allied to the high cost of commodities, and that is
> the scarcity of dwellings for our people. I know of quite a few families
> who have to quit their present abodes and are [on] the lookout for fresh
> quarters, alas, not to be found. Rents have increased enormously and [I]
> have heard of cases that look like extortion, one case where a tenant has
> been compelled to pay a rent at least two and one half times the real worth
> of the property. The cost of building and the scarcity of available sites in
> the city proper make it almost impossible for any but the well-to-do to
> build, or even think of building.[291]

The *Tribune* editorial of October 4 of that year supported the complaint that a housing situation existed in Nassau that was becoming "an acute problem." The paper cited examples of more than two families being forced to occupy one single-family house and living in very cramped and less-than-private quarters, "because it is absolutely impossible for each of them to obtain a dwelling, all for themselves."[292] The editor noted that certain unscrupulous landlords were indeed taking advantage of this fact to increase the already too-high rents, because they knew their tenants would be unable to find other housing. The cause of the housing shortage was attributed to the flow of people from the rural out-islands into Nassau seeking jobs and the Prohibition profits that had reportedly made the common laborer instantly rich.

In mid-1930, the *Tribune* editorial summarized the chronic situation facing the colony, creating a vexing, hydra-like problem of mass migration from the islands to the city and the subsequent demise of productive agriculture. Overcrowding was leading to a shortage in adequate housing and widespread unemployment that impacted local spending and debt service patterns:

> In recent years the various public works which have been carried out have provided ample employment at good wages for a large section of the community. Now that these available funds for continuing and developing these public utilities are exhausted, our legislators being alarmed because the budget fails to perform that difficult feat of balancing which is expected of it, prospective public works have had perforce to vanish into space like the conjurer's rabbit. Estimates of expenditure for the coming year, now already a quarter of its time expired, have been ruthlessly "axed" and the programme of public works, which it anticipated would provide employment to a considerable number of people, has been so cut down that many of these must inevitably look forward to periods of unemployment and its inseparable hard times during the ensuing months.[293]

The end of Prohibition and the resulting effects of the end of the unparalleled period of prosperity in Bahamian history became evident by 1930, when the editor of the *Tribune* admonished readers of the need to further develop tourism as a major industry for the Bahamas:

> It is generally believed that business conditions in the United States affected the tide of travel to Nassau last year and are likely to do so next year and what do we find? The Development Board forced to curtail its advertising campaign on account of a reduced grant owing to lack of funds in the Public Treasury. Any tourist resort in similar circumstances would be redoubling their efforts to attract visitors . . . . England and Scotland have launched thoroughly practical tourist development schemes, supported

by Tourist Associations whose funds are provided by subscriptions from members and associate members and corporations. Is it too much to hope that an organized movement similar to these associations . . . may be started in Nassau to supplement the efforts of the Development Board . . . and give Nassau a larger place on the map and a larger share of tourist travel?[294]

D. Gail Saunders, former director of archives for the Bahamas, describes the impact of Prohibition on development of the Bahamas:

The brief prosperity of the Prohibition years was marked by the consolidation of commercial enterprise and the improvement and modernization of public facilities and communication in Nassau. While concentrating on the expansion of the tourist industry, the legislators greatly neglected agriculture, and took an indifferent attitude to the faltering sponge fishing industry. The brief bonanza not only set the economic pattern but also delayed political and constitutional progress in the Bahamas. General neglect of the Out Islands, compounded by the devastating hurricanes, resulted in increased migration of destitute Out Islanders to the capital. When the Wall Street Crash came in 1929, many Bahamians were already experiencing desperate poverty once again.[295]

Indeed, with the demise of Prohibition and the global impact of the Wall Street Crash, the Bahamas once again settled into a familiar situation of social somnolence and economic destitution, but not without hope. The experiment with tourism was to become the savior of the colony and its economic mainstay far into the future. For the immediate ensuing years of the Great Depression, however, many Bahamians began to give increased thought and action to migration to the United States.

6. MIGRATION AND IMMIGRATION

The "Saltwater" Underground Railroad

The earliest recorded account of Bahamians migrating to what is now the United States of America happened in the late 1780s, when a group of fifty Bahamian refugees fled to Casco Bay in modern-day Maine to escape sporadic Spanish and French attacks against the islands. In the attacks, the residents were reportedly "spoiled by the Spanish of all their possessions and driven off naked and destitute."[296] The refugees were assisted by benevolent Brethren, who petitioned the Governor to provide the destitute Bahamians with land on which to settle and an advance in public funds to outfit and supply them. The Bahamians were apparently barely able to survive the bitter winter of 1786, complained to the authorities that the relief aid supplied was inadequate, and eventually returned to the Bahamas the following year.

The second recorded migration of a group of Bahamians to the United States occurred in the mid-1770s during the American Revolution, when refugees this time appealed to the British authorities to provide sanctuary against attacks by American rebels. Robin F. A. Fabel captures the event as follows:

> The coming of war to the Bahamas early in the American Revolution caused several inhabitants of New Providence, as Nassau was then called, to look for security in West Florida. On the 3rd and 4th March, 1776, the United States Continental Navy captured Fort Montague, artillery and governor Montfort Brown, among other officials. Fearful of repeated raids, the Bahamian planter Thomas Hodgson successfully petitioned for land on the Pearl River in West Florida. The following month he sponsored a more general petition on behalf of his fellow island[ers] which the West Florida Council received favorably, although how many refugees took advantage of it remains unknown.[297]

In the early 1800s, Bahamian Loyalists were encouraged by the Spanish authorities to return to lands many of them had abandoned in St. Augustine and New Smyrna, Florida, and engage in the production of sugar. A few Loyalists reportedly accepted the offer and "once again established themselves close by the southern reaches of the King's Highway, hoping to become wealthy sugar planters."[298]

One of the most intriguing yet largely underrepresented aspects of American-Bahamian migration history is the story of the Underground Railroad to the Bahamas. This era, which seems to have started in the late 1700s and continued through the 1800s, involved the migration of peoples of African, mixed African, and Native American ethnicity to the islands. This limited migration extended throughout the American Civil War years. In *Creeks and Seminoles* (1986), Wright outlines the variety of interactions that occurred along a multi-ethnic frontier in which Native Americans acted as buffers between European powers competing along the Gulf Coast and runaway slaves and free blacks. In this work, Wright notes that after Florida became a U.S. territory in 1821, the southern Native American groups increasingly became the emerging enemy of many white Americans who viewed them as a threat to the fulfillment of the American policy of Manifest Destiny.[299] The demand for their removal to the far West and perhaps even to Canada eventually became a matter of national policy. Some runaway slaves and blacks of mixed Native American and African blood, however, determined to migrate to the friendly nearby shores of the Bahamas.

During the American Revolution, many southern blacks and Native Americans associated freedom with the British government. For the blacks, in particular, the British made it a point to emphasize that most of the prominent American leaders, including George Washington, Thomas Jefferson, and Patrick Henry were hypocritical slaveholders who conveniently used the term "liberty and justice for all" for political and economic gain, and did not include consideration for the rights of blacks or Native Americans in that reference. On the other hand, the British enlisted thousands of free blacks and slaves into their armed forces with the promise of freedom and clear title to their own parcel of land. Wright notes that black males "joined the Royal Army and Navy, serving not only as musicians, body servants, and pioneers, but also as soldiers armed with Brown Bess muskets and foot-long bayonets . . . . [G]athering up his wife and children, a male slave could sneak off to British lines, be fed, clothed, armed, and freed. It was this rather than the philosophical musings of the Georgia trustees in London at an earlier period that made so many southern blacks associate the Union Jack with liberty."[300] Wright uses the career of Thomas Brown, a prominent land speculator, planter, and Indian trader, to illustrate how the experiences of blacks, whites, and Native Americans in the southern United States during the Revolutionary years were inextricably intertwined:

> When the Revolution broke out, he [Brown] became an outspoken
> Loyalist and for almost nine years led provincial troops in the bitter
> partisan fighting in South Carolina, Georgia and East Florida . . . . Brown

was commander of the East Florida Rangers, recognized as the King's
(Carolina) Rangers, and was also the southern Indian superintendent
for the eastern division, which included the Creeks, Seminoles, and
Cherokees; as a result, whites, blacks, and Indians all served under him.
When rebel slaves ran away to join British forces, Brown was sometimes
the [British] commander. His polyglot forces captured and carried off
rebel slaves, which contributed to the unprecedented infusion of free
blacks and slaves among the Muscogulges.[301]

The Bahamas became a focal point of contact between the southeastern Native
American peoples, runaway blacks living among them, and the British authorities.
William Augustus Bowles, Bahamian adventurer and self-proclaimed director-general
of the Creek nation, attempted to establish the Indian state of Muskogee as a
British protectorate. To accomplish this, he promised the Muscogulges and their
black dependents that Britain would protect their right to become a self-governing
state. He remained in contact with and initially received supplies from the British
authorities in Nassau until his death in 1805. While some blacks living in "Indian
territory," particularly those on plantations and in maroon settlements, generally
rejected adoption of aspects of the Native American cultural practices, most
conveniently learned several languages, including "English, Spanish, French,
Creek, Hitchiti, Yuchi, Alabama, Shawnee, Gullah, and Geechee. As a result they
became versatile linguists in great demand as interpreters and spies; this gave the
Negroes status and power."[302] In 1802, a Creek delegation made an unofficial visit to
the British authorities in Nassau. Prominent Nassau trader John DeLacy mentioned
the occasion to Augustus Bowles in a letter dated March 11th, in which he noted
how fortunate it was that Panton's black servant happened to be on the scene to
interpret the discussion between the Creeks and authorities.[303]

British military commanders, also encouraged blacks and disenchanted Native
Americans to rally around them as their most viable means of survival against the
mounting American encroachments. As a result, hundreds of black soldiers were
recruited, armed, and drilled at British forts in East Florida in preparation for
an all-out invasion of Georgia and New Orleans in hopes of disrupting American
stability in those areas and freeing slaves who would presumably join British ranks
in the process. Wright concludes:

> Britain's recruitment of and reliance on southern Negroes served to bring
> the Maroons among the Muscogulges into sharper focus. One hears about
> them, particularly from Americans concerned about runaway slaves,
> living at or near the British (Negro) fort on the Apalachicola River, at
> Miccosukee, Palatka, Tampa, and elsewhere. These Negroes, along with
> those in Indian villages and on Indian plantations, from time to time
> visited the Bahamas to beseech George III not to forsake them. [With]

the British flag flying over the fort commanding Nassau's harbor in the breeze, Negroes witnessed at first hand the implications of Britain's abolition of the slave trade. That black Muscogulges regarded George III as their friend, protector, and liberator worried Andrew Jackson, and this was one reason why he seized Pensacola in 1814 and swept deep into Florida four years later during the First Seminole War.[304]

According to Wright, "Between 1775 and 1815 British military commanders had freed tens of thousands of Negro slaves who ran away from their American masters and sought sanctuary with British forces. Some of these Negroes eventually became free black Muscogulges. White American slave-owners, however, vehemently [denounced] any British liberation."[305] The importance of these blacks to the British cause and subsequent impact on evolving American politics is illustrated in this statement by Wright:

> Whether fugitive plantation slaves or black Muscogulges, Negroes were to play an important role in Britain's southern campaign. The London government authorized enlisting five thousand Negroes from the deep South to serve in provincial regiments, and Colonel Nichols, Lieutenant George Woodbine, and other marine officers trained up to a thousand blacks at Pensacola, the British fort, and Cumberland Island. Black recruits evoked visions of a general slave insurrection, and their psychological threat was as great as their military potential. Invitations to desert their masters and come into British lines circulated throughout the South from Georgia and Tennessee to Louisiana . . . . Many of the Negroes enrolled in the British service came from Anglo planters and merchants in East and West Florida, especially from Forbes and Company.[306]

The losses sustained by the Forbes and Company were substantial, estimated at $30,000 for sixty-two slaves from the East Florida business, an estimated $100,000 in value for forty-four slaves, and significant numbers of cattle, horses, boats, gunpowder, and building supplies from the West Florida operations.[307] Coker and Watson, commenting further on John Forbes's economic woes, note that

> Losses in West Florida were significantly different from those in East Florida. No wholesale exodus of West Florida slaves followed the British departure from the province, although Forbes was later to accuse [British army] Captain George Woodbine of taking some of his slaves with him. For the most part, escaped West Florida slaves resided with the Indians, in the Negro villages on the Suwannee River, or at the British fort on the Apalachicola. By contrast, all the East Florida slaves left Cumberland Island on British ships.[308]

The black Muscogulges, realizing that Forbes and Company could no longer be relied on to protect their interests, encouraged Forbes's company slaves to join their ranks. As a result, blacks who were trained and armed to protect the company's interests deserted to the black maroon camps still equipped with their arms and uniforms. It was the breakdown in relations between Forbes and Company and the Muscogulges that opened the door for the auspicious (albeit brief) entrance of the adventurous Scottish-Bahamian, Alexander Arbuthnot. Arbuthnot, as mentioned in a previous chapter, opened a rival business in West Florida in direct competition with Forbes and Company. He became the *ex-officio* "advisor" to the Native Americans in the area, encouraging them and runaway blacks to rebel against American authority.

In 1816, American troops on orders from Andrew Jackson took advantage of an accidental but fatal explosion of ammunition supplies at the Negro Fort that killed many of its defenders and severely damaged the surrounding walls to address the vexing problem of black opposition to American authority in Florida. Formerly known as the Prospect Bluff fortification, the Forbes Company and American authorities were earlier informed that the British who had evacuated the fort "had left the Negroes [there] . . . in possession of a well-constructed fort, with plenty of provisions, arms and ammunition, and even cannon."[309] It was further reported that the fort was fast becoming a place of refuge for runaway slaves, and that the black refugees were well organized and securing armed vessels that were used to ferry runaway slaves to the fort and to the Bahamas and even to engage in piracy. The Americans, alarmed at the situation and eager to take advantage of the opportunity for pre-emptive military action created by the destruction to the walls and chaos caused by the accidental explosion, mounted an attack against the fort. They were convinced that the occupants were harboring runaway slaves and being defended by black Muscogulges and friendly Creeks. The American forces completely destroyed the fort and surrounding settlements and scattered the inhabitants, many of whom eventually sought refuge among the Miccosukee and in the Bahamas.

The question of fugitive slaves became a major issue of contention between the United States and Great Britain during and following the events of the American Revolution, and Congress grappled to arrive at a solution amenable to emerging American national policy, while at the same time acceptable to British foreign policy. Marion McDougall commented on the situation:

> Although no amendment could be procured to the Act of 1793, the government of the United States had repeatedly, by diplomatic demands and treaties, undertaken to recover fugitives, or their value, for Southern owners. The first Indian treaty negotiated under the Constitution, that of April 7, 1790, with the Creeks, required the return of negroes held as prisoners of war.[310]

A similar clause is contained in the treaty of 1814, made at the end of the Creek Wars, a war which incidentally was provoked in part by Creek support of fugitive blacks[311] In 1832, the United States government allocated seven thousand dollars in public funds to purchase "slaves and other property alleged to have been stolen" by the Seminoles.[312] Invariably, escape from a life of slavery in the United States through Florida to freedom in the Bahamas became the hope and subsequent action of many American blacks.

Fergus Bordewich, in his seminal work titled *Bound for Canaan* (2005), explains the significance of Florida in the 1820s as a gateway to freedom:

> Florida resembled the Texas frontier more than it did the interior of the cotton-growing South . . . . Florida had a population more Spanish and African than Anglo-Saxon. Almost half the territory's fifty thousand inhabitants were black, all but a handful of them slaves. Pensacola occupied a scant two dozen city blocks. Life focused on the port, one of the best on the Gulf Coast . . . the writ of law did not carry far beyond the city's thinly populated outskirts, however. Since the days of Spanish rule, the swamps that surrounded Pensacola had been home to bandits and renegades of every stripe. Although Florida had been a comparatively tolerant place under Spanish rule, in keeping with the policies of the slave states to the North, the territorial government had begun to enact more racially repressive laws that limited the movements and opportunities of the blacks, and forced many of them back into slavery as punishment for offenses as minor as the failure to pay fines.[313]

The sea, as Bordewich outlines in the following statement, became the great highway along which fugitive slaves and other blacks sought to escape racial discrimination in the United States to find refuge in the Bahamas:

> The sea was, in a sense, a commercial extension of the Northern states, and every Yankee ship that touched at a southern port like a piece of free territory that suddenly came within the physical reach of restive slaves. Merchants based in New York and Boston dominated commerce everywhere along the coast, while New Englanders, New Yorkers, and free black sailors crewed the thousand-ton brigs and low-slung coasters that shipped cargoes of plantation-grown tobacco and cotton, New Jersey bricks, Georgia turpentine, Pennsylvania coal, and Hudson river ice among the hundreds of Southern ports between Norfolk and Galveston. Ashore, they mingled with enslaved as well as free-blacks stevedores blurring the edges of segregation and providing potential fugitives with information about friendly captains, abolitionists, and life in the free states . . . . Escape

by sea [therefore] held an obvious appeal. A land journey that could take
months, and was unlikely to succeed, might by sea take only a week or two,
and from some ports, just days.[314]

In 1818, Iacohaslonaki (aka George Perryman), a Miccosukee chief from the
lower Apalachicola region, escaped from Pensacola aboard a British ship and, with
the aid of Bahamian supporters, sailed to England, where he petitioned the British
authorities to permit him and his people to immigrate to the Bahamas. The British
response was disappointing: "Giving him almost no presents and only few pounds
for expenses, the [British] government promptly dispatched him and his delegation
back to Florida, instructing naval commanders to bring no more Creek delegations
to the mother country."[315] One year later, eighty-year-old Kinache, a Muscogulge
leader, with a delegation of twenty-three attendants, boarded a Bahamian wrecking
ship at Plantation Cay and sailed to Nassau to seek British assistance for his people,
who were being severely pressured by American forces to leave their traditional
homelands. Over the years, Kinache had faithfully led his warriors in battle on the
side of the British, supported Bowles, and fought unsuccessfully against Andrew
Jackson, who in turn had systematically and unmercifully destroyed his villages.
Kinache told Bahamian governor William Munnings of the plight of his people and
of their expectation of British assistance. Unable to offer any significant assistance,
the governor nevertheless housed his visitors in facilities near the barracks, gave them
some gifts and supplies, and arranged for their safe passage back to Plantation Cay.[316]
Heartbroken and deeply disappointed in the lack of British support, the old warrior
died shortly after his return to Florida. Despite the absence of official British support,
however, Bahamians openly welcomed and assisted both runaway blacks and Native
Americans to their shores, thus establishing a veritable Underground Railroad.

Black Seminoles

Wright explains why many southeastern Native Americans, especially black
Seminoles, associated the Bahamas with freedom:

> At the end of the American Revolution and during the War of 1812 British
> officers who had promised Southern blacks liberty often came from or
> passed through the Bahamas. Aboard privateers, merchant ships, and in
> their oceangoing dugouts, black Seminoles who were sailors repeatedly
> sailed over to the Bahamas and back again. In the Bahamas they first
> heard about Britain's abolishing the slave trade in 1807, and it was there
> that they perceived specifically what was meant for blacks. As time passed,
> more and more black Seminoles stayed in the islands . . . . Fishermen,
> turtlers, privateers, soldiers of fortune trying to liberate Spanish America,
> and wreckers carried parties of harried Negroes over to the Bahamas.[317]

In the 1820s, Zephaniah Kingsley, arguably the owner of the most slaves in Florida, complained to authorities that two of his slaves had escaped from his north Florida plantation to the Bahamas.[318] A typical case of escape to Nassau was that reported by Mitchell Roberts, a black Seminole who in the 1850s testified about his ordeal to Bahamian authorities. According to his testimony, Roberts had served in the Royal Colonial Marines during the War of 1812 and was stationed at the British (Negro) fort on the Apalachicola River. In 1820, after the fatal explosion at the "Negro Fort," he escaped to the Bahamas, where he spent his remaining years.[319] Roberts' testimony included an interesting anecdote about the case of a fellow black Seminole called Ben Newton. Reportedly, Newton's mother was a free-black named Elizabeth who lived in the Tampa area. She unsuspectingly apprenticed young Ben out to an unscrupulous Bahamian ship captain who allegedly took Ben to Cuba and sold him into slavery. Despite his protests of being a free person, Ben was kept enslaved on a plantation in Cuba until his eventual escape in the 1850s, when he sought refuge in the U.S. consulate in Havana. Abolitionists in New York and the Bahamas championed Ben's cause and attempted to have him freed. According to documented accounts, Ben died before the courts ruled on his case. Grief-stricken, Elizabeth, his aged mother, immigrated to Andros Island in the Bahamas, where she lived out her last days still grieving the fact that she never saw her son alive again.[320]

One of the most widely researched and celebrated accounts of black Seminole escape to the Bahamas was recorded by Rosalyn Howard in her work titled *Black Seminoles in the Bahamas* (2002). Excerpts from that book tell the story of the betrayal and odyssey of that persecuted people:

> The British had promised to reward the Seminoles with military and economic support in return for their loyalty during the siege of New Orleans. Accordingly, the Florida Seminole leaders, desperate for assistance in their struggle against the Euroamericans, sought to take advantage of the British offer. A consensus was reached that Chief Kenadgie, a tribal elder, should travel "to New Providence [Bahamas] or Jamaica for the purpose of stating their grievances and soliciting assistance" from the British. Chief Kenadgie arrived at New Providence, via a dugout canoe on September 29, 1819, accompanied by several others, including an interpreter described as "an Indian of mixed blood." The interpreter may have been Abraham, a Black Seminole who often negotiated on behalf of the Seminoles with Euro-Americans and was Chief Micanopy's personal interpreter. They complained to the British that their people in Florida were being persistently tormented, and that "their greatest enemies were the Cowetas . . . who having made terms with the Americans [were] set upon them to harass and annihilate their tribe." When Chief Kenadgie appealed to the British for aid, however, the British reneged on their promises to buttress the Seminoles' cause. British officials in Nassau, New Providence, advised that because of

a recent peace treaty signed with the United States of America, the British
nation was not inclined to interfere in the Seminoles' current dispute.
Kenadgie and his fellow travelers were provided with food and shelter on
New Providence for one week, and summarily returned to Florida via the
British schooner *Primrose* with their canoe in tow.[321]

Howard recounts how another delegation of black Seminoles visited Bahamian
authorities in Nassau in 1821:

> Another party of Seminole Indians arrived in New Providence two years
> later. This time, however, the Seminoles had no express motive for their
> visit. Ten of them had arrived destitute and in need of food and clothing. In
> a futile gesture of loyalty, one member displayed his Certificate of Gallantry
> and Good Conduct, awarded for service with the British troops in Florida
> during the War of 1812. Once again, the British leaders offered only
> provisions to the Seminoles, and then sent them back to Florida. Several
> months after the second group of Seminole Indians returned to Florida in
> 1821, a third group made plans to depart for the Bahamas. This group was
> much larger and probably consisted mostly of Black Seminoles. After years
> of struggle to survive the increasingly hostile situation in Florida, they fled
> to the Bahamas, where they hoped to live as free men and women. They
> secretly congregated at Cape Florida and embarked in whatever transport
> they could secure, whether dugout canoes or wreckers . . . . The Seminoles'
> previous trips to the Bahamas had clearly demonstrated the futility of their
> efforts to secure aid from the British on New Providence, so they altered
> their strategy. This time they chose to land not on New Providence, but
> on the western shore of Andros Island, a large Out Island of the Bahamas
> approximately 25 miles west of New Providence and 150 miles from the
> Florida coast. A few landed in the Biminis and on Joulter Cay; many of the
> latter joined the majority of the Black Seminole and Seminole refugees,
> who had settled at Red Bays, Andros Island.[322]

Descendants of the black Seminoles continue to live in north Andros, where
they have distinguished themselves with their production of straw basketry and
woodcarving that is unique in style from other art forms typical of the other islands
of the Bahamas.

The Creole *Affair*

The case of the ship *Creole* is a classic example of slaves forcibly taking advantage
of the common knowledge that British antislavery policies were progressive to escape
slavery in the United States and seek asylum in a British territory where slavery

was not tolerated. The stage was set in 1807, when the British Parliament enacted laws to end the trade of slaves in its empire and summarily used its mighty navy to intercept ships on the high seas determined to be transporting slaves, regardless of nationality. These newly freed blacks were mostly released to safe custody within its global territories to be eventually assimilated into society. In 1834, the British antislavery laws were further advanced with enforcement of the Emancipation Act, providing freedom to all slaves living in British territories as well as asylum for runaways who sought refuge in any of those areas, such as the Bahamas.

In October 1841, the American schooner *Creole* and its crew of eight set sail from Richmond, Virginia, destined for New Orleans markets, carrying a cargo of tobacco and transporting five other sailors, six white passengers, and 135 slaves. The ship anchored on the evening of November 7, 1941, just outside the harbor at Abaco Island in the northern Bahamas, planning to stop at the island, perhaps with the intent to secure provisions the following morning. In the early morning hours while most aboard were asleep, nineteen slaves were led by the ship's cook, Madison Washington, in a revolt and took control of the ship. In the struggle for control, slave owner John Howell resisted; in the brief skirmish that followed, he was fatally stabbed. The mutineers discussed plans to sail to Liberia but had to abandon that plan because there were insufficient provisions for that long voyage. Instead, they agreed to sail the ship to Nassau, based on the knowledge that, a year earlier, the ship *Hermosa* was shipwrecked in the Bahamas, and Bahamian officials had granted asylum to all the rescued slaves who wished to accept the offer. Ironically, ninety of the slaves aboard the *Creole* belonged to Robert Lumpkin, owner of some of the slaves on the shipwrecked *Hermosa*. William Merritt, the white overseer of the slaves, was forced to plot a course and sail to Nassau. The ship arrived in Nassau harbor in early November. The events that followed created a global sensation and severely strained U.S. foreign relations with Great Britain.

Upon arrival in Nassau, both American consul John Bacon and colonial governor Francis Cockburn were advised of the presence of the ship and the general circumstances under which it came. Cockburn ordered a contingent of twemty-four soldiers of the 2nd West India Regiment to take control of the ship and all onboard until a decision on the fate of the vessel, crew, and passengers was made. It must have been a shock to the white passengers and crew of the *Creole* and a pleasant surprise to the slaves to learn that they were under the military authority of black soldiers commanded by a single white officer.[323]

Around noon that day, G. C. Anderson, the attorney general for the colony, noticed several boats filled with local blacks approaching the *Creole* as he was boarding the vessel and an even larger crowd of blacks on the shore, all in an apparent state of readiness to free the slaves should an attempt be made to repatriate them to the United States. Consul Bacon, fearing that the growing hostility of the crowd might result in danger for the white passengers and crew, requested the governor to restrain the local blacks. Cockburn complied.[324] With the ship secured, Cockburn convened an emergency meeting of the local executive council at which Bacon requested an audience to state the position of his country. The American consul requested permission to take custody of the *Creole* and all souls on board until an American warship could be summoned from Indian Key, Florida, to escort the vessel and all aboard back to the United States. He also requested that the nineteen slaves directly involved in the revolt be sent to the United States to be tried under American jurisdiction. The governor and council refused the requests.[325]

Frustrated and in a show of contempt for British authority, Bacon sanctioned an abortive attempt to "rescue" the *Creole*. With Bacon's complicity, the crew of an American schooner then in harbor, the *Louisia*, along with four sailors from the American brig *Congress*, also in port, plotted to take the *Creole* to Indian Cay. Before dawn, the men rowed to the *Creole* armed with muskets and cutlasses wrapped in an American flag and hidden on the bottom of the boat. While en route to the *Creole*, however, they were detected by the crew of one of the native sloops anchored nearby, who thereupon warned the black regiment of the intended assault. The would-be rescuers eventually rowed alongside the *Creole*, only to be confronted by twenty-five black soldiers with muskets armed with bayonets trained on them. The Americans wisely made a hasty retreat.[326]

On the morning of November 12, 1841, the blacks aboard the *Creole* were visited by two black clergymen, who assured them they were to prepare to be released. By noon, the slaves who had not taken part in the revolt were released into the custody of the clergymen and loaded into the nearby native sloops to the roaring cheers of the watchers on the shore. Onshore, hundreds of black supporters escorted the freed slaves to the office of the superintendent of police, where they were officially registered and released in the custody of the native blacks and free to resume lives in freedom. Anderson arranged to have the nineteen conspirators remain in custody to await a decision on their fate. Five slaves who had remained hidden on the *Creole* refused the offer of Bahamian asylum and were returned to the United States. Bacon accused the Bahamian authorities of overriding the American claims and releasing the slaves to the restive Nassau black community, which the governor vehemently denied. In his defense, Bahamian attorney general Anderson argued that he had informed the *Creole* slaves that he had no authority to hold those who had not participated in the revolt nor prevent any of them from leaving the vessel, whereupon many were urged and assisted by resident blacks to leave the ship.[327]

The arrival of the *Creole* in New Orleans on December 2, 1841, created a stir that prompted the Southern press to almost collectively denounce what was described as blatant interference in American maritime affairs and to demand that the British provide immediate compensation for the loss of the freed slaves.[328] The legislatures of Louisiana, Mississippi, and Virginia passed resolutions demanding restitution for the alleged British violation of American maritime rights.[329] U.S. Senator Thomas Hart Benton criticized Great Britain for encouraging mutiny and murder on the high seas, while Henry Clay warned of danger to American Atlantic trade. John C. Calhoun warned of a potential threat to the cotton trade.[330] Americans were temporarily disappointed and angered when the British authorities ruled that the nineteen mutineers should be released on a motion of lack of evidence.[331] The legal wrangling on both sides of the Atlantic raged for several more years until, in 1855, the case was settled and an Anglo-American Claims Commission awarded the owners of the freed slaves a total of $110,330 in compensation.

A number of black and white American antislavery sympathizers in Florida were prepared to serve as "conductors" along the saltwater Underground Railroad to freedom in the Bahamas. Such was the case involving Jonathan Walker and Charles Johnson. Walker was a white seaman originally from the bleak cold of Cape Cod who had relocated to the warm sunshine of Pensacola after many years at sea. His intention was to engage in the salvage of copper from a wrecked ship at the bottom of the harbor. He was an abolitionist and a disciple of Reverend Samuel J. May, an ally of William Lloyd Garrison, and acquainted with the plight and adventures of fugitive slaves. Charles Johnson, a slave and laborer on the docks of Pensacola, approached Walker and propositioned him to take himself and three other slaves in Walker's twenty-five-foot schooner to freedom in the north. The story of the encounter between the abolitionist and the slave underscores the strategic geopolitical significance of the Bahamas as a place of refuge from slavery in the minds of both slaves and abolitionists:

> Johnson told Walker that he and three other slaves wanted him to take them to the free states. Walker was willing, but knew that they could not travel the Atlantic seaboard without being discovered. Instead, he proposed a daring plan. He volunteered to take Johnson and his friends to the British-ruled Bahamas, where slavery had been abolished eleven years earlier. They knew that fugitives could expect a welcome there. Both men would have remembered how less than three years earlier 135 slaves had mutinied on the brig *Creole*, en route to New Orleans, and sailed it to freedom in the Bahamas 332.

Evidence suggests that ships running the blockade during the American Civil War at times conveyed fugitive slaves through Southern ports to the safety of Nassau. One such case is that of Thomas E. Taylor, arguably the best known and certainly one of the most successful of the blockade runners. At age twenty-one, Taylor was hired by a consortium of Liverpool merchants to run the blockade on a circuitous route from Liverpool to Nassau and to Southern ports, and to use his discretion to ensure the highest possible returns on the investments made. It was on one of Taylor's ships that an incident occurred that suggests that runaway slaves may have escaped the South as stowaways on blockade runners. On this particular occasion, a trip from Wilmington to Nassau, a black man was discovered hiding among the bales of cotton being off-loaded. According to British law, the stowaway was freed and given a hero's welcome by the sympathetic blacks of Nassau. The news of the escape and subsequent freedom of the slave was denounced by the Wilmington authorities, and Taylor was obliged to pay $4,000 in compensation for the property loss before being allowed to continue "business" with the South.[333] The migration of small groups of slaves from the United States to the Bahamas continued almost unabated until the strong influence of emancipation and the promises of enfranchisement promised by Reconstruction served to stem the flow. Some of the refugee slaves eventually became leaders in the Bahamian black communities, contributing specifically to the development of religion and self-help organizations.

The end of the American Civil War brought an end to blockade running and in effect ended that five-year period of prosperity Bahamians enjoyed from facilitating illegal trade with the Confederacy. Once again, The Bahamas faced serious a financial recession that bordered on near starvation. Nassau, the capital of the colony, faced widespread unemployment and insufficient and inadequate housing as a result of the emergence of the masses that migrated from the outer islands in search of that often illusive "piece of the pie" previously offered by prospects of blockade-running. Agricultural production in the islands had been virtually neglected and reliance on the steadily increasing importation of food and necessary commodities from the United States become a way of life not easily reversed. Bahamians, particularly in the northern islands, began to migrate first to the Florida Keys and later to the mainland in search of ways to sustain economic survival.

Bahamians and the Development of Florida

The Keys

Bahamian mariners were generally familiar with the Keys for a number of reasons. J. Leitch Wright Jr. summarizes the Bahamian connection as follows:

> Tory refugees or their descendents were among the first, if not the original, permanent settlers in the Florida Keys. Before finally arriving at Key West around 1821, these Tory exiles had changed their residences at least twice. At the end of the Revolution they moved from the St. Augustine-St. Marys region to the Bahamas, soon taking up the traditional island way of life by fishing, turtling, and wrecking. They began visiting the Keys and the southern peninsula seasonally, and after a long period, apparently in 1821, they permanently settled in the Keys. These Florida refugees were returning home, even though their new residence was not attached to the peninsula.[334]

George E. Merrick offers additional insight into the early Bahamian immigration to Florida in an address to the 1941 autumn meeting of the Association of Southern Florida:

> These Conchs began to come into the lower Peninsula in the early 1800s, and continued this occupation throughout the century, until their influence reached its peak from 1870 to 1890. The colonization reached from Key West to Lake Worth, the farthest point north of their occupation. These Conchs, as they and their descendents still are called, were descendent from American-British Tories who left the coastal parts of the thirteen colonies toward the end of the 1700's and who went to the Bahamas; were given grants there by King George III; and became a sea living, sea using, sea knowing people. At that time our region, the Florida Keys, and the whole lower East Coast of Florida was in essence a part of the Bahamas.[335]

Merrick notes the significance of the influence exerted by the early Bahamian immigrants on the development of southeast Florida:

> The West Indian Conchs . . . brought to the lower east Coast country the West Indian customs and West Indian fruits which were to have a lasting influence upon our mainland, planting around their houses many, many fruits that now are not so common with us, but which then were common with them, and for which much of their sustenance came. They brought their peculiarly West Indian vegetables, yams, cassava, eddys, pounders and benni.[336]

Bahamian incursions into the Florida Keys became a subject of complaint as early as the 1760s. In 1766, James Grant, governor of East Florida, complained that the "long-established practice" of Bahamians harvesting hardwoods in the Keys was detrimental to the development of the territory. In this regard, he outlined plans to "convince them still more of intentions to seize vessels which they load with Mahogany, tho' they are sent to the Keys under the pretense of fishing for turtles."[337] It was concern for the activity of Bahamian wreckers, however, that caused the U.S. government to take decisive preventive action. So the situation can be understood more clearly, it is necessary to provide a brief historical overview of the development of the Florida Keys, and Key West in particular.

In 1815, Key West became private property when the Spanish governor of Florida granted the island to Juan Pablo Salas as reward for military services rendered. After the annexation of Florida to the United States, however, Salas sold his rights to the island twice, first to a land speculator named John B. Strong in an exchange for a sloop valued at $500 and later, in 1821, to another investor named John Simonton for $2,000. Simonton used his superior political connections to win the litigation that ensued, whereupon he sold two-thirds of his rights to the island to various speculators and settlers. In the meanwhile, the new settlers and land owners began to complain to the new authorities about the unwanted activities of Bahamian interlopers in their waters and on their lands.

Wrecking

The Native American Calusa, the pre-Columbian pioneers of South Florida, were also the first to organize salvage operations in the Florida Keys, often plundering mostly Spanish ships wrecked along the numerous treacherous reefs and murdering the stranded seamen and passengers in the process. In 1513, Ponce de León, aware of the notoriety of the Calusa, and awed by the formation of some of the rocks in the Keys that reportedly resembled suffering men, dubbed the Keys los Martires, meaning "the Martyrs." Calusa control of the Keys declined in 1763 when the Spanish colonial administration directed the forcible relocation of most of the remaining Calusa residing on Matecumbe, Key Vacas, and Key West to Cuba to work as slaves. In the 1790s, the vacuum left by the Calusa wreckers was filled by Bahamian mariners who, despite their claims to be harmless turtlers and fishermen, were regarded as pirates by the Spanish, because their practices were allegedly often just as treacherous as those of their Native American predecessors.

Illegal wrecking and salvage became the most-often cited offenses committed by the Bahamians, to the frustration of the early Spanish administration, putting the later American residents of the Keys at a disadvantage. Hickey notes,

> The Bahamian wreckers cruised the Florida Keys from their islands but never seriously considered starting settlements; they came only for profit. All during the formative period of the Florida Key's settlement, the Bahamians continued wrecking. Their profits from the business did not benefit the United States in any way, but instead after they salvaged or saved a wrecked ship they immediately returned to Nassau with the Prize. The wreck would then be adjudicated in the British Admiralty Court under British maritime Law and the money earned would stay in the Bahamian economy.[338]

Traditionally, both black and white Bahamians were acutely adept at salvaging from wrecks, an industry that was established in the Bahamas for many years. *Hunt's Merchant Magazine*, in noting the expertise of the Bahamian divers, stated that they were capable of diving to depths of seventy feet.[339] In particular, for the black Bahamian immigrants, who were mostly unskilled laborers from the lowest economic and social levels in their islands of origin and in their new country of adoption, the benefits derived from the wrecking business were particularly rewarding. These people who unloaded the cargo salvaged from the wrecks onto wrecking boats and subsequently stored the items in various warehouses, managed to slowly achieve financial solvency. This position was verified by the Monroe County tax records of 1860, which stated that free blacks in that county owned property valued at $12,250, a substantial sum for blacks at that time.[340] By the 1920s, the money earned by the Bahamian wreckers was so important to the Bahamian economy that as many as fifty to sixty vessels and five hundred men participated actively in the trade, which provided support for many Bahamian families and a constant source of revenue for the government.[341]

John DuBose, an American official stationed at Key West, reported to his superior of on the encroachment by the Bahamians,

> I have been credibly informed that there are 120 sail of vessels, kept employed from the Bahama Islands within the Carrysford (Six) Reef, whose sole employment is wrecking and transporting over to [New] Providence, goods of this description, and that the amount of duties paid to the British government in Nassau by those wreckers may fairly be estimated at £15,000 yearly . . . . This trade has been [enjoyed] by the inhabitants of the Bahama Islands since the first settlement of those Keys—they appear to consider it as their right, and are determined to persevere in it until our Government by the adoption of some energetic measures, shall compel then to withdraw.[342]

In 1822, Lieutenant M. C. Perry, under direction of the United States Navy, raised the American flag on Key West and thereby officially established a federal presence in the Keys. Under the direction of Simonton, Key West was surveyed and mapped, and several lots were sold to new residents relocating mostly from South Carolina and St. Augustine. The new residents, resenting the competition from Bahamians for wrecking, fishing, and turtling rights in the Keys, filed a series of complaints to the territorial government to outlaw the illegal incursions by the Bahamians. In 1822, Congress responded by officially designating the southern coastal areas of Florida stretching from Cape Sable to Charlotte Harbor a federal tax collection jurisdiction. Additional legislation banned the export of resources salvaged within American territorial waters from adjudication outside the United States.[343] Governor DuVal urged American wreckers to cooperate with the federal authorities to control the illegal actions of the Bahamians: "avoid all amicable association with the foreigners," he urged, "refuse to furnish provisions or aid them in any manner, threw every possible obstacle in their way, enforce vigorously the revenue laws of the United States . . . and adopt many other expedients extremely vexatious to those against whom they operate."[344]

Bahamian wreckers were directly impacted, but many initially defied the new laws. Eventually, the severity of the laws and the existing poverty in the Bahamas caused many, primarily from the Abaco Islands, to relent and take up official residence in the Keys. Evidence of this new Bahamian migration is reflected in the 1830 census report, which for the first time recorded multiple entries of the predominantly Abaconian names of Lowe, Roberts, Bartlum, Russell, and Curry as some of the prominent citizens of the Keys. By 1840, the Bahamian immigrants had "helped to make Key West one of the richest cities in the United States."[345]

A quote from one of the series of articles written by Dr. Benjamin Stroebel, Key West army surgeon, during his tour of duty on that island, underscores the importance of the wrecking bonanza:

> One day I was very busily employed indoors for several hours, and took no cognizance of the passing events. On going, however, into the street, I at once discovered an unusual excitement in our little town . . . the world appeared to be turned upside down . . . I enquired of several what was the matter? At length, one man came running along, almost breathless. I seized him by the collar and demanded of him for God's sake what is the matter? You all appear to be mad! Let me go, Sir! Let me go! A wreck! A wreck![346]

By the late 1850s, it was estimated that the value of ships and cargoes annually passing through the Florida Straits was valued at between 300 and 400 million dollars.[347] Most residents of Key West benefited from the trade. Some used their clout to benefit more than others, as demonstrated in the case of the *Point a Petre*, wrecked on Carysfort Reef in February 1825. According to the *Pensacola Gazette*, the presiding judge adjudicating the case also acted as the magistrate who condemned the cargo from the wreck, the auctioneer who sold the goods, and one of the major purchasers of the condemned property.[348]

Soon after the Louisiana Purchase of 1803 and continuing after Florida became a territory in 1821, commercial interests in the newly acquired western territories and the East were pressuring Congress to establish navigational aids in Florida. By the 1820s, much of the commerce between the central areas of the United States and the eastern ports came down the Mississippi River, through New Orleans, then through the Straits of Florida, often passing through the Bahamas and Cuba before sailing northward up the Atlantic coast. The most dangerous parts of this voyage were passing the gauntlet of pirates and wreckers residing in the Bahamas and lurking in the Florida Straits, then having to navigate the narrows of the Straits, which were inundated with treacherous shoals and reefs, particularly around the Dry Tortugas and Cape Florida on Key Biscayne. In the 1860s, the federal government responded with the establishment of a series of "Houses of Refuge" along the shores of east Florida, stretching from the lower east coast up to Biscayne Bay and farther north beyond Cape Canaveral to St. Augustine. These Houses of Refuge, located an average of twenty to thirty miles apart, were the precursor of modern lighthouses. Ironically, these early lighthouses were manned predominantly by Bahamian immigrants, some of whose forebears most likely influenced the need for the signals.[349]

Salt

Beginning in the 1820s and continuing into the 1840s, Bahamians made important contributions to the development of the salt industry in Key West. Salt was already a well-established industry in the Bahamas, with numerous natural salt ponds operated throughout the archipelago, which included the Turks and Caicos Islands. In that age before refrigeration, salt was an important ingredient in the process of curing and seasoning. American businessmen took advantage of Bahamian expertise in the industry to introduce similar methods of production in Key West. In 1829, the *Key West Register* printed an article about William Adee Whitehead, an American developer who went to the Bahama Islands to view the salt production operations there with a view to adopting some of those successful methods in Key West. There, he observed the process by which water was dammed from shallow saltwater areas to create salt pans. The water gradually evaporated, allowing crystals to form, after which the salt was raked with large-toothed wooden rakes, collected, and shipped to markets mostly in the American North.

Richard Fitzpatrick is credited with attempting to develop the first commercial salt pans in the Keys. Apparently unsatisfied with the low production of salt by his inexperienced laborers, Fitzpatrick turned to the Bahamas to import experienced workers,. He hired a Bahamian black named Hart to oversee the business; subsequently, large numbers of black Bahamians were directly recruited or otherwise immigrated in search of work. These blacks were welcomed by local residents for their expertise in the field and for the anticipated economic benefits to the communities their labor in the pans would produce; however, they distrusted the Bahamians because blacks were free in that British colony, where at that time intolerance of slavery was the order of the day. Blacks were inclined to assert their freedom during the salt-raking off-season periods while living in an environment of racial discrimination.[350]

Walter C. Maloney, a prominent Key West resident, complained that the Bahamian black would encourage the local blacks to rebel against white authority, become vagrants during the off-season, and introduce vices to which local blacks were unaccustomed (or at least did not publicly exhibit).[351] The salt industry in Key West died because of consecutive very wet seasons that made it impossible to create productive pans, and the Keys fell into unsympathetic Union hands during the American Civil War, when the military concern that the salt could benefit the Confederacy outweighed the economic importance of the industry to the community. Bahamian blacks, however, then aware of the opportunities becoming available in the sponge fishing industry, quickly applied their knowledge of sponging to their benefit.

Live-Well Fishing

Bahamian immigrants are credited with revolutionizing the fishing industry in the Keys. Fresh fish was in greater demand in some markets than salted fish, but it was difficult to preserve and generally unsuitable for sale in markets that required more than a day in transportation. Bahamians solved this problem by introducing a "live well" in the holds of their sloops that was kept constantly filled with fresh saltwater that flowed in and out of this submerged holding pen even while the sloops were employed for several days at sea. This method of preservation exists today in the islands, allowing patrons to identify the exact fish they want simply by pointing to the desired item. The introduction of live-well fishing allowed New England fishermen the flexibility to market fresh fish on demand.

Sponging

William Kemp, a Bahamian immigrant, is credited with introducing sponging to Key West when he arrived in 1848 on his schooner *Mohawk* with a cargo of sponges; he hoped to eventually exploit the sponge-rich waters off the Keys. Finding no buyers in Key West, he took his goods to New York City and established lucrative markets there. In the 1800s, sponges provided a variety of uses, particularly as bath implements and in the medical industry, where natural sponges were prized because they were determined to have no lint and could be used as a prototype gauze that would not infect wounds. Key West emerged as the largest supplier of sponges during the Civil War era, providing 90 percent of them for American markets, and Bahamians were key players at all levels, making up a majority of the 1,400 men employed in the 300 boats engaged in the trade.[352]

Bahamians were veterans of the sponge industry and, unlike local blacks, accustomed to being away from the comforts of home and family during the two—and sometimes four—months excursions to the sponge fields. Typically, local blacks signed up to work on boats owned mostly by whites, but in a few cases by blacks. A line of credit was assigned to the captain of a vessel to purchase supplies, which included food and ship repair materials for use during the voyage. In the Bahamas, for example, credit was advanced to the families of the crew and redeemable at the local stores, which interestingly were owned mostly by investors. Frequently, the generally illiterate blacks were financially exploited as they had neither the means nor the enthusiasm to challenge the often questionable balance of payments maintained by the storekeepers, despite the regular service payments made after each voyage. As a result, many crew members remained perpetually indebted to the investors and consequently summarily obligated to continue to work on the ships. The credit advance, although not intended to include the purchase of liquor, quite often did not prevent that occurrence.[353] The predominantly all-black crews typically included a captain, a cook, a "skuller," and two divers. The larger vessels might accommodate a crew that included as many as twelve men. A share system was devised that, after expenses, gave a predetermined percentage of the returns to the investors, the owners of the vessels, and the captain and cook before provisions were granted to the crew.

Immigrant Bahamian spongers impacted legislation controlling the Florida sponge industry when they successfully agitated for environmental laws to prevent excessive exploitation of the sponge beds by Greek competitors. The Greeks used a rudimentary scuba system that equipped them with compressors that pumped air into helmets, allowing the Greek divers to remain submerged at greater depths and for longer periods than the Bahamian free-divers. The Bahamian spongers successfully argued that the Greeks wore lead-lined boots that allowed them to walk on the bottom, but that also destroyed fragile corals and the juvenile sponge beds. In 1837, the sponge industry in the Keys ended when a devastating disease destroyed the natural and cultured marine products.

Architecture

Perhaps in no other place is Bahamian colonial architecture and heritage more exquisitely demonstrated outside the Bahamas than it is in the Florida Keys. In 1941, Merrick noted that the "West Indian-like villages of the earlier Keys settlements, looking then as the Bahamian towns of today, such as those of Governor's Harbour and Spanish Wells [Eleuthera Island] and all the present day out-island towns of the Bahamas, sprang up along the Hawks Channel, along the Keys, in the middle of the 1800s and after. These villages reached up as far as Tavernier and Planter on Key Largo, [and] 'The Hole' on upper Matecumbe."[354] The Bahamians brought with them the knowledge of building with the abundantly available native coral limestone and conch shells, reducing the latter to powder in makeshift kilns to produce lime, the primary binding ingredient used in the construction of various types of masonry. Bahamians also introduced the extensive use of limestone to cheaply construct and repair local roads.

In her article titled "Key West's Conch's, 1763-1912: Outlaws or Outcasts?" Astrid Whidden provides insights into the way Bahamian immigrants to the Keys impacted "how their living space [and that of others] should be used."[355] Bahamian carpenters were often trained in the art of boat building and, as such, familiar with the use of wood as the primary material used in construction. She used the case of Bahamian immigrant Nicholas Pinder, who in 1829 advertised his professional skills in the local newspaper to include "house and ship carpenter, joiner, and cabinet maker."[356] In 1829, Bahamian immigrant Richard W. Coussans, an experienced carpenter and joiner, built what is now acknowledged to be the oldest house in Key West, at 322 Duval Street. The wooden structure is perched on an elevated foundation that protects against flooding, as a result of the numerous hurricanes with which Bahamians were historically familiar. It featured wood shingles and three dormers typically found in Bahamian homes and was designed to allow a flow of air through the upstairs bedrooms.

The Bahamian-designed architecture also featured large windows that allowed the maximum circulation of available cool breezes while releasing hot air through vents constructed under the eaves. Many Bahamian-style homes featured exterior kitchens that effectively removed odors and heat created by cooking and the storage of foods from the living quarters. Gables were added, designed to facilitate the capture of rainwater, which was redirected to cisterns common in most Bahamian homes as a constant supply of water. The wraparound verandas allowed for social meetings in a relaxed environment and also allowed families and visitors a view of the street and all the action taking place within view. Verandas almost never faced the sea, as the ocean was appreciated almost exclusively for its bounty and seldom for its intrinsic beauty.

From early occupation, Bahamian blacks provided an invaluable source of labor in the gradual taming of the wild frontiers of the Keys and the southeast mainland. Merrick captures the significance of the impact as follows:

> Now I come to an influence that had a marked effect on the Lower East Coast—that of the Bahamian negro. Through the 70s and 80s, and right through the 1890s, they were particularly the only available workers . . . . In this West Indian period all of our heavy laborers were Bahamian negroes. I believe these Bahamian negroes had a most distinct and important influence in that they brought inspiration to many of these first English, French, Northern and Southern planters; to all of those early settlers who at first were skeptical of the coral-rocky country, forbidding and desolate from the planting standpoint. In the Bahamas there is the same coral rock, and the Bahamian negroes knew how to plant on it; and how to use it: and they knew too all kinds of tropical trees would grow and thrive on this rock. They, too, had a vital influence upon our civilization in bringing in their own commonly used trees, vegetables and fruits. Soon, these supplemented all those that had been brought in by the Bahamian whites—the sea-living Conchs. Such things were introduced as the pigeon-pea, soursop, star-apple, Jamaica apple, and all the anons—caneps [geneps], sapotes, and dillies [sapodilla]. These fruits can still be found in best profusion in the Bahamian colored villages in Coconut Grove (which was first called Monrovia, and which was the first Bahamian negro settlement on the Bay) and also in their villages at Old Lemon City, Cutler, and Perrine.[357]

The early Bahamian black immigrants to the Miami areas, after having built houses in their islands of origin, replicated houses in their land of adoption using similar architectural styles and materials. As a result, some of the oldest buildings in Coconut Grove and Old Cutler, some more than two hundred and fifty years old, feature this style of construction. And although they were built without cement, they, like their architectural counterparts in the Keys, have withstood the many hurricanes that have ravaged Florida over the centuries.

Miami

In the late 1800s, Bahamian blacks began to flock to Miami, the so-called Magic City, in search of economic opportunity created by a series of capital investment projects under way there, not the least being the Flagler railroad project. The new immigrants came with the belief that "wonderful things were going on in Miami, and there was a great demand for labour there. Flagler's railroad was bringing in Northerners by the thousands, all anxious to stake a claim in southern Florida with its gentle climate. A remarkable boom was on, and any Bahamian who wanted a job could find it."[358] By the 1920s, Bahamian black immigrants had successfully established the "colored town" of Coconut Grove.

Raymond Mohl commented on the early migration of Bahamian blacks to Miami,

> Black immigrants from the Bahamas, in particular, gave immigration to Miami its special character in the early years of the twentieth century. As the building of Miami began after the mid-1890s, Bahamian blacks were attracted to South Florida by work opportunities in housing and railroad construction, the citrus and vegetable industries, and service jobs in the tourist hotels and restaurants. Some were migrant laborers coming to Florida six months of each year, but others settled permanently and began a black ethnic community.[359]

By 1920, approximately 5,000 black Bahamian immigrants comprised 52% of the black communities of Miami and an estimated 16% of the entire population of the city, creating the second-largest black immigrant population, after New York City, in the United States.[360]

The level of racial discrimination and segregation confronting the black Bahamian immigrants, who were generally used to more a relaxed racial environment back in the islands, was a cultural shock they were bound to challenge. The story of one black immigrant's first encounter with racial discrimination in Miami provides a microscopic insight into conditions typically encountered by the black immigrant to Miami:

> I took a carriage for what the driver called 'Nigger Town'. This was the first time I had heard that opprobrious epithet employed . . . . How unlike the land where I was born! There, colored men were addressed as gentlemen;

here as 'niggers'. There policemen were dressed in immaculate uniforms, carried no deadly weapons, save a billy; here, shirt-sleeved officers of the law carried pistols, smoked and chewed tobacco on duty.[361]

In the early 1900s, most of Miami's blacks lived in dilapidated conditions located to the northwest of the downtown area, in communities such as "Colored Town" (Overtown), Coconut Grove, and Old Cutler. The residents of these communities, as was the case of Grants Town and Bain Town, both located just south of the city of Nassau in the Bahamas, were generally employed as laborers in the predominantly white businesses located in the downtown areas. As investment opportunities in Miami increased, however, the areas of Colored Town were included in considerations of the "necessary" expansion of the business section. White merchants initiated plans to relocate the blacks to more distant, confined, and yet still labor-accessible areas "across the tracks." To achieve this grand scheme of mass relocation, a new housing subdivision project sardonically named Liberty City was developed. True to their traditional instincts, black Bahamian immigrants rebelled against this blatant discrimination and were generally tagged by Miami whites as troublemakers and instigators of racial tension. In the 1920s, therefore, it was not strange to find black Bahamian immigrants active in the vanguard of the emerging civil rights movement in Miami.

Arguably, the most significant precursor of the civil rights movement in Florida, the Universal Negro Improvement Association (UNIA) organized by Marcus Garvey, found fertile ground for growth among the increasing numbers of dissident black residents of Miami and the Keys. In 1920, the predominantly African American community of Colored Town and the predominantly black Bahamian immigrant communities of Coconut Grove, Lemon City, Old Cutler and Perrine collaborated in efforts to jointly protest communal congestion, inadequate and improper public utilities, the absence of or otherwise poorly maintained roads, lack of schools, areas of uncontrolled squalor, and the growing threat of infectious diseases. Additionally, blacks outlined the need for geographic expansion of community boundaries. The white authorities virtually ignored their requests, thus increasingly fueling anti-white sentiments. Early attempts by blacks to organize a protest came in the form of the Colored Board of Trade and the Negro Uplift Association of Dade County, each lobbying for improvements, but with limited success. The UNIA, however, became the vehicle that propelled black social protest to the forefront.

Bahamians and Social Protest

The Universal Negro Improvement Association movement was launched in Jamaica in 1914 by Marcus Garvey, a black charismatic civil rights champion. Garvey imported his movement to the United States in 1916. His messages demanding an end to lynching, Jim Crow laws, political disenfranchisement, and racial discrimination appealed mostly to the West Indian immigrant populations, who were familiar with organized protest in their native places of origin. The Bahamian-dominated branches, organized primarily in Colored Town, Coconut Grove, and Key West, were among the loudest saber rattlers.

Leon E. Howe, the Federal Bureau of Investigation agent assigned to investigate the UNIA movement in Florida, advised his superiors that the UNIA-Miami branch was indeed predominantly composed of and controlled by Bahamian immigrants, who, he also cautioned, were determined to undermine and even overthrow by force the white establishment of southeast Florida. According to Robert Hill, the FBI, which was convinced that the "large Bahamian and West Indian populations were poised for violence against the white community, plotted with the white forces to control the situation."[362] As early as 1908, Judge John Grambling of the municipal court had echoed this cautious view of Miami authorities toward the presence of black Bahamian immigrants in Miami. Judge Grambling praised the Miami police for their active role in altering the attitude of "Nassau Negroes who upon their arrival here consider themselves the social equal of whites."[363] Entering the foray as saviors of the white establishment, the KKK came at a gallop in a show of solidarity for the cause of white supremacy.

Throughout the 1920s, the KKK repeatedly paraded its members along the main thoroughfares of Miami, as many as two hundred at a time, fully uniformed in traditional white robes and hoods and on occasions mounted on horses equally draped in traditional KKK attire. This show of force was a not-too-subtle warning to blacks to desist from their protest or face the kind of reprisals the Klan was known to inflict. Black Bahamian dissidents were to eventually learn that these overt threats would be backed by covert action. In one case, the Reverend Reggie H. Higgs, a popular black Bahamian immigrant, was kidnapped from his home in Coconut Grove in the dead of night, right under the proverbial noses of his family, by several hooded men, taken to a deserted wooded area, tied face-down on the ground, and repeatedly whipped with knotted ropes. His kidnappers reportedly placed another rope around his neck, dragged him back to Coconut Grove and dumped on a street, but not before warning him to leave town within forty-eight hours. The *Miami Herald*, in covering the story, accused Higgs of having left himself exposed to violent reprisals as a result of his vehement protests preached from his pulpit and because of his active association in the UNIA.[364]

The wailing of his family, coupled with news of the kidnapping of Higgs, quickly echoed throughout the community, provoking residents to assemble in the streets of Coconut Grove intent on marching through the white communities in protest. The police reacted quickly and with force, shot one protestor when he "failed to halt upon command," and indiscriminately dispersed the crowd. Twenty-five protest leaders were hoisted off to jail and released the next day. Needless to say, Higgs feared for his life, and with the assistance of fellow-Bahamian immigrants, he fled to the safety of the Bahamas. In 1975, Albert Gibson, in an interview with the *Miami*

Herald on the affair, described how he and fellow Bahamian immigrants assisted Higgs to escape. He claimed that the rescuers arranged for Higgs to escape aboard a British-registered steamer bound for Nassau: "We put him on the boat, gave him a couple hundred dollars, and let him get lost."[365] Gibson reported that Oscar Johnson, another Bahamian immigrant and the financial secretary of the Miami branch of the UNIA, joined Higgs in escaping to Nassau.

In July 1921, the *Miami Herald* published an exposé of the UNIA that focused on an alleged letter purportedly written by Reverend Higgs to the Reverend T. C. Glasden, president of the Key West branch of the UNIA. The letter was reportedly intercepted by the FBI and made accessible to the newspaper. The document allegedly exposed a UNIA-supported plot to poison all the residents of Key West and take possession of the island. While the *Miami Herald* reported possession of the letter, and noted its existence as evidence of a viable threat of violence against white citizens, it failed to make its contents public. Interestingly, the newspaper apparently ignored the fact that Key West was home to a formidable squadron of federal Coast Guards and also home to many residents, both black and white, of Bahamian descent with possible social and perhaps blood connections. Ironically, the report appeared on July 3rd, just hours before the annual celebration of the independence of the nation from the colonial tyranny of the British. Equally interesting was the allegation that the "letter" was reportedly made available to the newspaper via the pro-segregation, overtly discriminating Miami Police Department.[366]

Anti-UNIA repression was further punctuated twelve days after the kidnapping of Higgs, when eight hooded men kidnapped the Reverend Phillip S. Irwin, the white pastor of the St. Agnes Episcopal Church in Colored Town. Irwin was reportedly handcuffed, gagged, blindfolded, and taken to a deserted place in the woods, where he was strapped to a log and stripped of his clothes, repeatedly whipped, tarred, and feathered, and summarily dumped battered and naked on the grounds of the courthouse in downtown Miami. Irwin left Miami two days later. The *Miami Herald*, in its report on the matter, sardonically identified Irwin as a sympathizer of the UNIA and possibly an officer in that organization who justly deserved his fate.[367] The KKK, still flush with the euphoria of success in its mission against the Bahamian blacks and emboldened by the support of the white community, erected an obelisk at the county courthouse where Irwin had been dumped, with a legend stating, "On this Spot a few years ago a white man was found who had been tarred and feathered because he Preached Social Equality to Negroes." The obverse read, "Note: If you are a Reckless Negro Chauffeur or a White man who believes in Social Equality be advised Dade County don't Need You."[368]

The reference to "Chauffeur" inscribed on the obelisk was related to a series of reprisals by white chauffeurs against potential black interlopers for attempting to participate in the predominantly white chauffeur monopoly. The events began in 1917 when black Bahamian immigrant Fred Andrews opened a chauffeur service in Miami and publicly encouraged other blacks to participate in the trade. Several white chauffeurs physically and verbally assaulted Andrews and severely damaged his vehicle. Andrews later stabbed Randolph Lightbourne, one of his assailants; he was fined, arrested, tried, and convicted for the unthinkable act of assault against a white man. None of Andrews' assailants, however, were questioned by the police or charged. Blacks reacted angrily, and rumored threat of black armed uprising caused whites to strike first.

In the early hours of July 15th, a band of white men were seen leaving Colored Town. Within minutes of their departure, the Odds Fellow Hall, the largest building in the black community, was dynamited. A race riot became imminent as many blacks, awakened by the massive blast, emerged armed with an assortment of weapons. The quick action of several black clergymen who called for calm and refraining from violence along with an assurance by the police that they would investigate the incident and apprehend the culprits temporarily eased tensions. Ten police officers were dispatched to Colored Town, and a reward of $50 was posted by the police for information that might lead to the arrest of the perpetrators. Eventually, while no white offender was ever charged with the dynamiting, black leaders, after a series of meetings with white authorities, were given permission to open a chauffeur business, but only to operate within the black communities. The black leaders had threatened mass migration from Miami, which would have aggravated an already chronic situation at a time when the development of Miami was faced with a labor shortage.[369]

Kidnappings and beatings intended to intimidate mostly black Bahamian immigrants and force their repatriation continued almost unabated throughout the 1920s. In April 1920, a white fireman went on a shooting rampage through Colored Town, killing one man and injuring several others. In May of that year, fifty white men drove through that community and indiscriminately shot at buildings, cars, and even people in the disputed Highland Park area claimed by whites, but where several black families had defiantly relocated. On June 29th, a group of white vigilantes tossed dynamite from a speeding car into an abandoned home in Highland Park as a definitive warning to blacks not to settle in that area, thought to be too close to white communities. White and black leaders met to resolve the latest disputed breach of the "color line" without success. A rumor that blacks were preparing to march on white communities was discouraged when a force of three hundred armed soldiers were dispatched to patrol Colored Town and enforce martial law.[370]

Racial tensions between Miami whites and blacks reached a boiling point on July 30, 1920, when Henry Brooks, a black Bahamian, was accused of raping a white woman. Brooks was arrested and jailed, then whisked out of town by train to prevent his inevitable lynching by an angry mob of an estimated three hundred armed whites. Members of the vigilante followed the train carrying Brooks, intent on forcibly removing him and lynching him. Terrified, Brooks allegedly jumped from the train and was killed by injuries suffered from his fall. Reportedly, "several hundred blacks, mostly Bahamians, convinced that Brooks' death was the result of mob action, gathered in Colored Town and angrily discussed ways of avenging it."[371] The overwhelming numbers of armed white forces patrolling the community dissuaded actual reprisals. Brooks's body was eventually shipped to Nassau for burial.

White authorities argued that the civil rights agitation of the black Bahamians was to blame for provoking the once relatively docile African American Miamians to engage in civil unrest. Soon afterward, prominent black Bahamians received threatening letters warning them to return to the Bahamas or face reprisals. The recipients, all prominent civic leaders, including Dr. A. P. B. Holly, Baptist Reverend Vincent Moss, and John Bethel, were branded as "traitors" and "dangerous to any community" in the letters, signed "the Committee that waited on Higgs and Irwin."[372] Police Chief Raymond Dillon, when confronted by some of the affected blacks about the matter, denied involvement of the Klan or any other whites; instead, he insisted that the intimidating letters were the work of other blacks who had become personal enemies because they were jealous of the emerging civic role played by Bahamians in the black communities.[373]

There was a militant side of the UNIA that perhaps gave some justification to the fears of the white establishment that the local blacks, led by Bahamian agitators, were preparing to resort to reprisals, or at least to protect against violent discrimination. The African Black Legion was organized and commanded by a black Bahamian immigrant, James Nimmo. In some primitive respects, this 1920s agency foreshadowed the imminent rise of the militant Black Panthers of later years. Nimmo had immigrated to Miami in 1916 at the age of sixteen, intending to enlist in the U.S. armed forces, after his application for recruitment in the British army was rejected because he was under the age of eligibility. He served with the American forces in France during the First World War and, upon discharge, returned to his adopted home in Miami. He joined the UNIA; because of his military experience and general militancy, he was made leader of the uniformed branch of the African Black Legion. Along with two subordinate officers, he was given command of an estimated two hundred "defenders of the cause," including many veterans of the Great War.

In the indomitable style of their national leader, Marcus Garvey, the troops wore blue uniforms adorned with brass buttons, red-striped pants, and military-style caps with the ensign of the UNIA emblazed across the front. The officers wore plumed hats and sported ceremonial swords. While each recruit discreetly possessed firearms reportedly smuggled in from the Bahamas, they wisely paraded in public using wooden rifles made by local carpenters. Occasionally on Sundays after church ended, the troops paraded in local Dorsey Park dressed in full regalia and in open view, to the consternation of white residents. On the other hand, residents of the black communities would gather in complete appreciation of the drills in progress.

Needless to say, the police would intervene, confiscate the wooden weapons, knock in a few skulls, and unceremoniously disperse the gathering.[374]

Still, despite the dragnet cast by the white authorities over the black communities, incidents of black reprisals, mostly by Bahamians, did occur. In October 1924, three blacks, later identified simply as migrant Bahamian agricultural workers, engaged in a shootout in Colored Town with two white police officers. Two months later, a Bahamian black, in the indomitable traditional combat style of his heritage, avoided arrest by striking a policeman on the head with a brick and fleeing into the heart of the community, remarkably avoiding a hail of bullets discharged by the assailed white officer. In January 1926, a battle erupted between fourteen blacks and a white patrolman that led to the death of the officer and injuries to six of his assailants. The blacks had determined to forcibly prevent the officer from patrolling their turf. As was often the case, Bahamians were blamed for fuelling the racial unrest.[375]

In the 1920s, the protest actions of the Bahamian-led, Florida branches of the Universal Negro Improvement Association helped to create a more focused challenge to the opposition to racial discrimination against blacks in southeast Florida than had existed prior to that date. Additionally, the concerted resistance set the stage for the emergence of the later civil rights movement of the 1950s. Many of the members and leaders of the Florida UNIA became active associates of the protest movement led by Martin Luther King, Jr. Civil rights leaders, including Marcus Garvey, Adam Clayton Powell, and Dr. Martin Luther King, Jr., were apparently at ease in the Bahamas and in the company of Bahamians of like persuasion. Perhaps it was the search for this solace that was the reason King, with a premonition of impending doom, reportedly experienced his epiphany in a boat just off the shore of Bimini in the Bahamas, in the company of a Bahamian fisherman, and where he reportedly penned his now famous "I Had a Dream" speech!

Bahamians in Migrant Labor

For many decades now, the United States has engaged in the importation of seasonal migrant labor for employment, primarily in agriculture and to a lesser degree in other sectors of the economy. As earlier, Bahamians were recruited for employment in several sectors of the economy of the developing Florida Keys, including the production and harvesting of pineapples, sponge diving, and the emerging hospitality industry. Bahamians also benefited from work as stevedores on American steamers embarking and disembarking from ports in the southern Bahamas and sailing to the Caribbean and Central and South America.

7. THE INTERCHANGE OF CULTURAL INFLUENCES

Bahamian Labor Migration and American Influence

From the early 1900s up to the 1960s, the wage-labor migration of Bahamians was primarily to the United States and secondarily to Central and South America and the Caribbean. Just before the beginning of the twentieth century, hundreds of Bahamians migrated to south Florida, where they contributed principally to the development of Miami and the Keys. Early in the 1900s, scores of Bahamians from the southern Bahamas found employment on mostly American vessels as stevedores loading and unloading cargoes in Central and South America and the Caribbean.

Albury states that in 1902, 143 steamers and 85 sailing vessels stopped at islands in the southern Bahamas and recruited an estimated 2,888 Bahamians on monthly contracts to work as laborers.[376] The number of recruits decreased to just 160 by 1929, and by 1950 such migration had ceased when a geographic reversal of affairs found most Bahamians favoring employment in the United States, instead.

In 1919, more than 2,000 recruits primarily from the central and northern Bahamas were employed to work in U.S. Navy installations in Charleston, South Carolina. The short-term contract lasted for only three months, with most recruits arriving in August 1919 and leaving just before Christmas. In all cases, Bahamian labor migration was influenced by American perspectives on life and society, which they in turn imported back into the Bahamas. Perhaps no other labor-migration experience helped to shape the evolution of the Bahamian cultural identity more than the "Contract".

Beginning in 1943, thousands of Bahamians and persons from other parts of the British West Indies were recruited to work in the United States under an agriculture labor program negotiated by the governments of the United States and Great Britain on behalf of its colonial citizens. The controversial policy of the United States to recruit migrant workers is worth noting.

A review of the origins of the World War II Emergency Farm Labor Importation Program that spawned the H-2 labor program in the eastern United States and the Bracero labor program in the western United States will show that the U.S. government never believed that there was a national agriculture labor shortage due to the war during the war years; rather, it was due in part to pressure exerted by the nation's powerful agriculture sector, which demanded an abundant supply of cheap and compliant labor, forcing officials to establish a national program to facilitate the importation of foreign migrant labor. The review dispels a position commonly presented in West Indian historiography that the West Indian laborers were chosen because of their value in productivity and reliability. Instead, it attempts to prove that the eventual recruitment of the foreign migrants was purely a matter of political expediency that incidentally produced aspects of American-Bahamian connections that helped shape the Bahamian national identity.

Perspectives on the "Contract"

At the advent of global conflict in 1939, agriculture in the United States was struggling to cope with the challenges faced by that sector of the economy during twenty years of depression. The Roosevelt Administration's "New Deal" exacerbated the problem when it introduced a controversial program that paid farmers to grow less and allowed the subsidized farmers to evict sharecroppers from private lands on which the latter had historically eked out meager earnings. Very limited federal assistance was offered to alleviate the plight of the disenfranchised sharecroppers. The Federal Emergency Relief Administration, the National Labor Relations Act, the Social Security Act, and the Fair Labor Standards Act, programs especially designed to provide assistance to the underprivileged, all failed to provide relief to destitute sharecroppers. In effect, an estimated 65 percent of all African Americans and many other poor whites and Mexican migrant workers were further plunged into economic depression, creating even more homeless and poor Americans.[377] The only federal assistance was provided through the initiatives of the Farm Security Administration's Migratory Camp Program.

The Migratory Camp Program created permanent and mobile camps that provided shelter, bathroom facilities, daycare centers, and health clinics to the thousands of indigent sharecroppers willing to participate in the program. In 1939, permanent camps sheltered some seven thousand predominantly Mexican families living along the Pacific coast. The program, however, was just a minor solution to a very large problem. Similar types of assistance facilities were slow to be introduced in the South, where the sharecroppers were mostly African Americans.[378] Interestingly, authorities in California and Florida, the largest agricultural states in the union, established border patrols to keep displaced migrant workers from flooding their states. John Steinbeck's novel *The Grapes of Wrath* provides a succinct perspective on the plight of the typical migrant laborer employed in agricultural programs during this period.[379]

The boom years of the burgeoning war economy positively impacted production and the demand for labor in most other sectors of the economy, but they did little to alleviate the challenges confronting the agricultural sector. In fact, only two years after the outbreak of the global conflict, the Department of Agriculture continued to be challenged by what officials called the "superabundance of labor power on American farms," concluding that even if more than 1.5 million of the national pool of farm workers were recruited for employment in areas of war production and the armed forces, agricultural production in the country would not be disrupted.[380] Unscrupulous farmers, like the cotton producers, invested their federal subsidies in the purchase of cotton-harvesting machines, further increasing the pool of unemployed sharecroppers. And while some sharecroppers and day laborers enlisted in the armed forces or migrated to the urban centers, many thousands more remained homeless, jobless, and hopelessly destitute.[381]

Following the attack on Pearl Harbor, and despite repeated federal insistence to the contrary, rumors began to circulate that a scarcity in available farm labor was threatening the future of the agriculture sector. Growers in California and Florida, the largest producers in the country, were allegedly the primary instigators of the rumors. Motives for the rumors may have been fear by California farmers that assistance for the federal Migratory Camp Program subsidizing the employment of mostly cheap Mexican farm labor was to be decreased.

California and Florida farmers generally rejected the federal demands for increased agricultural production, which would have required increased investment of their personal resources and fewer government grants or perhaps encouraged competition in a highly monopolized industry. Members of the American Farm Bureau Federation and the California Associated Farmers responded by orchestrating a deluge of protest letters to local political representatives, state and federal administrators that threatened to boycott agricultural production if their supply of cheap surplus labor was in any way jeopardized. Federal administrators were faced with a perplexing situation in which a viable option was to ignore their own intelligence and publicly confirm the rumor that there was indeed a shortage of available farm labor, despite the fact that the farmers paying the lowest wages were the ones protesting the loudest.

The decision to go along with the position of the large farm interest groups was not a difficult one for federal authorities, who were burdened with a Migratory Camp Program that demanded millions of dollars in federal funding to pay for the amenities provided to the laborers. Additionally, authorities were faced with the prospect of a confederation of farmers historically used to an ample supply of first slave then cheap Mexican and African American labor at lower than affordable rates. The most serious problem lay with the southern farmers, who paid an average of twelve cents per hour, compared with farmers in the northeast, who paid as much as thirty-one cents per hour. In the end, the U.S. Department of Agriculture and the U.S. Department of Labor's Inter-Bureau Coordinating Committee acquiesced to mounting public pressure and concluded that the farmers were accustomed to "a great over-supply of workers . . . which some had come to consider a normal supply, and to consider any reduction in the surplus supply as a shortage."

The official position of the agriculture administration was to agree with the farmers that there was indeed a labor shortage. The authorities feared that the farmers would make good on their threats and create harvest labor shortages that would undermine war production goals. A concerted effort was made to assure farmers that there was a federal response to the "labor shortage." To accomplish this feat and pacify farmers while at the same time protecting national agriculture interests proved to be a political juggling act. In response, the federal government reluctantly expanded the Majority Camp Program to support eighty-nine camps that stretched from coast to coast. Forty-three were mobile camps that facilitated the movement of migrants to areas of critical demand and importance to the success of the national agricultural program. An additional one hundred and four others were designed for immediate construction. Once again, federal authorities were faced with increasing costs to transport laborers, house them, feed them, provide daycare for their children, and attend to their medical needs. On the other hand, farmers were relieved that the federal government had spared them much of the expense associated with the industry. Matters arose, however, that forced the federal government to make tactical decisions to assure the success of the national agricultural program.[382]

Farm states vehemently protested the recruiting of eligible workers from their limited pools to satisfy labor demands emanating from other states. The governor of South Carolina, for example, threatened to arrest any federal agent who attempted to recruit laborers in his state. The farmers in Florida called the recruitment of hundreds of workers from that state to work in New Jersey "the most high-handed act of piracy ever perpetrated in this state." Southern states, in particular, were outraged when many of their mostly African American laborers refused to work for Depression-era wages and bargained with their white bosses for equitable wages. This was unheard of (and unacceptable) in the South, where whites were unaccustomed to overt resistance by blacks.

In the Jim Crow South of the 1940, farmers found it extremely demeaning to have to even consider negotiating with people of color for anything. Historically, such acts of "insolence" were rewarded with decisive force. Many threatened to leave the crops unharvested rather than negotiate with an established underclass. In cases in Florida, local law enforcement agencies collaborated to force workers who were unattached to the federal programs to work off fines levied for trumped-up crimes. Sheriff Willis McCall of Lake County, Florida, for example, would raid black communities and arrest any able-bodied man "suspected" of vagrancy.

In one case, the Justice Department charged McCall with forcing sixty gainfully employed longshoremen to work on his farm. Blacks, especially those in the federal employment program, however, knew that their jobs were protected by federal laws and that they were the principal source of labor, and as such did not have to fear acts of injurious reprisals. Many refused to work for less than market rates and negotiated labor conditions and wages with other farmers, sometimes in other states.

In the meantime, between 1935 and 1939 there was widespread social and political unrest in the British West Indies. The crash of the Stock Market in 1929 and the challenges of the Depression that followed were a source of frustration for many British West Indian immigrants prevented from gaining employment on farms in America by the passage of the Quota Act passed by Congress in 1924. Many others previously employed were forced to return to their native lands where the prospect of continued employment was very slim. Amid the maelstrom of economic and political problems confronting them, American politicians did not want to have to deal with colonial territories in their backyard that were mired in unrest and possibly susceptible to Nazi anti-British influences or anti-American Marxist-Socialist propaganda. The American base construction program in the circum-Caribbean was in the pipeline and had thus created an urgent need to remove any possible security threat to that strategic Anglo-American military initiative that could be caused by uncontrolled unrest in the territories.[383] Caught in a seemingly untenable vise—grip of challenges from all sides, American authorities decided to implement a bold policy designed to appease the farmers, free themselves from the huge financial burden of the Migratory Camp Program, and gain an advantage in foreign politics by striking a deal with their Mexican and British allies to recruit migrant workers from Mexico and the British West Indies.[384]

The new policy, called the Emergency Farm Labor Importation Program—commonly known in the Bahamas as the "Contract"—was designed to use foreign migrant workers in a carefully controlled program that would ensure a cheap, consistent, controlled, and effective labor supply that would please the farmers, ensure consistent harvests, and promote U.S. foreign policy arrangements with the United Kingdom and Mexico.[385] Not to be easily overlooked was the fact that the new program would be effective in controlling illegal migration into the United States.

In 1942, Secretary of Agriculture Claude Wickard made a secret trip to Mexico to negotiate for the new foreign migrant workers program to begin on the West coast. An initial contingent of four thousand Mexicans were imported to conduct harvests on farms in California and Arizona.[386] East coast farmers demanded similar concessions. In response, Congress passed Public Law 45, allowing for the expansion of the farm labor supply program with the proviso that no federal funds would be used to improve the wages or conditions of American farm workers. In essence, the new law was a blow primarily against African American workers, who were forced to accept the wages offered and could not leave their home states to work elsewhere without the authorization of their local agricultural extension agents, who in many cases were at the same time white farmers or more likely sympathizers wishing to preserve the Southern white status quo.

In 1943, into this political, economic, and social quagmire were imported the first contingent of West Indian migrant workers, first from the Bahamas, and then from Jamaica, Barbados, and other parts of the British Caribbean. With the stroke of the federal pen, conditions were developed for confrontation between African American farm workers, historically accustomed to a monopoly on most farm jobs in the South, then forced to compete with black West Indians from depressed economies for jobs and spaces in the federal migrant labor camps. As one federal staff member noted, the arrival of the Bahamians resulted in the exclusion of many local farm workers from day work they had come to expect as their inalienable right.[387] Perhaps more than any other, the personal experiences of these Bahamian migrant workers, their encounters with Jim Crow laws, and interactions with people from other West Indian sending societies became significant determining factors that helped to shape their political and social ideologies and, in turn, influenced the creation of the national identity of the evolving Commonwealth of The Bahamas.

Independence and the Search for Self-Identity

Thomas Wagstaff notes that "in the mingled optimism and frustration of the 1960s, Black Nationalism, the radical alternative to integration, a constant, if muted theme in the history of the Negro protest thought in American, made a powerful appeal to the Black community."[388] Scores of black Bahamians, ever moving back and forth between the "states" seeking and taking advantage of employment opportunities, at times experienced or become aware of violent acts of racial discrimination that included kidnapping, whipping, and even lynching. Such acts of discrimination were unheard of in a Bahamas which was also grappling with racial issues of its own. In the 1960s, many black Bahamians were drawn to the messages of hope promoted by the African American Black Nationalist movement, just as many of the elders among them or their forebears and acquaintances were stirred by the promises of Garveyism of the 1920s. The appeal of the Bahamian "Garvey," the locally dubbed "Black Moses," Lynden Oscar Pindling and his Progressive Liberal Party advocating increased enfranchisement for local blacks, became a forceful rallying cry for change, and nothing short of total Bahamian sovereignty was acceptable.[389]

In preparation for independence from Great Britain scheduled for effect in July 1973, the Progressive Liberal Party, the predominantly black national governing administration, collaborated with leading Bahamian church leaders and selected members of the black intelligentsia to discuss and determine a public interpretation of the national identity to be endorsed by the new nation. Generally, the United Bahamian Party, the largely white Bahamian constituency representing racial, social, and economic disenfranchisement, was largely ignored. This author remembers his many discussions with the late George Mackey, venerable political activist, one of the mentors of the Bahamian Independence movement, and up to the time of his death, chairman of the board of the public corporation of which I had the honor to serve as executive director for more than a decade. Among other things, he informed me that it had been determined among his peers that cultural heritage identity comprised three elements distinctive to the self-image of the emerging Commonwealth of The Bahamas: a sense of geography, a general historical perspective, and, most significantly, the African origin of the nation because of its overwhelming black population.

The sense of geography recognized the cultural and political position of the new nation within the British West Indies, but reiterated the historical denial that the country was geographically a part of the circum-Caribbean. The sense of history identified the new nation as distinctly divergent from the predominantly agrarian plantation economy characterizing the Caribbean, promoting the new country instead as an economic and social appendage of the United States with a distinctive traditional reliance on the sea for existence. The racial identity in self-definition was intended to demonstrate a rejection of the colonial Anglo-identity that had marginalized the role of blacks in favor of a new social and economic policy—a policy that reflected aspects of the Black Power movement in vogue in the United States and promised increased black enfranchisement.

To achieve this last goal, a national television station was introduced that featured, among other things, Alex Hailey's *Roots* mini-series and African-American sitcoms, including *Good Times, The Jeffersons, Julia*, and *Benson.*[390] In addition, a Department of Archives was established in the then Ministry of Education and Culture with a mandate to collate and preserve national documents. This agency was also to feature a "black history research center and reading room."[391] Interestingly, the first in a series of public exhibitions mounted by the Department of Archives focused on the subject of "Aspects of Slavery." The centerpiece of national cultural expression, however, was to be the development of a Bahamian National Museum and Research Centre to be located in the Art and Craft Center of the Afrocentric cultural facility called Jumbey Village, which incidentally (but not accidentally) was situated "over-the-hill," away from the white suburbs and near the highly touted, newly developed model low-cost housing subdivision named Yellow Elder Gardens.[392] This subdivision featured houses architecturally styled as concrete huts to evoke a sense of pride in a national African identity in the masses struggling to free themselves from the repressive influences of the white oligarchy.[393]

Ironically, generally absent from the tables of discussion on national identity were representatives of the Haitian community, the largest ethnic group in the country, and arguably the bedrock of the Bahamian labor force. Because of a sense of superiority, Bahamians then as now disregard the *kweyole*-speaking Haitians and Bahamians of Haitian descent as a subclass necessarily tolerated as a very convenient source of labor. Instead, the children of English-speaking Caribbean immigrants assumed control of the new government and key elements of administrative authority and used these mediums to express their own unique sense of national self-identity.[394]

Caught up in the euphoria of independence, Bahamian-born Lisle Alleyne, Jr., son of Barbadian immigrants to the Bahamas, wrote the following comments on Bahamian self-identity from Pace College in New York City; it reflects the values of many other black Bahamians of that era:

> Our Bahamian identity is a unique identity, because it is based on our African experiences and our Bahamian experiences. I know the coloured people are saying that they have never been to Africa to have such an experience, but these are the experiences of our forefathers that produced Junkanoo, Goombay, etc. These are the experiences that that make up our identity and culture; these are the experiences that make Bahamians unique.[395]

Alleyne, perhaps like so many black Bahamians of that era, failed to consider the undisputable significance of the American immigrants, both black and white, in the shaping of the Bahamian national identity beyond the obvious pan-African influences, but instead favored endorsement of the primary influence of the African-American Black Power movement that promoted the afro, platform-heeled shoes, *Shaft*, and Motown.

Impact of White Loyalists

White Loyalist immigrants reluctantly came to the Bahamas as a result of political forces that deprived them of homes, citizenship, social status, and other things of tangible and intangible value. For the most part, they dreamed and schemed of eventually returning to their former stations in life in the vastly more sophisticated, familiar environs of the American South. To most, the Bahamas was a convenient, albeit challenging and temporary refuge geographically close to the northern mainland but sparsely populated by groups of uncivilized thieves and plunderers devoid of societal values and identified by the ignoble appellation of "Conches." The soil was generally unsuitable for meaningful agriculture, and the local blacks were presumptuously overly familiar. While the white Loyalists were in their temporary refuge, changes had to be made to make their existence more meaningful and comfortable, and these changes had to include a more rigid code of discipline for the often insolent blacks. And so with the white Loyalist migration came the introduction and enforcement of stricter slave laws and more rigid social and racial boundaries suitable for the introduction of a cotton-plantation economy that relied almost exclusively on slave labor.

Large land grants were given to these white immigrants to allow them to attempt to carve out a plantation lifestyle in the agriculturally hostile islands. As a result, the demography of the once vastly underpopulated outer-islands in particular was significantly and permanently transformed by the migration of a handful of whites commanding the unswerving fidelity of hundreds of slaves forced to reproduce aspects of the plantation life their masters enjoyed back home. Traditional squatter rights to the land that the few inhabitants enjoyed gave way to carefully articulated and calculated land titles that forever restricted land use and ownership in the islands. Fences and boundary lines demarked what was once free range accessible to all, regardless of color or social status, to use for subsistence farming and construction of rudimentary shelters. In no other area, perhaps, was the influence of the white Loyalist immigrants more effectively demonstrated than in the area of architecture, which reflected the Georgian style that came to dominate Bahamian architecture of the late eighteenth and early nineteenth centuries. But as Saunders and Craton (1998) surmise, "it was probably the slave and free black majority of newcomers who most indelibly shaped the social history of the Bahamas,"[396] and a good starting point for research on this early African American influence would be an examination of the impact of the creolized African Gullah-Geechee culture on the evolution of Bahamian black self-identity and the culture of the masses.

Gullah-Geechee Influences

The Gullahs are a people of largely Senegambian descent who live in the Low Country region of South Carolina and Georgia, in particular, both along the coastal plain and in the Sea Islands. Their historical territory once extended northward to the coastal areas of Cape Fear in North Carolina and southward to the vicinity of Jacksonville in north Florida. Their language is called Geechee, which some scholars speculate is derived from the Creek name for the Ogeechee River near Savannah, Georgia. The Gullah have preserved aspects of their African heritage well, and they speak a language that is a creolized form of English containing many West African loan words and demonstrates the influence of African grammatical structures. The Gullah language is closely related to the English patois spoken in Sierra Leone, Jamaica, Barbados, and the Bahamas. Their storytelling, food-ways, music, folktales, craft and farming, and fishing traditions all exhibit the strong influence of West and Central African cultures. Aspects of the Afro-Bahamian cultural identity are in many ways reflected by the historical connections between the Gullah and Afro-Bahamians.

According to John Holm, "the syntax of Bahamian is very close to that of contemporary Gullah," and they were sister languages of eighteenth-century plantation creole transported from the South to the Bahamas.[397] Prominent Bahamian amateur folk-historian Dr. Cleveland Eneas noted the similarities between the Gullah and Afro-Bahamians during his initial trip to the Low Country:

> When I first went to Liberty County . . . I was amazed to find that they didn't only look like the people of Bain Town, but they talked like them.

> Their accent was almost identical with that of the people among whom I
> grew up . . . [I asked myself], why should one see Bain Town faces on the
> streets of Charleston and

Savannah, or why one's ears should be graced by the over-the-hill patois that
comes out of these faces?[398]

Elsie Clews Parsons, a folklorist who collected tales from the Bahamas and the
South Carolina Sea Islands, confirmed the strong cultural connections between
the two areas: "It is interesting to recognize in Sea Islands lore many riddles and
tales that have been recorded in the Bahamas and told not only like them as to
pattern, but like them as to phrase or little turns of expression which suggests
historical connection with the Carolinas."[399] Some examples of these linguistic
similarities include use of words and phrases like "too" in reference to "very"; "day
clean", referring to day-break or dawn of day; "yinna" for "all of you"; and, "beni"
for "sesame".

Thousands of my generation of Bahamians growing up in the 1950s and 1960s
were delighted by the folk stories orally shared by our elders and teachers of the
con-games played on each other by the consummate tricksters Bro. Bookee, the
fox, and Bro. Rabbie, the trickster rabbit. In Senegambian culture "Bro. Bookee" is
articulated as "Bouki", the trickster hyena of Wolof culture. "Bouki" becomes "Brer
Fox" in Gullah folktales. Keith Cartwright, lecturer at the College of the Bahamas,
spent two years in West Africa researching the cultural similarities of his native land
and West Africa. He drew on the research of Elsie Clews Parsons to illustrate those
cultural connections:

> Parson's *Folk-Tales of Andros Island, Bahamas* (1918) and her *Folklore
> of the Sea Islands, South Carolinas* (1923) provide plenty evidence to
> support her belief that Bahamian tales and language were shaped by the
> Loyalist immigration. Interestingly, a number of these shared tales have
> clear Senegambian sources. "The Animals Who Ate Their Mothers," a
> Senegambian tale that thrived in the Carolinas and the Bahamas, features
> the decision of Lion, Hyena, and Hare to form a rice cooperative in which
> members agree to make their mothers into sauce to be eaten with the
> rice." After Lion and Hyena kill their mothers, who are unable to pass
> the test of recognizing the group members' code names, Hare saves his
> mother by drumming his colleagues' names as they work in the fields . . . .
> In Andros, Bookee, Rabbit and Elephant change their names and agree
> to eat their mothers if the mothers can't break the code. Rabbit, of course,
> finds a way for his mother to decode their song.[400]

Carolina planters demonstrated a specific preference for slaves originating
from the coastal and marsh areas of Senegal and Gambia in West Africa. In the

1750s, Henry Laurens, operator of the largest slave-trading firm in America, stated, "The slaves from the River Gambia are preferr'd to all others with us [Carolina planters] . . . next to Them the Windward Coast are preferr'd to Angolas."[401] This ethnic preference was based on the knowledge that Senegambian slaves were historically accomplished rice planters and mariners, and aptly suitable for labor in the Low Country and coastal areas of the Carolinas and Georgia, where the cultivation of rice was arduous and exacted a high mortality rate from laborers in that industry. Many of the slaves imported from Senegambia were converts to Islam, as were a small group carried from the Bahamas to the American South. In the Bahamas, the assumption of the presence of many African converts to Islam was supported by the report of a missionary to the Bahamas in 1802, who noted that he had encountered many slaves who "called themselves the followers of Mahomet."[402] Together with those directly imported, it was presumably these slaves who contributed to the early establishment of the Islamic faith in the Low Country.

Shared Senegambian Heritage

Historically, Senegambia was not the 1981 geographical confederation comprising modern-day Senegal and Gambia. It was, instead, a vast territory stretching between two river basins, the Senegal and the Gambia. It began at the sources of these rivers on the Futa Jallon plateau and meandered to the Atlantic Ocean. The region was bordered by the Atlantic Ocean to the west, the Sahara Desert to the north, and savanna grasslands and the equatorial forests to the east and south. The diversity of Senegambians included the Wolof, Peut, Tukulor, Manding, Sereer, Soninke, Susa, Joola, Nalu, Baga, Beafada, Bainuk, and Basari peoples.[403] Cotton, rice, and salt were important trade commodities for the Senegambians, who thrived among a myriad network of mangroves, swamps, forests and waterways, a region that closely mirrored the geography of the Low Country.[404]

Islam was introduced into the Senegambian region in the early fifteenth century. Barry notes,

> By the fifteenth century, Senegambia . . . had a secular experience of Islam, thanks to the influences coming from both the Sudan and the Sahara. From the Sahara, it was the Zawaya families of Berber marabouts who converted populations in northern Senegambia to Islam. In the beginning . . . Muslim trading communities were simply tiny enclaves in the environment of political structures peculiar to Senegambia . . . . It was tolerated and accepted in royal courts . . . Islam emerged clearly as an ideology of political [and social] change around the time when Europe was imposing its mode of capitalist production on the domestic societies of Senegambia.[405]

Interestingly, the rise of Islam in the United States was a part of the Black Power movement that echoed the protest of their African forebears against oppression perpetrated by adherents of the cross in favor of the crescent.

Barry notes that the Senegambians were expert rice farmers and mariners: "they excelled in rice farming . . . . It was much more profitable to transport cola, indigo dye and iron goods produced in the forests for sale in the savanna to the north by canoe along the coasts and up the Southern Rivers, than to have head-porters haul them overland across the Fula Jallon plateau."[406] Senegambians kept domestic slaves to work their farms and to produce a variety of handicraft goods. It was from among these people that many of the slaves imported into the Low Country and the Bahamas came, bringing exquisite skills in fishing, sailing, rice cultivation, indigo dye production, and handicrafts, industries that became important Southern and Bahamian industries. In particular, rice, a traditional food plant in Africa and a large part of the world, was introduced to the Carolinas in the early 1700s with seeds from Madagascar. Senegambians introduced traditions of rice planting methods like working in organized gangs and hoeing in unison to the tunes of work songs.[407]

One of the earliest records of an African Muslim brought to the Bahamas was the 1831 case of Abul Keti, a liberated African freed from a slave ship and sent to New Providence, where his fate was to be decided by the local vice-admiralty court. While in a Bahamian slave-clearing center, he appealed to the Bahamian colonial governor, James Carmichael Smyth, for clemency on the grounds that he was already a free man undeserving of enslavement. His letter, written in Arabic, caused quite a stir in local circles.[408] In the early 1800s, Loyalist Thomas Spaulding of Sapelo Island, Georgia, returned to the mainland from the Bahamas, bringing with him several Senegambian slaves. One such slave was Bilali Muhammad, the Pulaar-speaking overseer of his Sapelo plantation.

John Couper, another Bahamas-repatriated Loyalist, brought his Senegambian slave called Salih Bilali back to his Georgia plantation and, like Spaulding, made him overseer of his plantation of several hundred slaves. According to Holloway, Southern planters valued Senegambians not only because of their agricultural skills, but also because of their conversion to Islam, which, it was assumed, made them more assimilated to a civilized culture than slaves from other regions, who were essentially considered "uncivilized heathens" and as such more difficult to acculturate to European behavior. Many Senegambians were entrusted with positions requiring a degree of responsibility and civility, such as overseers, cooks, house servants, craftsmen, and nurses. Some of the more physically attractive Senegambian women reportedly became the mistresses of the socially indiscreet Southern gentlemen.[409]

Personal Reflections

At midnight on July 10, 1973, the Union Jack, a key symbol of British national pride and colonial might, was lowered and replaced by the flag of the newly born

Commonwealth of The Bahamas. At age nineteen, I was one of many Bahamians standing on the bluff overlooking the ceremony unfolding. Fort Charlotte, the imposing fortress of colonial repute, formed the backdrop. Like most Bahamians, I did not fully understand the significance of the event, but I was happy the ceremony was happening at night and not during the day as in the case of Empire Day ceremonies, when uniformed school children and government officials stood in the shadow of that same fort, in the woeful heat of the midday sun, wishing the boring ceremony extolling the colonial authority of Great Britain to govern the affairs of the Bahamian people would end and the holiday the event accorded would begin. But even as the respective flags were being replaced, questions concerning the Bahamian national identity remained unresolved.

As with most Bahamians, my early education was immersed in the culture of the motherland. I learned of the legendary chivalry of Sir Walter Raleigh, who, according to lore, had spread his coat over a puddle of water on a muddy London street to allow his "Good Queen Bess" to pass without getting her shoes wet. I was ever covertly reminded that the British were a superior people who ruled an empire so vast that the sun never set on it. I was familiar with the history of that island nation—the Tudors, Stuarts, and Windsors; its literature—Shakespeare, the Lake Poets, and Alfred, Lord Tennyson. Our textbooks, standard throughout the Commonwealth, included the *Student Companion* and *Royal Readers,* both designed to promote British cultural identity and values. Members of the judicial system wore powdered wigs (as they still do today) and argued aspects of British common law; law enforcement officers wore uniforms designed in Great Britain that included light woolen cloaks and khaki outfits unsuited for the tropical environment. The teaching of Bahamian history was very limited as it was yet largely unresearched and unwritten. This was the environment in which Bahamian independence emerged; however, "things British" were already being challenged by new thoughts of national identity largely influenced by the Black Power movement that was gaining popularity across the United States.

In the late 1960s and early 1970s, many young Bahamians who were not obligated by the narrow constraints of national scholarships opted not to pursue British-influenced tertiary education at the various campuses of the University of the West Indies established in Jamaica (Mona), Trinidad (St. Augustine), and Barbados (Cave Hill). Instead, scores chose to attend schools in the United States, where the quality of education was in many cases superior, the bright lights of the big cities were alluring and the distance away from the rules of parents and guardians was in many cases appealing. In many respects, the students were supported in their choice of American colleges by parents, guardians, and friends who had became familiar with aspects of American tertiary education while employed on the "contract" or in other sectors in the various states. And invariably, these students came into direct contact (and perhaps conflict) with African American ideas of self-identity. In many cases, students returned to the Bahamas sporting afro hair styles, a few had even made the sojourn to Ghana, many others religiously read *Jet, Esquire,* and *Ebony* magazines, knew all the latest Motown hits, and in some cases had their own tales to share of racial discrimination and black resistance. The vernacular lexicon acquired such words and phrases as "right on" to denote agreement, "I'm hip," which denoting a general understanding of a situation, and "kool," which declared a thing or person to be remarkably acceptable.

Parents and guardians made the twice annual pilgrimage to "the states" during the summer months and at Christmastime to visit with friends and relatives and stock up for the new school year and Yuletide festivities. They frequented the established department stores like Burdines, McCrory's and Woolworths, where the purchase of "American style" clothes, such as dungaree pants, "jockey" underpants, and Fruit of the Loom tee-shirts had become a tradition. No pilgrimage was complete without a meal at the McCrory's or Woolworths lunch counter, or a hamburger from Burger King, where the sandwiches were reportedly "as large as small plates," and a Dairy Queen ice cream sundae was a must, as was a bucket of Colonel Sanders' delightful fried chicken to take home.

From these experiences, taste for American cuisine and apparel began to replace that for English-manufactured goods, and they became a staple in the emerging Bahamian culture. This was perhaps best exemplified in the establishment of the Bahamian version of Burger King, called "Keith's," and Father Allen's Chicken Shack, the popular local response to Kentucky Fried Chicken, where the featured sale of fried "chicken-in-the-bag" was also complemented by the sale of made-to-order hamburger sandwiches. By the time of Independence, however, Burger King, Dairy Queen, and Kentucky Fried Chicken franchises had sprung up in a number of areas primarily in Nassau as a direct result of the compelling influence of the "American" lifestyle that Bahamians had come to admire and enjoy. Bahamians watched American television programs via antennas erected on rooftops on sets featuring networks like ABC, CBS, and NBC beamed in from Miami, and they were far more acquainted with the ebb and flow of the Vietnam War, the Watergate scandal, and the New York Knicks' unlikely defeat of the Los Angeles Lakers in the 1970 NBA Finals than with events occurring in England, or for that matter, in the British Caribbean just to the south. Ironically, while Bahamian Independence was finally attained, the search for self-identity continued to be earnestly conducted in the shadow of the "American Dream"—the acquisition of things and attitudes from "the states"—that Bahamians continue to chase even to the present.

INDEX

NOTES

1. Most historians generally accept the place of the 1492 landfall as San Salvador. Other claims persist, however, that the site was elsewhere in The Bahamas, including Cat Island and Samana Cay in the central Bahamas.

2. Some historians point to multiple visits to the Americas years before that of Columbus. One claim suggests that the English visited the Americas in 1481.

3. Howard Mumford Jones states that "about two thirds of the continental United States owes something to Spanish culture." *O Strange New World: American Culture, the Formative Years* (New York: Viking, 1964), 80.

4. In an apparent attempt to appear gender-correct, David Weber further notes, "With few exceptions, the preponderance of those Spanish explorers were males. Gender roles, as all Europeans imagined them, rendered exploration an inappropriate activity for women." *The Spanish Frontier in North America* (New Haven, CT: Yale University Press, 1992).

5. Weber, *The Spanish Frontier.*

6. The island is now officially named Eleuthera.

7. Sandra Riley, *Homeward Bound* (Miami: Island Research, 1883), 31.

8. S. E. Morison, *The Eleuthera Donation,* Harvard Alumni Bulletin 32 (1930), 107.

9. Ibid., 107.

10. Barbados, measuring slightly more than 500 square miles in area, is a relatively small island comparable in size to the Bahamian capital island of New Providence, which measures just 21 miles in length and 7 miles in width.

11. *Journal of the Barbados Museum and Historical Society* 13, pp. 125-36.

12. Ibid, 140.

13. Nathan Miller, *Sea of Glory: A Naval History of the American Revolution* (Charleston, SC: Nautical and Aviation Publishing, 1974), 49.

14. Ibid., 93-99.

15. Barbara W. Tuckman, *The First Salute: A View of the American Revolution* (Annapolis, MD: Naval Institute Press, 1974), 56.

16. It was widely believed that Fort Nassau and Fort Montague, the principal British fortifications on New Providence, held considerable amounts of gunpowder and arms which if captured could prove to be useful to the rebel cause.

17. William M. Fowler, Jr., *Rebels under Sail: The American Navy during the Revolution* (New York: Charles Scribner's Sons, 1976), 92. Marines were traditionally trained for close combat and amphibious landings. They were also responsible for the control of sailors; as such,

their quarters and place for meals were separate from those of the crewmen, but not equal to those of the officers.

[18]   It is apparent that Hopkins misjudged his timing; as a result, the fleet just narrowly avoided disaster when the ships sailed into port in the direct wake of the preceding vessels.

[19]   The site of the landing is most probably the beach now called Long Wharf, which today is a popular spot for American college students to enjoy Spring Break and where locals frequently beach.

[20]   Word of the arrival of Hopkin's fleet anchored off Abaco was conveyed by the residents to the authorities in Nassau.

[21]   The merchant seamen were stranded in Nassau as a result of the capture of their ship by privateers.

[22]   Frank H. Rathburn, "Rathburn's Raid on Nassau," *United States Naval Proceedings* (November 1870), 40-47.

[23]   Tuckman, *The First Salute,* 63.

[24]   Ibid, 66.

[25]   John Maxwell to Lord George Germaine, New Providence, May 14, 1782, in John Almon, ed., *The Rememberance,* 2:148-49. PRO, CO 26/16/1-3, General Assembly, April 20, 1784.

[26]   South Carolina's Confiscation Act (passed March 20, 1782) declared Andrew Deveaux to be *persona non grata* for organizing and leading his band of Loyalists in attacks against persons loyal to the United States. *South Carolina Weekly Gazette* (Charles Town), May 24, 1783.

[27]   *Charles Town South Carolina Weekly Gazette,* May 24, 1783.

[28]   *Charles Town (SC) Royal Gazette,* March 20, 1783.

[29]   Roderick MacKinzie, *Tarleton's Strictures* (London, 1787).

[30]   Thelma Peters, "The American Loyalist and the Plantation Period in the Bahama Islands," (Dissertation, Ph.D., University of Florida, 1960) 127.

[31]   John J McCusker, "The American Invasion of Nassau in The Bahamas," *American Neptune* 25 (July 1965), 189-217.

[32]   Ibid., 214.

[33]   Ibid, 221.

[34]   Ibid.

[35]   Claude H. van Tyne, *The Loyalists in the American Revolution* (New York, 1902), 280.

[36]   Tonyn to Evan Nepean, October 1, 1783, CO 5:560, 717-19.

[37]   "The Petition of the British American Loyalist who took refuge in East Florida," October 28, 1784. East Florida Papers, b195, m15.

[38]   Tonyn to Vicente Manuel Zéspedes, July 10, 1784, East Florida Papers, b40, 11-12.

[39]   Tonyn noted several reasons why the evacuation was a slow process in his "Reasons for the Long Evacuation Period," Tonyn to Nepean, May 2, 1786, CO 5:561, 849-852

[40]   Thomas Courtney claim, East Florida claims, AQ 12; 3, 18:21.

[41]   Ibid.

[42]   Benjamin Springer claim, East Florida claims, AQ 12:3, 182-87.

[43]   Peter Edwards claim, East Florida claims, AO 11-17, 100-1.

[44]   Robert Robinson claim, East Florida claims, AO 12:3, 13-18.

[45]   Ibid.

[46]   Edgar Legare Pennington, "The Reverend James Seymour, S.P.G. Missionary in Florida," *Florida Historical Quarterly* 5 (April 1927), 198-99.

[47]   "Extract from a letter from Mr. Johnson to a friend in London," July 14, 1783, in Thomas Nixon to Nepean, n.d., CO 5:560, copy in the Lockey Collection.

[48]   James Edward Powell to Tonyn, June 9, 1785, enclosed in Tonyn to Sidney, August 29 1785, CO 5:561, 721-23.

[49]   Lydia Austin Parrish, "Records of Some Southern Loyalists, Being a collection of manuscripts about eighty families, most of whom immigrated to the Bahamas during the American Revolution," unpublished manuscript. Copy located in the Yonge Library of Florida History, University of Florida. Regrettably, Parrish's research does not include reference to blacks, soldiers, or the thousands of uneducated immigrants, most of whom did not come to the Bahamas from the Carolinas or Georgia via St. Augustine but via New York.

[50]   Thelma Peters, "The American Loyalists In The Bahama Islands: Who Were They?" *Florida Historical Quarterly* 34 (1961) 226-27. The name" Conch" was a derisive reference by the newly arrived immigrants to the diet of the "Old Bahamians," which included the large conch mollusk.

[51]   Ibid., 230.

[52]   J. Leitch Wright, Jr. *Britain and the American Frontier, 1783-1815* (The University of Georgia Press, 1975), x-xi.

[53]   Ibid., x.

[54]   The Old Northwest was a loose reference to that area of the western United States situated generally above and below the Ohio Valley and west of the Appalachians.

[55]   Wright, *Britain and the American Frontier,* 46.

[56]   *Nassau Bahama Gazette,* February 25, 1786.

[57]   Wright, *Britain and the American Frontier,* 46-47.

[58]   In the 1780s, Britain maintained significant alliances with various American Indians, who generally fought against the American rebels during the Revolution. The term "Indian" loosely refers to the Six Nations of the Iroquois Confederacy in the northwest, the Shawnees and Algonquin peoples, the Creek and Muskogean in the south. Ironically, none of these native people whose ancestral lands were directly affected participated at the 1782-83 Paris peace negotiations where, among other things, Indian lands were partitioned without their knowledge or authority.

[59]   Wright, *Britain and the American Frontier,* 13.

[60]   *London Times,* March 28, 1788.

[61]   "Kings, chiefs, and head warriors of Creek and Cherokee Nation," Coweta, second windy moon, 1789, C.O. 42/87.

[62]   Spain had defeated the British in minor arenas in the Bay of Honduras, Nicaragua, and in the areas of the southwestern United States.

63 Lord Dunmore to Lord George Germain, Charleston, March 30, 1782, C.O. 5/175 (transcript, Library of Congress). Dunmore to Thomas Townsend, London, August 24, 1782, C.O. 5/175 (transcript, Library of Congress).

64 Benjamin Quarles, *The Negro in the American Revolution* (Chapel Hill, NC, 1961), 19-32.

65 Dunmore to Henry Clinton, Charleston, February 2, 1782, C.O. 5/175: John Cruden's proposal . . . for employing 10,000 black troops, Charleston, January 5, 1783, C.O. 5/175.

66 Ibid.

67 William Wylly was a wealthy and influential Loyalist émigré to the Bahamas who disagreed with the Bahamian Assembly on the question of the rights of blacks. In 1817, he was accused of obstructing justice by way of his public position as Solicitor General and ordered arrested to stand trial for his alleged crimes. Attempts to arrest him at his plantation at Clifton (western New Providence Island) were thwarted by the action of blacks armed with flintlocks and bayonets, who blocked the gate to the estate and prevented access to Wylly with the threat of force.

68 Thomas F. Abernethy, *Western Lands and the American Revolution* (New York: 1937), 93-94.

69 Most of Dunmore's associates in the land speculation hailed from West Florida and were members of the Bahamian Council or held other high public office, positions sanctioned by the governor.

70 John Ferdinand Dalziel Smith, *A Tour in the United States of America,* 2 vols. (London, 1784), vol. 2, 227-69.

71 Dunmore's claims to lands in the Ohio Valley and elsewhere on the Gulf coast are outlined in Schedule of Losses Sustained by the Earl of Dunmore, Audit Office Group, Class 13, bundle 78, Public Record Office (photostat, Library of Congress).

72 Dunmore to William Pitt, Manchester St., October 7, 1797, Gifts and Deposits Group, Class 30-8, vol. 131, Public Records Office.

73 Great Britain, Privy Council. Copy of council minutes on enquiry regarding marriage of Prince Augustus Frederick and Lady Augusta Murray, January 27 and 28, 1794, Melville Papers, Clemens Library; *The Gentleman's Magazine* 64 (January 1794), 87.

74 The Board of American Loyalists, under the presidency of James Hepburn, was organized to "preserve and maintain those Rights and Liberties for which they left their homes and possessions," Registry Office Records, Nassau, Bahamas, O, 299.

75 Ibid., 149.

76 Douglas C. McMurtie, "The Beginnings of Printing in Florida," *Florida Historical Quarterly* 23 (October 1944), 67.

77 *Bahama Gazette*, November 28, 1793. A cotton gin (short for cotton engine) was a machine that quickly and easily separated the cotton fibers from the seeds. Previously, the separation of cotton fiber from the seeds was labor-intensive and required a large number of slaves. Whitney's gin, which was invented in 1793, did not receive a patent until 1794, after the Bahamian model was already in action.

78 Ibid., 94.

[79] Ibid., 95.

[80] Ibid.,100.

[81] Parrish, "Records," 31.

[82] Daniel Mc Kinnon, *A Tour through the British West Indies, in the years 1802 And 1803, giving A Particular Account of the Bahama Islands* (London, 1804), 225.

[83] Parrish, "Records," 24.

[84] Johann David Schoeph, *Travels in the Confederation, 1783-1784,* trans. and ed. Alfred J. Morrison (Philadelphia: William J. Campbell, 1991), 240.

[85] Ibid, 350.

[86] Edwin J. Perkins, *The Economy of Colonial America* (New York: Columbia University Press, 1980), 145.

[87] Ibid., 145.

[88] In The Bahamas, what came to be known as the "truck system" epitomized this commercial arrangement.

[89] Perkins, *Economy of Colonial America,* 129.

[90] Gary Cash, "Urban Wealth and Poverty in Pre-Colonial America," *Journal of Interdisciplinary History* (Spring 1976), 545-84. Nash stated that he found only three Boston merchants who had left estates valued at slightly more than £6,000, compared with thirty-one Philadelphia merchants who had left estates valued in excess of £15,000.

[91] John J. McCusker and Russell R. Menard *The Economy of British America, 1607-1789,* Institute of Early American History and Culture (North Carolina: University of North Carolina Press, 1985), 359-60.

[92] George Woodbury, *The Great Days of Piracy in the West Indies* (New York: W. W. Norton, 1951), 9.

[93] Calendar of State Papers, 31/209, Captain Woodes Rogers to Council of Trade and Plantations, March 29, 1719. Rogers reported that up to that time, the Spanish and French had invaded and sacked Nassau and the outlying islands at least thirty-four times.

[94] Sandra Riley, *Homeward Bound* (Miami: Island Research, 1983), 41.

[95] Ibid., 43.

[96] Colin Woodard, *The Republic of Pirates* (Orlando, FL: Houghton Mifflin Harcourt, 2007), 12.

[97] Ibid., 12.

[98] Ibid., 86.

[99] Colonial Office Records, 137/12, folio 90 (iii): A List of Some of the Many Ships, Sloops, and Other Vessels taken from the Subjects of the King Of Great Britain in America by Subjects of the King Of Spain since the Conclusion of peace, Jamaica, c. 1716.

[100] Woodard, *Republic of Pirates,* 87.

[101] Ibid., 88.

[102] "Boston News Item," *Boston News-Letter,* April 29, 1914, 2.

[103] Anne and Jim Lawlor, *The Harbour Island Story* (Oxford: Macmillan, 2008), 4.

[104] Ibid., 47.

[105]   Ibid., 48.

[106]   Ibid., 48.

[107]   Peter Earle, *The Pirate Wars* (New York: St. Martin's, 2003), 161.

[108]   Ibid.

[109]   Ibid.

[110]   Terrance Zepke, *Pirates of the Carolinas* (Sarasota, FL: Pineapple Press, 2005), 24.

[111]   Charles Eden was appointed Governor of North Carolina on May 18, 1713.

[112]   Zepke, *Pirates of the Carolinas,* 27.

[113]   Ibid., 28.

[114]   Nathaniel Wright Stevenson, "The Romantics and George Washington," *American Historical Review* 39, no. 2 (January 1934), 274-83. Also see Wilson Miles Carey, *Sally Carey: A Long Forbidden Romance of Washington's Life* (New York: The DeVine Press, 1916).

[115]   Walker's letters: CO5/1265, no 17: Thomas Walker to the Proprietors of the Bahamas, New Providence: March 14, 1715.

[116]   King's instructions to Rogers: His Majesty's Commission to Woodes Rogers to be Governor of the Bahama Islands, Court of St. James, London: January 16, 1718 in *CSPCS*1717-1718, no. 2201, 110-12.

[117]   Zepke, *Pirates of the Carolinas,* 100.

[118]   McCusker and Menard, *Economy of British America,* 362-63.

[119]   Robert H. Patton, *Patriot Pirates: The Privateer War for Freedom and Fortune in the American Revolution* (New York: Pantheon, 2008).

[120]   George Washington to Philip J. Schuler, November 16, 1775, *The George Washington Papers at the Library of Congress, 1714-1799.*

[121]   Patton, *Patriot Pirates,* 39.

[122]   Ibid., 40.

[123]   Ibid., 40. In 1776, Congress established three courts in Massachusetts to adjudicate privateer captures, with the most active one at the Middle District, comprising Boston, the North Shore ports, and Salem.

[124]   Ibid., 48.

[125]   Ibid., 49.

[126]   Ibid., 48-49. Patton states that in May 1775, thirty-seven-year-old Deane, the Connecticut representative in Congress, "borrowed" funds from the Connecticut treasury to finance the purchase of artillery used by the patriots against British forces at the battle of Ticonderoga. He left promissory notes to back the £300 he used in reckless disregard of proper financial ethics.

[127]   Ibid.

[128]   Ibid., 48.

[129]   Ibid., 50

[130]   Ibid., 51. Patton notes that Beaumarchais was a playwright famed for *The Marriage of Figaro* and *The Barber of Seville.* He became Deane's contact and broker in Paris.

[131]   Ibid., 59.

[132]   Ibid., 61.

[133] Lord Stormont to Lord Weymouth, July 2, 1777, NDAR, vol. 9, 452.

[134] John Bradford to John Hancock, March 20, 1777, NDAR, vol. 8, 155.

[135] Patton, *Patriot Pirates*, 189.

[136] J. Leitch Wright, Jr. *Creeks and Seminoles: Destruction and Regeneration of the Muscogulge People* (Nebraska: University of Nebraska Press, 1986), xii-xiii.

[137] Ibid., 42.

[138] Ibid., 59.

[139] Lyle N. McAlister, "William Augusta Bowles and the State of Muskogee," *Florida Historical Quarterly* 40 (April 1962), 317-28.

[140] Bowles moved freely and frequently between the islands and the mainland, which made his exact domicile difficult to pinpoint.

[141] William S. Coker and Thomas D. Watson, *Panton, Leslie & Company and John Forbes and Company, 1783-1848* (Pensacola: University of West Florida Press, 1986), 148.

[142] Wright, *Creeks and Seminoles,* 147.

[143] Ibid, 154.

[144] (Bahamas) Registry Office Records, Nassau, Bahamas, M, 146.

[145] Coker and Watson, *Panton, Leslie & Company*, 150

[146] Melvin H. Jackson, *Privateers in Charleston, 1793-1796.* Smithsonian Studies in History and Technology, no.1 (Washington, DC: Smithsonian Institution Press, 1969).

[147] Ibid., x.

[148] Hunter to Bowles, March 5, 1800, *Greenslade Papers,* Florida Historical Society, Tampa.

[149] DeLacy to Bowles, Selkirk's Papers, National Archives of Canada, vol. 22.

[150] Coker and Watson, *Panton, Leslie & Company*, 45.

[151] Power of Attorney for Indian chiefs to Arbuthnot, Ochlockonee Sound, Creek Nation, June 17, 1817, *New American State Papers, Indian Affairs,* 1:726:27.

[152] Arbuthnot to governor of Havana, June 17, 1817, *British and Foreign State Papers,* 6:444-45.

[153] Nicholas to J. P. Morier, Eltham, September 25, 1815,War Office Records, 1/143.

[154] Cappachimico, McQueen, Charlie Tastonosky, et al., to Charles Bagot, with enclosures, Sawahanee Town, November 8, 1816, Colonial Office Records 23/66.

[155] Stephen R. Wise, *Lifeline of the Confederacy: Blockade Running during the Civil War* (University of South Carolina Press, 1988), 23.

[156] Mary Ellison, *Support for Secession* (Chicago, 1972), 1.

[157] Ibid.

[158] Frank Lawrence Owsley, *King Cotton Diplomacy* (Chicago, 1959), 97.

[159] Ibid.

[160] Francis B. C. Bradlee, *Blockade-Running during the Civil War* (Salem, 1925), 64.

[161] Alice Strickland, "Blockade Runners," *Florida Historical Quarterly* (March 1955), 28.

[162] Horatio L. Wait, "The Blockade of the Confederacy," *Century Magazine* 56 (1898), 194.

[163] Ibid.

[164] A. Roberts, *Never Caught* (Martinsburg, West Virginia,1867), 41.

[165] *Nassau Guardian*, November 2, 1864.

[166] Keith Tinker, "Nassau and Blockade Running, 1860-1865 (master's thesis, (Florida Atlantic University, 1982), 17.

[167] James M. Starks, *History and Guide to the Bahama Islands* (Boston: 1891), 243.

[168] Samuel Whiting to William Seward, June 8, 1862, U.S. Consular Despatches, vol. 2.

[169] Thomas Yoseloff, ed., *Jefferson Davis: Rise and Fall of the Confederate Government*, (London, 1959), 156.

[170] Brunch to Lord Lyons, October 6, 1862, U. S. Consular Despatches, vol. 9.

[171] C. Hawley to William Seward, March 16, 1863, U. S. Consular Despatches, vol. 13.

[172] Ibid.

[173] Ibid.

[174] W. C. Thompson to William Seward, November 6, 1863, U.S. Consular Despatches, vol. 10, Bahamas Archives, Nassau.

[175] *Nassau Guardian*, September 2, 1863.

[176] Benjamin Kirkpatrick to William Seward, September 24, 1864, U.S. Consular Despatches, vol. 3, Bahamas Archives, Nassau.

[177] *Index* (Nassau: 1861-1865), Bahamas Archives, Nassau.

[178] Craton, *A History of the Bahamas*,(Macmillian Caribbean, 1990), 24.

[179] *Nassau Guardian*, November 23, 1940.

[180] C. J. Bayley, *Report on the Bahamas for the Year 1860*, January 5, 1861, Governor's Despatches, Bahamas Archives, Nassau.

[181] Ibid.

[182] Craton, *History of the Bahamas*, 224.

[183] Ibid.

[184] Ibid.

[185] Frank I. Wilson, *Sketches of Nassau* (Raleigh, NC, 1864), 13.

[186] James H. Stark, *History and Guide to the Bahama Islands* (1891), 97.

[187] Bayley to Newcastle, January 14, 1863.

[188] Ibid.

[189] Ibid.

[190] Ibid.

[191] Bahamas Census Report for the Year 1860-65, 1870, *Governor's Despatches*, Bahamas Archives, Nassau.

[191]

[192] It should be noted that a yellow fever outbreak in 1864 resulted in the death of 1,250 residents and visitors in Nassau, 893 of whom were whites, and 742 of whom were foreigners.

[193] Bayley to Newcastle, January 15, 1861.

[194] Ibid.

[195] Ibid.

[196] Ibid.

[197] Rawson W. Rawson, Report on the Bahamas for the Year 1865 (London, 1866), 54.

[198] Anonymous, "The Bahamas," *Harper's* 49 (1874), 761-62.

[199] Moseley, "Centenary Issue," *Nassau Guardian* (1940), 68.

[200] *Bahamas Handbook and Businessman's Annual* (Nassau, 1980), 330.

[201] Ibid.

[202] *Nassau Guardian*, May 8, 1863-July 7, 1896.

[203] Ibid., February 1863.

[204] Ibid.

[205] Peters, "Blockade-Running in the Bahamas during the Civil War," *(Tequesta, no. v., 1945)* 27.

[206] *Nassau Guardian*, March 24, *1863*.

[207] Wilson, *Sketches of Nassau,* (Raleigh NC. 1864), 14.

[208] *Nassau Guardian*, November 1862. The bulk of the coal was imported from England, but some anthracite (hard coal) came from Pennsylvania. This type was reportedly reserved for the critical run through the blockade.

[209] Ibid., March 13, 1853.

[210] Ibid., April 14, 1863.

[211] Ibid., January 8, 1864.

[212] Ibid., August, 1862.

[213] "The Oreto Affair," Harper's 49 (January 7, 1874), 37.

[214] Moseley, "Centenary Issue," 68.

[215] Thomas E. Taylor, *Running The Blockade* (New York: 1896), 87.

[216] *Nassau Guardian* December 24, 1864.

[217] Bayley, *Governor's Despatches,* January 10, 1864.

[218] Ibid., March 13, 1862.

[219] Ibid., "Report on the Bahamas for the Years 1860-1863."

[220] Ibid.

[221] Ibid., May 2, 1864.

[222] Ibid., January 14, 1863.

[223] J. T. W. Bacot, *The Bahamas: A Sketch* (London: 1869), 94.

[224] Craton, *History of the Bahamas,* 238.

[225] Bacot, *The Bahamas,* 50-51.

[226] G. J. H. Northcroft, *Sketches of Summerland* (Nassau, 1900), 304.

[227] Mark Lender and James Martin, *Drinking In America: A History* (New York: Free Press, 1987), 2-3.

[228] H. L. Mencken, *The American Language,* Supplement I (New York: Knopf, 1993), 266.

[229] Frederick Marryat, *A Diary in America.* Second part, vol. 1 (London: Longman, 1839), 124.

[230] W. J. Rorabaugh, *The Alcohol Republic: An American Tradition* (New York: Oxford University Press, 1979), 20-21.

[231] Robert Carse, *Rum Row: The Liquor Fleet that Fuelled the Roaring Twenties,* (Mystic, CT: Flat Hammock Press, 1959), 3.

[232] Ibid., 5.

[233] Ibid., 12.

[234]   Ibid.

[235]   Harold Waters, *Smugglers of Spirits: Prohibition and the Coast Guard Patrol* (New York: Hastings House Press, 1971), 42.

[236]   Ibid., 52.

[237]   Ibid., 55. The Coast Guard applied the code name "Blacks" to all rum runners, regardless of size.

[238]   Ibid., 41.

[239]   Ibid., 42.

[240]   *Nassau Guardian*, February 4, 1920. By late 1920, thirty-one bonded warehouses, storing some 37,400 cases and 13,700 barrels of liquor, had been constructed in Nassau.

[241]   Frederic F. Van de Water, *The Real McCoy* (Garden City: Doubleday, Doran & Company, 1931), Van de Water's work recounts the exploits of William "Bill" McCoy, the rum runner turned national hero whose quality of liquor and fair business practices immortalized the phrase "It's the real McCoy."

[242]   *The Times* of London, March 3, 1921.

[243]   David Gray, "Bootlegging from the Bahamas," *Collier's* (June 24, 1922), 94.

[244]   *Bahamas Blue Books*, 1923-1924, p. 178. The "Blue Books" are a compilation of colonial government statistical reports.

[245]   Carse, *Rum Row*, 13, 19.

[246]   *Tribune*, September 1922.

[247]   Van de Water, *Real McCoy*, 64.

[248]   Carse, *Rum Row*, 20.

[249]   Van de Water, *Real McCoy*, 64.

[250]   Ibid.

[251]   *Tribune*, February 10, 1922; January 22, 1925; September 11, 1926.

[252]   Ibid., 65.

[253]   Carse, *Rum Row*, 20-21.

[254]   Van de Water, *Real McCoy*, 66.

[255]   Ibid., 67.

[256]   *Wall Street Journal*, September 18, 1923.

[257]   *Los Angeles Times*, December 25, 1923.

[258]   *New York Times*, January 13, 1924.

[259]   Netley Lucas, *Crooks: Confessions* (Hurst & Blackett, 1925), 12.

[260]   Gertrude "Cleo" Lythgoe, *The Bahama Queen: Prohibition's Daring Beauty* (New York: Exposition Press, 1964), 163.

[261]   Keith Tinker interview with anonymous informant, December 27, 2010. The author has known the informant for a number of years and can note that the involvement of his family in rum running is widely accepted by the Bahamian public of that generation.

[262]   Waters, *Smugglers of Spirits*, 139.

[263]   Ibid., 140.

[264]   Ibid., 142.

[265]   *Miami Metropolis*, October 4, 1920.

266 "A Bootlegger's Paradise in the Bahamas," *Literary Digest* (September 10, 1921, vol. 7), 36, 38.

267 Carse, *Rum Row*, xxx.

268 Quentin Reynolds, "Whisky Ships," *Collier's* (May 12, 1934), 38-39.

269 "The Wet Way from Bimini to Florida," *Literary Digest* 104 (February 15, 1930), 17.

270 *New York Times,* July 23, 1923.

271 Ibid., April 17, 1923.

272 Ibid.

273 Park Trammell to Charles Evans Hughes, April 3, 1922, U.S. State Department, Decimal File, 811.114.

274 *Miami Herald*, January 24, 1924; Great Britain, Foreign Office, *British and Foreign State Papers, 1924,* part I, vol. 119 (London:, 1927); *Papers relating to the Foreign Relations of The United States, 1924,* 2 vols. (Washington, 1939), vol. 1, 157-61.

275 Lythgoe, *Bahama Queen,* 162.

276 Carse, *Rum Row,* 82.

277 Ibid, 84.

278 Waters, *Smugglers of Spirits*, 151.

279 Ibid., 152.

280 Ibid., 156.

281 Olga Culmer Jenkins, *Bahamian Memories: Island Voices of the Twentieth Century* (Gainesville: University Press of Florida, 2000), 243.

282 Ibid., 243.

283 Ibid., 244.

284 *Nassau Guardian*, October 1, 1928.

285 *Tribune*, September 2, 1922.

286 Ibid., July 17, 1926.

287 Ibid., September 20, 1922.

288 Ibid., December 30, 1927.

289 Ibid.,1922.

290 Keith Tinker interview with anonymous informant, December 13, 2010. Anonymous white Bahamian businessman's father reportedly was a "business associate" of the operator of the Bahamian Club, a supplier of liquor to that establishment as well as to a "select clientele" in Miami.

291 *Tribune*, September 9, 1922.

292 Ibid., October 4, 1922.

293 Ibid., June 28, 1930.

294 Ibid., September 17, 1930.

295 D. Gail Saunders, "Prohibition, A Mixed Blessing for The Bahamas," *Journal of The Bahamas Historical Society* (Fall, 1992), 46.

296 Riley, *Homeward Bound,* 41.

297 Robin F. A. Fabel, *The Economy of British West Florida, 1763-1783* (Tuscaloosa: University of Alabama Press, 1988), 64.

[298]   Mark F. Forbes, "The Seminole War: Its Background and Onset," *Florida Historical Quarterly* 30 (1951): 58-60.

[299]   James H. O'Donnel, Southeastern Frontiers: Europeans, Africans, and American Indians, 1513-1848, (Michigan, 1956)166.

[300]   Wright, *Creeks and Seminoles,* 90.

[301]   Ibid., 91.

[302]   Ibid., 96-97.

[303]   John DeLacy to Bowles, March 11, 1802, Lockey Collection, University of Florida Library.

[304]   Wright, Creeks and Seminoles, 93.

[305]   Ibid., 98.

[306]   *Ibid.*, 98. The Nassau-based Forbes and Company were increasingly aligning their economic interests with that of the Americans and as such were losing slaves to the British who at the very least promised them freedom from slavery.

[307]   William Coker and Thomas D. Watson, *Indian Traders of the Southeastern Spanish Borderlands,* (Pensacola: University of West Florida Press, 1986), 296-97.

[308]   Ibid., 297.

[309]   James Innerarity to John Forbes, August 12, 1815, GP; *Florida Historical Quarterly* 12 (1934), 128-29. James Innerarity and his brother John were senior officials in the John Forbes and Company enterprise.

[310]   House Journals, 17 Congress, I session, 1379, Annals of Congress, 1379, 1415, 1444, Appendix B, no. 8.

[311]   Ibid., Appendix B., no. 11.

[312]   Ibid., Appendix B, no. 19.

[313]   Fergus M. Bordewich, *Bound For Canaan: The Underground Railroad and the War for the Soul of America* (New York: HarperCollins, 2005), 269.

[314]   Ibid., 272.

[315]   [321] Ibid, 273.

[316]   William Munnings to Earl of Bathurst, Nassau, September 30, 1819, CO23/168.

[317]   Wright, *Creeks andSseminoles* 314.

[318]   William P. Duval to Calhoun, St. Augustine, September 23ʹ 1823, Letters Received, Second War, Microcopy 271, roll 4:536-37.

[319]   *Bahamas Royal Gazette,* October 2, 1819.

[320]   David Wood, *A Guide to Selected Sources for the History of the Seminole Settlement at Red Bays, Andros, 1917-1980,* appendix 3, Nassau, Bahamas: Department of Archives.

[321]   Rosalyn Howard, *Black Seminoles in the Bahamas* (Gainesville: University Press of Florida, 2002).

[322]   Ibid.

[323]   G. C. Anderson to Cockburn, November 13, 1941; Bacon to Cockburn, November 12, 1841.

[324]   Raised in 1795 from among the slave population of the British West Indies, the West India Regiments comprised trained soldiers who proved invaluable to the British cause

during the Napoleonic Wars. The soldiers served throughout the Caribbean and British West African territories as protectors of the colonies and included many ex-slaves freed from slave ships by the British Navy among their ranks.

[325] Deposition by Gifford, December 2, 1841.

[326] Ibid., 44-45.

[327] Cockburn to Bacon, November 15, 1841, Senate Documents, 27 Congress, 2 Session, II, no. 51, 8, Anderson's report to Cockburn, November 13, 1841, Ibid., 9-10. Most slaves from the *Creole* released in Nassau eventually settled in Jamaica.

[328] *Washington National Intelligencer*, December 15, 1941; *Charleston Mercury*, December 14, 1841; *Mobile Register & Journal*, December 6, 1841; *Nashville Union*, December 15, 1841; *Jackson* (MS) *Southern*, December 9, 1941.

[329] *Baltimore Sun*, December 20, 1842.

[330] *Congressional Globe,* 127, Congress, 2 Session 47, 116, 203-4.

[331] *London Times,* January 14, 19, 1842; *Boston Liberator,* April 1, 1842.

[332] Bordewick, *Bound for Canaan*, 271.

[333] Thomas E.Taylor, *Running the Blockade* (New York, 1896), 82.

[334] Wright, Jr., *Britain and the American Frontier, 1783-1815 (University of Georgia Press,*1985), 147.

[335] In 1941, George E. Merrick was President of the Historical Association of Southern Florida, Founder of the City of Coral Gables in Miami, and one of the founders of the University of Miami.

[336] George E. Merrick, *The Making of Miami,* Florida Historical Quarterly, vol. 12, 1941, 9

[337] James Grant to Lords of Committee of Trade, East Florida, August 26, 1766, Extract in Florida Collection, Hadley Library, Islamorada, Florida.

[338] Jefferson Brown, *Key West: The Old and the New* (St. Augustine, FL: Record Company, 1912), 27.

[339] *Hunt's Merchant Magazine*, 1852.

[340] Sharon Wells, *Forgotten Legacy: Nineteenth Century Key West,* (Key West: Historic Florida Keys Preservation Board, 1982), 20.

[341] Dorothy Dodd, "The Wrecking Business on the Florida Reefs," *Florida Historical Quarterly* 22 (April 1944), 174.

[342] John DuBose to John Rodman, May 21, 1823, FTP, 684.

[343] United States Senate, *Executive Journal*, III, 312, 313.

[344] William P. DuVal to E. Livingston, October 7, 1981. State Representative, 242, 30th Congress, 1st session (512), p. 94.

[345] Dodd, "The Wrecking Business", 180. Dodd notes that according to the early reports of the wrecking industry, between December 1824 and December 1825, an estimated $293,253 in wrecked property was sold in Key West, yielding revenue valued at $35,000 and federal taxes valued at just over $5,000.

[346] E. A. Hammond, "Wreckers and Wrecking on the Florida Reef, 1829-1832," *Florida Historical Quarterly* 41 (January1963), 251-52.

[347] William Marvin, *A Treatise on the Law of Wreck and Salvage* (Boston: Little, Brown, 1858), 2.

[348] *Pensacola Gazette*, August 20, 1825.

[349] Merrick, *Making of Miami,* 3.

[350] *Key West Register and Commercial Advertiser,* February 12, 1829.

[351] Ibid.

[352] *Key West Citizen,* December 1915, Centennial Issue.

[353] In the summer of 2009, this author interviewed several veteran spongers at various locations in the predominantly black settlements of Central and South Andros Island in the Bahamas as a part of a new research initiative that is ongoing. In most cases, and with very few exceptions, the black spongers had very few tangible financial assets to show for years of dedicated participation in the sponge industry, despite the fact that all boasted of how lucrative the industry was and how well they all profited from employment in the trade.

[354] Merrick, *Making of Miami,* 3.

[355] Astrid Whidden, "Key West's Conchs, 1763-1912: Outlaws or Outcasts?" *Tequesta* 10 (1984), 36-39.

[356] Ibid., 36.

[357] Merrick, *Making of Miami,* 4.

[358] Albury, *Story of the Bahamas,* 169.

[359] Raymond Mohl, "Shadows in the Sunshine: Race and Ethnicity in Miami," *Tequesta* 49 (1989), 67.

[360] Ibid., 70.

[361] Ira De A. Reid, *The Negro Immigrant: His Background, Characteristics and Social Adjustments, 1899-1937,* (New York: Columbia University Press, 1939), 189.

[362] Robert Hill, ed. "Reports by Bureau Agent Leon E. Howe, Miami, Florida, 7/6/21," *Marcus Garvey Papers and the Universal Negro Improvement Association Papers,* vol. 6 (Berkeley: University of California Press, 1984), 514.

[363] *Daily News and Metropolis,* August 23, 1908

[364] *Miami Herald,* April 18, 1921.

[365] Ibid., February 12, 1975.

[366] Ibid., July 3, 1921.

[367] Ibid., July 17, 1921.

[368] *Miami Sunday News,* July 24, 1949.

[369] *Miami Herald,* July 19, 1917.

[370] Ibid., June 30, July 1, 1920.

[371] *New York Times,* August 3, 1920.

[372] *Miami Herald,* July 26, 1921.

[373] Ibid., July 26, 1921.

[374] Interview with James Nimmo, *Negro World,* May 22, 1926.

[375] *Miami Daily News and Metropolis,* September 24, 1926. The hurricane of 1926 devastated Miami. White authorities ordered the conscription of every able-bodied black to participate in the reconstruction initiative. Miami Sheriff Henry R. Chase declared in the execution of this order, "The Negroes, many of them, are lying idle. We are going to put

them to work." Naturally, many blacks and most Bahamians resisted. Several Bahamians escaped to the safety of their island of origin.

[376] Albury, *Story of the Bahamas*, 198.

[377] Wayne Rasmussen, *History of the Emergency Farm Labor Supply Program, 1943-47*, Agricultural Monograph no. 13 (Washington, DC: U.S. Department of Agriculture Bureau of Agricultural Economics, 1951); *Yearbook of Agriculture*, 1940, 908-10.

[378] Sally M. Miller and Daniel A. Cornford, *American Labor in the Era of World War II* (Westport, CT: Praeger, 1995), 2. The authors state that during the war years, approximately 15 million Americans moved from one city, state, or region to another in search of work, while about 13 million enlisted in the armed forces.

[379] Record Group 83 (records of the Bureau of Agricultural Economics, Department of Agriculture, 1923-1946), Folder Farm Labor (1941-1946), Box 239: Entry 19, "Reports on Farm Labor Shortages and the Works Projects Administration," prepared by the War Production Agency for the House Committee Investigating National Defense Migration, July 1941, 10-11.

[380] Ibid., 912-13.

[381] *Norfolk Journal and Guide*, Saturday 17, 1943. African Americans protested the possible use of African Americans enlisted in the armed forces to work on farms.

[382] Cindy Hahamovitch, *The Fruits of Their Labor: Atlantic Coast Farmworkers and the Making of Migrant Poverty, 1870-1945* (Chapel Hill: University of North Carolina Press, 1997), 78-83.

[383] Record Group (RG) 59 (US State Department): Box 6022, Folder 5: 844.00/8-2045: "Social and Political Forces in Dependent Areas of the Caribbean: Part III: Population and Migration in the Caribbean Area", December 1944, 527-29. Charles Taussig, one of President Franklin Roosevelt's advisors on the Caribbean, made several visits to the region during the war.

[384] Fitzroy Baptiste, *War, Cooperation and Conflict: The European Possessions in the Caribbean, 1939-1945* (New York: Greenwood Press, 1988), 141-69.

[385] Miller and Cornford, *American Labor*, 4-7.

[386] Ronald L. Goldfarb, *Migrant Farm Workers: A Caste of Despair* (Iowa State University Press, 1981), 116. Goldfarb notes that in 1944, the U.S. government spent $24 million to import 62,170 braceros (strong-armed men) into the migrant labor program.

[387] General Correspondence, Employment, 1-4 Farm, Office of Information Press Release, May 24, 1943-44, box 51, file C2-R36-Florida, RG 224, NARA.

[388] Thomas Wagstaff, *Black Power: The Radical Response to White America* (Beverly Hills: Glencoe Press, 1969), 3.

[389] Pindling was the son of a Jamaican immigrant to the Bahamas.

[390] *Good Times* and *The Jeffersons* featured leading black actresses Esther Rolle and Roxie Roker, respectively, who were of Bahamian descent.

[391] *Nassau Guardian*, February 28, 1973.

[392] In 1973, the Yellow Elder (*Tecoma stans*) was adopted as the national flower of the Commonwealth of The Bahamas.

393   The Yellow Elder Gardens subdivision featured oval-shaped houses designed to resemble an African-styled kraal, intended as tourist attractions.

394   The first prime minister, some members of his first cabinet, and others who held key positions in government were the offspring of West Indians who migrated to The Bahamas in the 1920s in search of employment opportunities. Most of the earlier immigrants came from former British colonies where the level of education was superior to that of The Bahamas. Together with money earned as migrant workers elsewhere, these pioneer immigrants invested their earnings, superior educational acumen, and social and economic networks in ways that allowed them to accumulate land, develop middle-class businesses, and access the best affordable education for their children. It was these well-educated and financially secured children who influenced the politics of the Bahamas of the 1970s and 1980s.

395   Interview quoted in the *Nassau Guardian*, March 1, 1973.

396   Michael Craton and D. Gail Saunders, *Islanders in the Stream: A History of the Bahamian People*, vol. 1 (Athens: University of Georgia Press, 1998), 179.

397   John A. Holm, "On the Relationship of Gullah and Bahamian," *American Speech* 58, no. 4 (1983), 303-18.

398   Cleveland Eneas, *Bain Town*, (Nassau: Timpaut Press, 1976), 52, 54. Bain Town is a quintessential historical community founded by former slaves and Africans liberated from slave ships following the abolition of the British slave trade, where Afro-Bahamian folkways are significantly influenced by residents' African heritage.

399   Elsie Crews Parsons, "Folk-Tales of Andros Island, Bahamas," *Memoirs of the American Folklore Society* 13 (1918), xiii.

400   Keith Cartwright, "Loyalist, Geechees & Africans: North American Roots of Afro-Bahamian Culture," *YINNA: Journal of the Bahamas Association of Cultural Studies* 1 (2000), 50-52.

401   Phillip May Hames, George C. Rogers, and David R. Chestnut, eds., *Papers of Henry Laurens* (Columbia: University of South Carolina Press, 1972). Laurens's Charleston firm reportedly sold more than eight thousand slaves to markets throughout the Americas.

402   C. F. Pascoe, *Two Hundred Years of the S.P.G.: An Historical Account of the Society for the Propagation of the Gospel in Foreign Parts, 1700-1900* (London, 1901).

403   Boubacar Barry, *Senegambia and the Atlantic Slave Trade* (Cambridge: Cambridge University Press, 1998), 3.

404   Ibid.

405   Ibid., 34.

406   G. Brooks, *Kola Trade and State Building in the Upper Guinea Coast and Senegambia, 15th and 17th Centuries*, African Studies Center Working Papers, no. 38, 1980, 15.

407   Karen Hess, *The Carolina Rice Kitchen: The African Connection* (Columbia: University of South Carolina Press, 1992), 34. Europeans dubbed the region of Senegambia the "Rice Coast".

408   D. Gail Saunders, Slavery in the Bahamas, 1648-1838,(Nassau: Nassau Guardian, 1985), 13.

409   Joseph E Holloway and Winifred K. Vass, *Africanisms in American Culture: Blacks in the Diaspora* (Indiana University Press, 1994), 12-13.